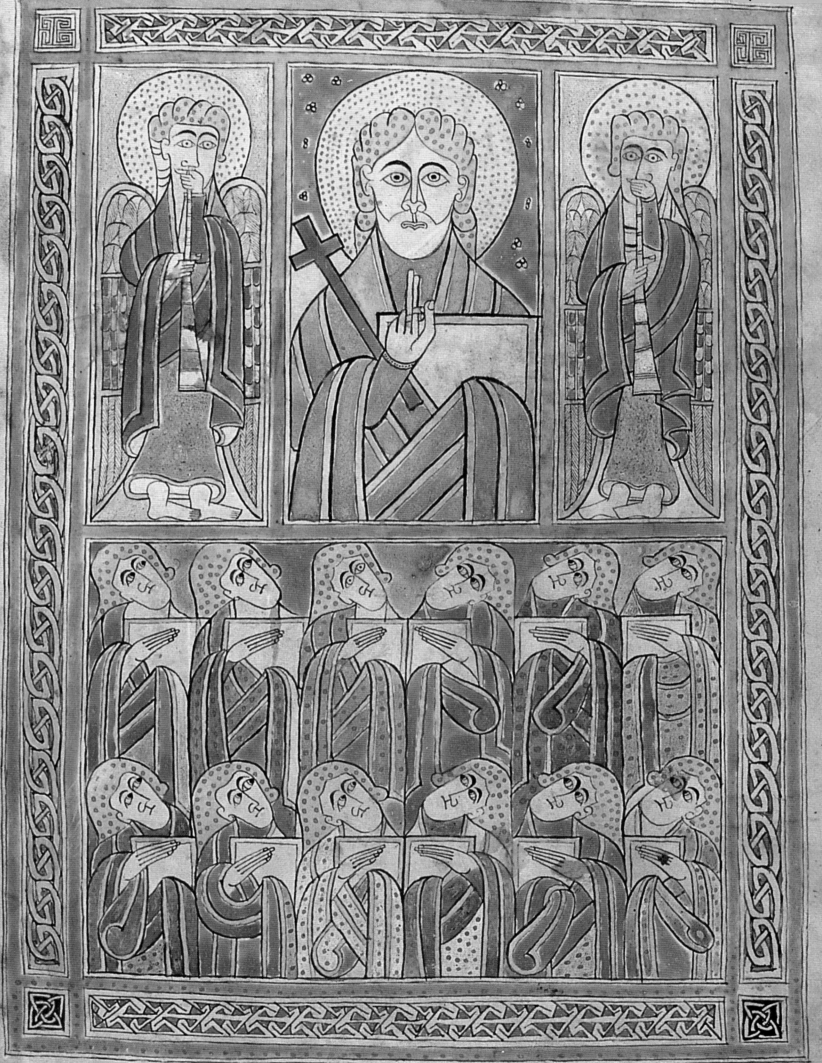

ANCIENT
IRELAND

OXFORD

UNIVERSITY PRESS

ANCIENT

FROM PREHISTORY

JACQUELINE O'BRIEN

NEW

OXFORD UNIV

2 0

IRELAND

TO THE MIDDLE AGES

AND PETER HARBISON

YORK
ERSITY PRESS
0 0

CONTENTS

THIS IS THE THIRD VOLUME IN A TRILOGY WHICH COMPRISES:

1. GREAT IRISH HOUSES AND CASTLES
JACQUELINE O'BRIEN AND DESMOND GUINNESS 1992

2. DUBLIN: A GRAND TOUR
JACQUELINE O'BRIEN WITH DESMOND GUINNESS 1994

3. ANCIENT IRELAND: FROM PREHISTORY TO THE MIDDLE AGES
JACQUELINE O'BRIEN AND PETER HARBISON 1996

PHOTOGRAPHER'S NOTE
HAVING PHOTOGRAPHED THE MONUMENTS OF IRELAND OVER MANY YEARS
I HAVE NOT ALWAYS USED THE MOST UP-TO-DATE IMAGE
IF AN EARLIER ONE WAS MORE PLEASING

EDITED BY COLIN GRANT
DESIGNED BY HARRY GREEN
MAP BY TECHNICAL ART SERVICES

FIRST PUBLISHED IN 1996 BY GEORGE WEIDENFELD & NICOLSON LTD
THE ORION PUBLISHING GROUP, ORION HOUSE
5 UPPER ST MARTIN'S LANE, LONDON WC2H 9EA

PUBLISHED IN NORTH AMERICA BY OXFORD UNIVERSITY PRESS, INC.,
198 MADISON AVENUE, NEW YORK, NY 10016, USA

OXFORD IS A REGISTERED TRADEMARK OF OXFORD UNIVERSITY PRESS

LIBRARY OF CONGRESS CATALOGING-IN-PUBLICATION DATA
O'BRIEN, JACQUELINE (JACQUELINE WITTENOOM)
ANCIENT IRELAND: JACQUELINE O'BRIEN, (PHOTOGRAPHER) AND PETER HARBISON, (AUTHOR).
P. CM.   ISBN 0-19-521268-1
1. IRELAND--ANTIQUITIES--PICTORIAL WORKS. 2. ARCHITECTURE, MEDIEVAL--IRELAND--PICTORIAL WORKS.
3. HISTORIC BUILDINGS--IRELAND--PICTORIAL WORKS. 4. HISTORIC SITES--IRELAND--PICTORIAL WORKS.
5. MONUMENTS--IRELAND--PICTORIAL WORKS. I. HARBISION, PETER. II. TITLE.
DA920.025 1996   96-14398   941.5--DC20   CIP

ISBN 0-19-521268-1
PRINTING (LAST DIGIT) 9 8 7 6 5 4 3 2
PRINTED AND BOUND IN ITALY

PAGE 1
LUNULA, AN IRISH BRONZE AGE NECK ORNAMENT,
INCISED WITH TRIANGULAR AND ZIGZAG MOTIFS

ENDPAPERS
LEFT HAND SIDE, THE CRUCIFIXION; RIGHT HAND SIDE, THE SECOND COMING OF CHRIST;
BOTH FROM MANUSCRIPT 51, MONASTIC LIBRARY OF ST GALL, SWITZERLAND

FOREWORD

By Jacqueline O'Brien

Ancient monuments redolent of past civilizations are still to be found in every corner of rural Ireland. They stand often in hauntingly beautiful landscapes: in the rich green fields of meadow grass, high above mountain streams or bounded by inaccessible cliffs dropping hundreds of feet into the turbulent Atlantic; nothing can be more breathtaking than to round a corner in some remote parish and come face to face with the tumbled ruins of a medieval monastery or a round tower soaring heavenwards with its doorway raised ten feet above the ground as if still in constant expectation of a dreaded Viking raid. However Vikings also made positive contributions to the country by founding townships which have been built over by successive centuries of development, the stones of earlier monuments constantly re-used. A glimpse of Dublin's extensive Viking past was revealed some twenty years ago but sadly was engulfed once more under tons of concrete. Monuments spread around Ireland's rural areas have fared much better and give us an extraordinary richness of antiquities.

Fortunately public and government awareness of the value of Ireland's rich heritage is growing swiftly and strenuous efforts are being made to save what still remains. The Office of Public Works in Dublin and the Northern Ireland Department of the Environment are trying valiantly to prevent decay and destruction, to preserve with sensitivity and even recreate with imagination. As always, work is handicapped by insufficient funds. The threats are real: time, the weather, weeds and vandals wage constant war. Monuments for so many centuries a feature of the Irish countryside are now being destroyed at a frightening pace by acid rain – something I can confirm by comparing photographs taken less than ten years apart. One solution is to place the most important monuments under cover as has happened with the great High Crosses at Clonmacnoise. Good imitations have replaced them but the magic of the site must, perforce, be diminished. The crosses at Monasterboice still stand, as they have for a thousand years, silhouetted against an ancient landscape. But not for long as they must surely be uprooted soon and taken inside. I feel we are so very privileged to see the monuments in their original positions, as so many are today, and urge visitors to come quickly!

In an economy dependent in large measure on tourism, places of interest must be signposted, kept clear of encroaching weeds and public facilities provided. But the difference between the manicured landscape and the wild, yet atmospheric, is obvious in so many places. As each location is conserved and tidied for future generations, the very orderliness of such work destroys the sense of age, of the ineluctable march of time. Disturbing, too, is to find newly erected headstones polished to a high gloss with attendant plastic flowers lapping the lichen-covered walls of ancient sites, but at least this shows that the sites are not merely museums. It is that magical sense of the numinous – an overwhelming feeling of mystery or awe – which visitors come to experience, yet its destruction is sad, but inevitable.

Nonetheless most local bodies and communities throughout Ireland care tenderly for their ancient sites and it is of great importance that monuments attract visitors. The small village of Upperchurch in Tipperary, for example, has made great efforts to care for and publicize its remote dolmen, Knockcurraghbola; the little town of Clones is dominated by a venerable High Cross now sheathed in scented roses and its ancient graveyard, filled with fascinating antiquities, is a delight to discover. Much is being done at a national level, too; in the south the new National Monuments legislation, enacted in 1994, gives comprehensive legal protection to all Recorded Monuments. The full list of these, almost 200,000 sites, is expected to be completed by the end of 1996.

The great institutions care for an extraordinary richness of archaeological treasures. The National Museum of Ireland and the Ulster Museum, the Royal Irish Academy, The National Library of Ireland and Trinity College, Dublin have been so fortunate in having secured marvellous antiques. These have been gathered down the years by generations of zealous collectors who appreciated the vital importance of the artifacts and manuscripts for Ireland's heritage. The pre-Christian gold in the National Museum of Ireland, for example, is unique in Europe.

I must thank Dr Peter Harbison for the superb text he has written covering Ireland's history up to 1700. He has an intimate knowledge of the ancient archaeological sites of Ireland and, even where there is little to see today, he has been able to describe how the buildings would have looked originally. Early Irish history is a complex story but he has unravelled the threads to provide a lively text, scholarly yet packed with information, accessible to general readers, and expressed occasionally with a sense of humour. A very long bibliography has been included which, it is hoped, will be of value to scholars and those faced with research, not only in the period generally, but with the individual sites.

We owe a great debt of gratitude to numerous institutions and individuals who have been of assistance during the preparation of this book. To the following institutions and their respective staffs we would like to express our thanks for help of various kinds: The Commissioners of Public Works, the most co-operative staff of the National Monuments Service, especially William Cumming and Aighleann O'Shaughnessy; The Northern Ireland Department of the Environment, Historic Monuments and Buildings Branch; and in particular Dr Ann Hamlin, Director of the Northern Ireland Archaeological Survey; to Dr Patrick Wallace at the National Museum of Ireland for his invaluable co-operation and kindness, Valerie Dowling for helping with the photography, and Raghnall Ó Floinn and Mary Cahill for setting it up; The Council of the Royal Irish Academy for permission to reproduce two of its manuscripts (the *Cathach* and the *Stowe Missal*), and to its library staff (Siobhán Uí Raifeartaigh, the Librarian, Íde Ní Thuama, Marcus Browne, Kim Hunter and Dymphna Moore) for all their help; Dr Cornel Dora, the librarian and Carsten Seltrecht, photographer, at the beautiful Monastic Library of St Gall for permission to photograph the superb Irish manuscripts and for their assistance; The Irish Architectural Archive (David Griffin and Colm O Riordan, as well as Ann Henderson, Hugh Doran, Simon Lincoln and Aidan O'Boyle), The Royal Society of Antiquaries of Ireland (Siobhán de hÓir and Orna Somerville), and Dr Pat Donlon and all her helpful staff in the National Library of Ireland; The British Museum for permission to photograph St Cuilean's Bell and the 'Londesborough' Brooch, and Susan Youngs who made the photography possible.

Among the individuals we would like to thank are Mrs Edelgard Soergel-Harbison and Mrs Sheelagh Harbison; Dr Katharine Simms and Dr Terry Barry of Trinity College, Dublin; George and Dr Maccon Macnamara of Corofin, Co. Clare, as well as Letitia Pollard, Editor of *Ireland of the Welcomes* magazine, and Pauline Byrne of Bord Fáilte. Charles Colthurst and Mervyn Johnson of Blarney Castle, the Rev. Sean Bourke of Boher for permission to photograph St Manchan's Shrine; Gretta Byrne of the Céide Fields Interpretative Centre; Cian O'Carroll of Bunratty Castle; Tom Cassidy of Craggaunowen; Maureen and Paul Derby; Professor George Eogan; the Rev. Joseph Garvey of Curraha; Mr and Mrs Michael Green of Newtown; Alan Hayden for information about his as yet unpublished excavations at Trim Castle; Thomas Kinsella for permission to reproduce the poem on page 180; Mrs Libby Ponsonby of Kilcooley Abbey; The Rev. Daniel Ryan of Upperchurch; Christopher St Lawrence of Howth Castle; Mrs Nesbit Waddington of Beaulieu;

and the very co-operative staffs at all the monuments including Boyle, Clonmacnoise, Ennis, Glendalough, Jerpoint, Newgrange (especially Claire Tuffy), and the Rock of Cashel.

This handsome volume has benefited greatly from the editing skills of Colin Grant, the imaginative design of Harry Green and the assistance of Caroline Earle and Richard Atkinson at Weidenfeld, to all of whom homage is due. Our publisher, Michael Dover, has been very helpful throughout the publication of this book and its two predecessors in the trilogy on Ireland: *Great Irish Houses and Castles* and *Dublin: a Grand Tour*.

For permission to include the churches and for the tremendous kindness shown in photographing them, I would like to express my appreciation to all who patiently put up with the photography – lights, ladders, tripods and cameras cluttering the aisles – particularly the following: the Augustinian Fathers of The Abbey, Fethard; the Rev. Michael Nuttall, Rector of Adare; Dr Frank Moriarty, Parish Priest of Adare; the Rev. Frank Fahey of Ballintober; the Carmelite Fathers at the Friary, Loughrea; the Rev. Wayne Carney, Rector of Clonfert Cathedral; John Paterson, Dean of Christ Church, Dublin and Allen Figgis; the Rt. Rev. Monsignor Sean Swayne of Duiske Abbey, Graiguenamanagh; Dermot Clifford, Archbishop of Cashel and Emly and the Rev. Mathew McGrath of Holy Cross Abbey; Ernon Perdue, Dean of St Flannan's, Killaloe; Donal Murray, Bishop of Limerick for permission to include the O'Dea mitre and crozier, and the Rev. Michael Wall for his help; the Very Rev. Dr Robert McCarthy of St Nicholas of Myra Collegiate Church, Galway, and the sexton Christine Hunt; Robert Townley, Dean of St Brigid's Cathedral, Kildare, and Kenneth Dunne; Norman Lynas, Dean of St Canice's, Kilkenny, and George and Muriel Bell; Cecil Orr, Dean of St Columb's Cathedral, Derry; Dr Norman Gamble of St Doulagh's, Balgriffin, and Robert Geelan; Morris Sirr, Dean of St Mary's Cathedral, Limerick; the Rev. Peter Rhys Thomas, Rector of St Mary's Church, Youghal; Maurice Stewart, Dean of St Patrick's Cathedral, Dublin and Joyce Wynne, and Anthony Previte, Dean of St Mary's Cathedral, Tuam.

John Derby was of tremendous assistance with a large part of the photography and organized the results most efficiently. I will always be grateful to him for having passed on so much of his extensive knowledge of Ireland and its history. My gratitude also to photographer John Slater who participated in some photographic expeditions with great enthusiasm showing me Ireland through the eyes of a Yorkshireman; to Eleanor O'Neill from Ballydoyle, my companion on many trips, who has looked after me and my extensive equipment most diligently for many years; to Gerry Gallagher and Alan Rapier who helped with the driving over hundreds of miles and to Brian Carpenter, John Swan and Robert Goodbody of Westair Aviation at Shannon for their help with the aerial photography.

Finally my heartfelt thanks to Peter Harbison's family who must have missed him during his prodigious periods of work and my own family who patiently endured many absences and who must be glad that the trilogy on Ireland is now complete.

CHAPTER ONE

IRELAND BEFORE HISTORY

THE STONE AGE

The medieval monuments of Ireland, which are the main focus of this book, inform us about and bring to life the first thousand years and more of the country's history, ranging from the time of St Patrick in the fifth century down to the decline of Gaelic Ireland in the seventeenth. But the native Irish who erected many of these monuments did not suddenly appear out of nowhere along with the national apostle: their antecedents had been established in the country for millennia, and the blood genes that flowed in their veins had an Irish ancestry going back many thousands of years. This is why the medieval monuments are introduced here with a selection of their prehistoric predecessors, taking us back to the Stone Age when the Irish were already demonstrating their masterly use of stone.

It may come as somewhat of a surprise to learn that the historic period in Ireland – from St Patrick to the present – encompasses less than one-sixth of the time that mankind has settled the soil of Ireland. For the other five-sixths, the country's inhabitants lacked the capacity to set down their history in writing and, to help us gain some idea of what transpired in those thousands of years of prehistoric time, we must resort to what archaeology and related sciences have managed to recover in recent decades, and glance at the stone monuments that survive from those primeval far-off days.

Travelling by car or bus today along the country roads of Ireland, with lush green pasture or extensive bog on either side, it is difficult to realize that a mere twenty thousand years ago it would have been impossible to traverse the same terrain even on foot, for most of the country was covered by the kind of glaciers still visible in Iceland or the upper reaches of the Alps today. Only a small strip of land along the south coast remained ice-free, and there archaeologists have long sought in vain for traces of Old Stone Age men, the rough contemporaries of those artists who decorated the cave-walls of France and northern Spain with their brilliant animal paintings. A thaw in the northern hemisphere's weather meant that things were to change gradually and even, at times, rapidly. The glaciers retreated pole-wards over the European landmass till reduced to the size of their present-day successors among the mountains of western Norway. By 8000 BC, and probably before, Ireland no longer groaned under their weight and was free to receive the first human footsteps to tread upon the country's soil. Whether those feet got wet in coming from Britain we cannot say, as it has

not yet proved possible to determine with any precision whether the land-bridge with Britain, that dry umbilical cord linking the smaller island with its larger neighbour to the east, was finally severed before or after the arrival of Ireland's first families.

What can be stated with reasonable certainty is that human traces are known in Ireland from around 8000 BC, or about ten thousand years ago. They belong to Mesolithic – or Middle Stone Age – people whose economy was largely that of the hunter and fisher. What are now green fields in the eastern half of the country were a mixture of forest and scrubland, and it would have been up the rivers and streams that these first inhabitants would have penetrated inland from their first beach-heads. Being forced to hunt and fish for their daily proteins, they had to be constantly on the move to catch their prey for dinner, and could not afford to tarry too long in any one place. They had no time to erect permanent monuments to their dead, and all that the archaeologists' spades have been able to discover of their traces are their temporary camps, discernible by discolourations in the ground where the upright posts of their flimsy cabins once stood, along with some of the stone artefacts that they fashioned to reduce the drudgery of their daily chores.

For almost half the duration of Irish human prehistory, amounting to about four thousand years, these hunter and fisher folk eked out their perilous existence in small family groups, and a break of around a thousand years in the archaeological record of the period could suggest that they may even have perished without trace, to be replaced later by new arrivals to continue the unremitting struggle for life at a similarly primitive level of hand-to-mouth existence.

The sunnier climes of western Asia and elsewhere had, however, already made life easier by facilitating the cultivation of crops and creating the possibility of permanent settlement in one place. This development of the earliest civilization in the Fertile Crescent gradually spread to the European continent, where villages were established by farming communities living not far from the great rivers of the Danube and the Rhine. They not only tilled the soil but also domesticated cattle and sheep, which provided a more readily accessible meat source for the daily diet, without having to go out and hunt for it. When, eventually, these farming communities crossed the English Channel to Britain, they brought their seeds and livestock with them, but seem to have largely abandoned their village concept in favour of individual houses scattered throughout the landscape. It was only a matter of time till these new developments reached Ireland's shores, some six thousand years ago.

It is at this stage that Ireland made the decisive leap into the New Stone Age, or Neolithic period, which provided the island with its first sedentary farming communities, able to clear the forest with stone axes so as to make way for the raising of livestock and the cultivation of crops such as wheat and barley. An advantageous climate, with the temperature on average about two degrees Fahrenheit above today's, enabled agriculture to be practised on higher ground than is feasible in modern times. The people began to settle down in favoured areas such as the shores around Lough Gur in County Limerick, where they built houses, round or rectangular in shape, and with a roof supported by upright wooden posts. In time, the houses were given solider wall foundations made of stone. These recently arrived people would have intermingled with the earlier Mesolithic population groups, thereby creating an extended basis for the blood-genes of the Irish

LEFT Early farmers were attracted to the rich soils of south-east Limerick and buried their dead in this megalithic tomb near Lough Gur some four thousand years ago.

people today. What language they spoke is, of course, unknown to us but, rather than being the 'noble savages' envisaged by some of our own more immediate ancestors within the last two centuries, they were a highly intelligent people who harnessed nature brilliantly to their own needs, which were no longer just purely of the materialistic kind.

This becomes clear when it is realized that these Neolithic farmers were the first to erect the remarkable stone monuments to their dead which we know today as megalithic tombs. The name, derived from two Greek words meaning 'great stone', is well deserved, for these graves consist of large chunks of stone which stand up and out in the landscape as a remarkable achievement by a Stone Age people who obviously paid more attention to the permanent resting places of their ancestral dead than they did to the construction of their own long-vanished homes. These notable markers in the countryside may have served to establish rights to the surrounding land, possession of ancestral bones having possibly been construed as providing proof of ownership to newly won territory.

One of the most famous types of megalithic monument is the 'passage-grave', or 'passage-tomb', which has a stone-lined passage leading from the rim of a usually circular mound to a burial chamber roughly at its centre. It was certainly built by a people intent on making a permanent mark on the landscape, for they frequently sited their burial places on eminences which

could be seen for miles around. Among the most obvious of these is what is called Queen Maeve's (or Medb's) Grave on top of Knocknarea, which provides a truly breathtaking panorama over Sligo Bay and looks dramatic when seen from Carrowmore megalithic cemetery below. A smaller example is the so-called 'Mound of the Hostages' on the Hill of Tara in County Meath, from which, it is said, seven counties of Ireland can be seen on a clear day. But by far the most famous group of such passage-graves is to be found occupying prominent positions on a ridge overlooking the River Boyne 5-6 miles (8-10 km) upstream from Drogheda. The trio of tombs comprises Knowth, Dowth and, most renowned of all, Newgrange, the last with its restored front wall of white quartz which makes it almost as conspicuous from afar as the Taj Mahal.

These three great monuments can be taken as the high point of

BELOW The massive and unopened passage-tomb on top of Knocknarea overlooking Sligo Bay is traditionally known as the tomb of the warrior Queen Medb, whose exploits in urging Connacht men to conquer Ulster in the old Irish epic, *Táin Bó Cuailnge*, the 'Cattle Raid of Cooley', may conceivably mirror actual events some time before the dawn of Irish history.

LEFT Strong religious beliefs and social circumstances must have motivated the creation of the 36 ft (11m) high megalithic monument on top of Knocknarea in County Sligo – an undertaking as difficult to achieve as trying to work out how many Stone Age man hours went into its making.

RIGHT Carrowmore, 2 miles (3km) west of Sligo town, had a cemetery complex of eighty-five megalithic tombs, one of the largest and – if the results of Swedish excavations are accepted – also one of the oldest anywhere in Europe. Its passage-tombs and dolmens in stone circles, with Knocknarea in the background, create an unforgettable megalithic experience.

LOWER RIGHT Knowth is one of the three great burial mounds erected in the 'sacred landscape' of the lower Boyne valley in County Meath. Extensive excavations by Professor George Eogan brought to light two very different passage-tombs back to back with one another under the great tumulus, probably erected before 2500 BC. Many of the stones, both inside and out, are richly decorated with abstract designs of great beauty and complexity. Visitors are welcome to inspect the recently reconstructed smaller 'satellite' tombs that cluster around the main mound like chickens round the mother hen.

megalithic construction in Ireland, not only because of their sophisticated building techniques and their masterly decoration but also because, chronologically, they seem to be the culmination of a series of tombs stretching back many hundreds of years. The same county of Meath in which they stand also has a veritable necropolis of passage-graves on the Lough Crew Hills, collectively known as Sliabh na Caillighe ('Witch's Hill'), which bear decoration that is fine though not quite as brilliant as that of the Boyne Valley. Other cemeteries, most notably in Sligo, also add interesting bumps to the hill-top skyline, as exemplified by the undecorated tombs at Carrowkeel, overlooking Lough Arrow.

The passage-grave may not, however, have been the earliest type of megalithic tomb in Ireland, though this cannot yet be verified in the current state of our knowledge. One class of tomb which has claims to be earlier is the 'court-tomb', or 'court-cairn', such as that at Ballymacdermot, County Armagh. Around four hundred court-cairns are known from Ireland, all – with few exceptions – lying north of a line from Galway to Dundalk, with the heaviest concentration in the north-western quadrant of Ireland. Unlike the passage-tombs, they are almost entirely lacking in decoration, a feature that led the folklorist and archaeologist Estyn Evans to envisage them as belonging to a 'northern region, eschewing iconography', in contrast to the passage-tombs which he saw as adhering to 'a more artistic, flamboyant, sun-worshipping south'. The burial rite is mostly cremation, and the finds are simple in character – pieces of worked flint and Stone Age pottery bowls. These, taken together with the shape of the court-tombs, suggest that they belong to a wider north-west European type of chambered tomb, built by some of the earliest farming communities in the fourth millennium BC and probably remaining in use for several generations. Built on lower, often flat, ground, in contrast to the more elevated location of the passage-tombs, they usually occur singly rather than in

cemeteries, their sites marking the burial place of ancestors which gave the tribe their visual focal point and claim to the surrounding lands.

Difficult to date in comparison to the passage-graves and court-cairns, but certainly more eye-catching than the latter, are the dolmens, which consist of a number of uprights bearing a capstone on top. To our eyes they

ABOVE Lean, scrawny but elegant, the dolmen at Legananny, Co. Down, seems to anticipate visually by thousands of years the occasionally recorded Irish custom of resting coffins momentarily on upright stones at the entrance to a graveyard, as a final prayer is said before interment.

LEFT The half-circular forecourt flanked with large stones graded in size is typical of Irish court-tombs and is well exemplified here at Ballymacdermot where the Stone Age builders chose an attractive site overlooking the plain of Meigh in south Armagh. Unusually, the burial chamber at the back of the forecourt had a corbelled rather than the more customary flat stone roof.

LEFT The reconstructed white quartz facing of the great tomb at Newgrange makes it radiate a brilliance in the modern landscape, as it presumably also did when originally erected some five thousand years ago. Around the massive heart-shaped mound enclosing the tomb are remnants of a circle of large stones and a 'wood henge', discovered in the excavated rectangles in the foreground, but these were erected about a thousand years later, probably long after the tomb itself had gone out of use.

BELOW Behind the intricately carved entrance stone at Newgrange lies the doorway to the tomb passage, with movable door-slab to the right and, above the lintel, the so-called 'roof-box' through which the sun's rays shine into the burial chamber at each year's winter solstice.

have the great advantage of simplicity, combined with a sculptural quality which renders them among the most visually appealing of all the megalithic tombs, as exemplified by the dolmen at Legananny, County Down.

NEWGRANGE
Co. Meath

Newgrange is one of Ireland's, but also Europe's, best-known prehistoric monuments, made internationally famous because of the orientation of its tomb passage towards the rising sun of the winter solstice. Together with the neighbouring tombs at Knowth and Dowth, it forms a megalithic cemetery of major proportions, strung out along a low ridge of hills north of the River Boyne about 6 miles (10 km) above where it flows into the Irish Sea. It was the Boyne, a river sanctified by its own goddess Bóann, and the rich land around it, which must have attracted Newgrange's Stone Age builders to settle in this fertile region. The fact that none of their flimsy wooden habitations has ever been found demonstrates how much more important for them was the construction of houses for the dead, which must have taken millions of man-hours to build.

Newgrange, the largest of the three great mounds of this necropolis, is roughly heart-shaped in plan; it rises to a height of about 36 feet (11m), and measures about 300 feet (90m) in diameter. The mound is made with a mixture of earth, turves and stones, placed neatly one above the other like

LEFT The 20ft (6m)-high corbelled roof of the Newgrange burial chamber is a masterly and timeless piece of construction that has kept the interior dry for five millennia.

RIGHT As the sun climbs above the horizon on the shortest day of the year, its pencil-thin rays penetrate along this passage to illuminate the central chamber before stealthily disappearing seventeen minutes later, leaving those who have returned to the womb of mother earth to ponder on its eternal annual message.

layers in a cake. The horizontally laid and partially decorated kerb-stones placed around the foot of the mound proved insufficient to retain the vast volume of material in the mound, which inevitably spilled out over them. According to Professor M.J. O'Kelly, who excavated at Newgrange from 1962 until 1975, the same fate awaited white stones, which, he believed, provided a special facing along the front of the mound on either side of the entrance to the tomb. He found these white stones spread out in a slight slope at the foot of the mound. On his advice and that of an engineer who worked out where these quartz stones must have been placed originally to have fallen into the position where Professor O'Kelly found them, the Office of Public Works, the owners of the monument, reconstructed the white facing which we see today. While this procedure has not been without its critics, it adds a shining brilliance to Newgrange which makes it stand out visually from a distance.

This effect was doubtless also intended by the prehistoric builders who placed their tombs on geographical eminences so that the message of the mound's importance would be appreciated far and wide. Because of its great diameter, Newgrange occupies not only the top of the ridge but part of the slopes around it as well. This fact is brought home to us today as we climb the incline towards the entrance to the tomb, marked by the magnificent stone decorated with spirals (one triple) and diamond-shaped lozenges – one of the finest carved stones of prehistoric Europe. When we pass through the doorway, noticing the original movable stone door on the right, we can feel almost imperceptibly the continuation of the slope as we climb gently up the 62-foot (19m)-long passage-way to the centre of the tomb itself. Here, what seems like a round chamber is roofed to a height of almost 20 feet (6m) by large corbel stones, tilted slightly downwards away from the centre – one of the tomb's clever devices to drain off water sideways and prevent it percolating down into the burial chamber from the mound above.

Leading off the main chamber are three burial niches, giving the tomb-plan a cruciform shape. The niche straight ahead has one of its side walls decorated with a triple spiral, akin to that on the entrance stone. But the most ornamental of the tomb's stones is that forming the roof of the niche on the right, which also has a ritual stone basin on the floor. It may be worth noting that the Treasury of Atreus in Mycenae which, like Newgrange, is also a passage-grave though more than a thousand years younger, has its only side niche on the right, showing the importance of this location in the tomb-area.

When he entered the tomb at the winter solstice in 1968, Professor O'Kelly noticed that the sun, when it crept above the horizon to the south-east at 8.58 a.m., cast a pencil-thin ray of sunlight into the centre of the burial chamber, only to disappear again, as quietly as it had come, a mere 17 minutes later. The rays of the sun, as it comes up above the sky-line, are almost horizontal, and the gradual slope upwards of the passage towards the tomb meant that that the rays coming through the doorway only penetrated about half-way along the incline of the passage. In order to allow the rays in at a level high enough to reach the tomb at the upper end of the passage, the unknown architect of the mound inserted an opening, called the 'roof-box', above the entrance, and through it the sun could then penetrate to the centre of the chamber, to shine there for just over a quarter of an hour on the shortest day of the year, 21 December, and a few days on either side of it.

This discovery not only provided an explanation for the 'roof-box' (which had previously been thought to have been designed to allow the living to pass in food for the dead after the door had been closed) but also demonstrated that the line of the passage had been intentionally orientated towards the place on the horizon where the sun rose on the shortest day of the year. Doubtless intended as much for the living as the dead, this device proclaimed the message that, in the same way that nature began a new period of growth after the nadir of mid-winter had been reached, so too the dead could look forward to a new life after death – surely one of the earliest testimonies to a belief in the afterlife in prehistoric Europe.

All of this shows the great care and attention paid by the builders to provide a suitable home for the deceased in their new life after death. Indeed, one might imagine that many of the geometrical designs which decorate the stones of Newgrange were copied from patterns carved in wood or woven in textile – as ornaments in the houses of the living, which have proved so ephemeral in comparison to the eternal creation that is Newgrange.

Newgrange is by no means the earliest of Ireland's passage-tombs, but it can be regarded as the climax of a series of such tombs because of its size, decoration and clever attention to constructional detail. In this it is joined by the neighbouring passage-tomb at Knowth, where the excavator, Professor George Eogan, has discovered not one but two passage-tombs, back to back, under the same mound. The fact that the tomb chamber at Newgrange does not reach the centre of the mound has given rise to speculation that Newgrange may also contain a second tomb though, despite the best efforts of Professor O'Kelly, this has yet to be located. Instead of being back to back with the known tomb, as at Knowth, could it be located at right angles, connected possibly with the rise of the mid-summer sun?

Newgrange may be compared with the pyramids of Egypt in that it is also a man-made mound with a passage leading to a burial chamber within, but while the pyramids appear to have been designed as the final resting place of a single, divine Pharaoh, Newgrange seems to have been

LEFT The triple-spiral motif in the deepest recess of the Newgrange tomb reiterates that occurring on the entrance stone, but its meaning for those who carved it is now lost.

BELOW Of the three side niches off the main tomb at Newgrange, that on the right has a smoothly carved stone basin, which doubtless played a role in the burial ritual, perhaps as recipient of the cremated bones of the individuals interred there.

created as a communal vault. The cremated remains of the three or four individuals discovered among the finds in the tomb do not allow us to ascertain if they all belonged to the same family. However, as the calibrated date of the radiocarbon specimen taken from the passage roof at Newgrange worked out at around 3100 BC, it suggests that Newgrange may be as much as five hundred years older than the pyramids, thus making it into one of the world's first great pieces of architecture.

A number of 'satellite' tombs, smaller in scale, have come to light around the perimeter of the mound at Newgrange, clustering like chickens around the mother hen, and the locations of some of their stones are indicated by modern concrete replacements set in the ground where they stood. More impressive for the visitor, however, are the massive unhewn stones forming part of a circle which once surrounded the mound at a distance. Yet excavation by David Sweetman has proved these to be unrelated to the original construction and to have been added about a thousand years later by the

CREEVYKEEL
Co. Sligo

The megalithic tomb at Creevykeel, beside the Sligo-Bundoran road, is of a very different kind to Newgrange – and probably older as well. Like Newgrange, it is one of the more 'exotic' and developed examples of its type, which in this case is a court-tomb. The basic ground-plan of a court-tomb is that at the broader end of a long stone cairn or mound there is an open-air forecourt, which is little more than a half-circle in shape – a form which gave rise to an earlier name for this type of tomb, the 'lobster-claw cairn'. Opening off this forecourt, and reaching back into the mound along its central axis, is a burial chamber, usually covered with heavy capstones and frequently subdivided into three or four sections by low sills above ground and jambs projecting from the walls. This basic form can be varied by placing two similar tombs back to back

Beaker people, probably Ireland's first metal producers who were unrelated to the tomb-builders. Somewhat to the south-east of the tomb, down the slope towards the river, these Beaker people built a round wooden enclosure consisting of upright stakes (also replaced by modern concrete footings) and containing a number of burial pits, demonstrating that Newgrange retained its importance as a burial centre long after it had ceased to provide interment for its builders. The tomb itself was not rediscovered until 1699 but in the intervening thousands of years the tomb must have been regarded almost as one of the 'Seven Wonders' of the local world, as evidenced by the finding of Bronze Age gold torcs there and coins deposited by Romans, who, even if they did not invade Ireland, at least came like the modern tourists to marvel at the Stone Age splendour that is Newgrange.

ABOVE LEFT The importance of the right-hand burial niche at Newgrange is emphasized by the rich abstract designs of its ceiling stone, copied perhaps from wood or weavings in the houses of the living to make the dead feel more at home.

ABOVE The open oval area in the court-tomb at Creevykeel, Co. Sligo, gives access to the burial gallery.

within the same stone mound or by having what we see at Creevykeel, namely the forecourt completed to form an oval entered from the end opposite the doorway to the tomb and, in this instance, with small unrelated burial chambers in the body of the mound.

Creevykeel itself was excavated in 1935 by the Harvard Archaeological Expedition to Ireland under Hugh O'N. Hencken. The expedition carried out a number of exemplary explorations in various parts of the country that were to be a great training ground for a young generation of Irish archaeologists.

DOLMENS

Dolmens are, for their size, the most dramatic and graceful of all the megalithic tombs of Ireland, leading one authority to describe them as examples of the earliest public sculpture in Europe. They consist of between three and seven uprights which support a massive capstone, usually tilting upwards towards the entrance, where a large stone sometimes acted as a door.

The word itself – which lent its name to one of the best-quality printing presses in twentieth-century Ireland – comes from two Breton words meaning 'stone table'. Early antiquaries, fascinated by their primeval form, imagined them to have been druids' altars, but excavations have unearthed human bones interred within, which indicated that they were burial places. They were placed in long, low mounds, which would suggest that they were in some way related to, though not necessarily derived from, the court-tombs with which they may have been roughly contemporary – one of the most famous dolmens, Poulnabrone in County Clare, providing a radiocarbon date somewhere between 3800 and 3200 BC. One of their chief characteristics is the almost weightless way in which they carry their cap-

RIGHT The dramatic outline of Poulnabrone dolmen makes it look as if it is about to take off for outer space from the already lunar limestone landscape of the Burren in north Clare.

BELOW As if having shrugged off the wearisome weight of their capstone, the uprights of the dolmen in the grounds of Howth Castle, Co. Dublin, enclose what tradition says is the grave of Aedeen, who died of grief at the loss of her husband Oscar during the battle of Gabhra in AD 284: 'Meet spot to sepulchre a queen', in the words of the nineteenth-century poet Sir Samuel Ferguson.

BELOW It is no wonder that a race of giants was credited with the erection of this massive capstone on the dolmen at Browneshill in County Carlow.

RIGHT The natural simplicity of the dolmen at Proleek, Co. Louth – in the grounds of the Ballymascanlon Hotel – give it the appearance of a three-legged toadstool.

stones, which must have required considerable skill and manpower to raise and place in position. One example, at Browneshill in County Carlow, is said to weigh 100 tons, but the capstone at Proleek, Co. Louth, can't be too far behind. In the absence of a modern block-and-tackle mechanism, the stones must have been tediously hauled up an earthen ramp, which was heaped up against the uprights and subsequently removed.

THE BRONZE AGE

One other type of megalithic monument remains to be mentioned. It once went by the name of 'wedge-shaped gallery grave', but this nomenclature proved to be such a mouthful that it was shortened to 'wedge-grave', or 'wedge-tomb', the titles deriving from the wedge-shaped ground-plan of the burial gallery. It expands from the back towards the entrance at the front, and the massive covering stones also rise in height as the gallery expands, though not all of these have necessarily survived, as witnessed by the example at Knockcurraghbola in County Tipperary. But what distinguishes the wedge-tombs from the others is that they probably belong to the Bronze Age, a period which followed the Stone Age some time in the second half of the third millennium BC and lasted about two thousand years. It gets its name from the main material used to make implements (chiefly axe-heads) and weapons, which were easier to shape and mould than the less malleable stones used during the preceding Neolithic period.

As far as Ireland is concerned, the Bronze Age is almost a misnomer, because it was during this period that Ireland produced its sparkling range of gold ornaments which can be seen to best advantage in the display cases of the National Museum in Dublin and the Ulster Museum in Belfast. Indeed, the products of the Bronze Age are best studied in museums, because there are not many notable field monuments which can be reliably fitted into the Bronze Age along with the wedge-tombs, as burials of the period are frequently underground or placed in low earthen round barrows which do not normally rise much above ground level.

Some other stone monuments of the Bronze Age are intriguing because of the mystery surrounding their function. Prime among these are the stone circles, such as at Drombeg, Co. Cork, possibly used to record the movements of celestial bodies, and the simple rows of stones, or stone alignments, mini-versions of those which are found stretching for miles over the heath at Kermario in Brittany. Then there is the standing stone, or menhir, occasionally with a Bronze Age burial at its foot, as at Punchestown, Co. Kildare, where the stone reaches a height of 23 feet (7m).

The warm climate which enabled Stone Age farmers to cultivate crops even on hill-tops seems to have deteriorated towards the end of the Neolithic period, and the continuing decline during the Bronze Age led to the spread of bog in various parts of Ireland. The peat began to cover areas previously inhabited and cultivated, as demonstrated by the Céide Fields in north Mayo, where very extensive field walls – and even an intact megalithic tomb – have come to light many feet beneath the bog surface. This creeping growth of the sphagnum made travel hazardous, and recent excavations in the midland bogs have revealed the presence of a series of

LEFT Among the rich collection of Irish prehistoric gold in the National Museum in Dublin is this bar-torc from County Mayo, cleverly twisted into shape around 1200 BC.

BELOW The gold gorget from Gleninsheen, Co. Clare, now in the National Museum, dates from around 700 BC, when Ireland's prehistoric goldsmiths reached the zenith of their craft. This brilliant neck ornament was taken to be an old coffin-fitting when first discovered in 1932.

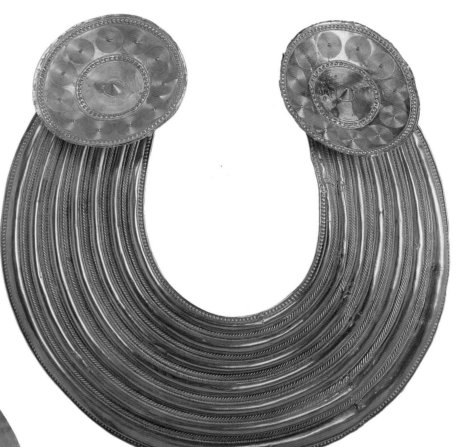

Gold glistened on Irish Bronze Age breasts in the form of wafer-thin lunulae (half-moon shapes), incised with triangular and zigzag motifs.

wooden trackways, as at Corlea in County Longford, some of which must have been laid down as early as the Bronze Age to enable wheeled vehicles to cross the bogs.

The population at the time must have been worried by the spread of this natural phenomenon against which they were powerless to act, and the Bronze Age experienced a rise in the deposition of sacrifices in water, doubtless in a vain effort to appease the weather gods. Driven off their ancestral lands, some of the people may have been forced to encroach on their more fortunate neighbours' territories, thereby giving rise to a new tension which can be sensed in the increasing number of bronze weapons produced – and probably also in the apparent development of new fortifications. Neolithic folk had been known to ring a hill-top with an occasionally interrupted earthen wall, as at Lyles Hill or

23

Donegore in County Antrim. But the appearance of earthen or stone forti-fications has only recently come to be recognized as a possible Bronze Age development, and most of these have hitherto been dated to the ensuing Iron Age which, by comparison, has far fewer weapons to show for itself.

Stone fortifications can take many forms, and are largely confined to the western half of the country. They can best be examined in their various guises, such as at Ballykinvarga in the Burren, Co. Clare, or on the Aran islands in Galway Bay, where there is so much stone available that it was an obvious building material. There, the forts can be round, as at Dún Conor, oval or even a semi-circle abutting onto a cliff-face, as at Dún Aengus or Cahercommaun, Co. Clare. Stone was further used to fortify promontories, as at Dún Dúchathair on the largest of the three Aran Islands and elsewhere along the mainland coastline, as at Dunbeg on the Dingle Peninsula in County Kerry. It was Claire Cotter's recent

RIGHT Away back in the mists of time, the Aran islanders of Inishmore in Galway Bay expended huge amounts of energy in building the stout barricade of the Black Fort (Dún Dúchathair), to defend their now barren promontory of stone.

BELOW A ring of closely spaced, upright stones known as *chevaux-de-frise* defended the stone fort at Ballykinvarga, near Kilfenora, Co. Clare – but when it was built, and for or against whom, remains a mystery.

RIGHT The Clare farmers who built the imposing stone fort at Cahercommaun more than a thousand years ago saved themselves the trouble of completing the full circle by building their defence on the side of an almost unclimbable cliff.

excavation at Dún Aengus and her discovery of remains of the period within the stone fort there which raised the possibility of a Bronze Age date for such defences.

However, this does not actually prove that the fort was built during the Bronze Age, and merely provides a possible starting date for use of the place. It would be premature to presume that all stone forts were of such an early date, and it may well be that some of them – including the round forts at Staigue in County Kerry and the Grianán of Aileach in County Donegal – may not have been constructed before the commencement of the historic period. The fact is that we have little reliable basis on which to date these imposing structures, and it is best to leave it to further excavations to help decide the matter in each individual case.

WEDGE-TOMBS

The final expression of the megalithic tomb idea in Ireland was the wedge-tomb. These tombs, as mentioned earlier, consist of long stone-lined and roofed galleries, wedge-shaped in plan, often with a further setting of stones running outside them, and all erected in a round or D-shaped mound. Finds of Neolithic (New Stone Age) pottery have been discovered in some of the tombs, but others have produced

LEFT Knockcurraghbola on the hilly uplands of County Tipperary is an impressive representative of the Irish wedge-tombs built around 2000 BC.

RIGHT A wonderful yet mysterious aura emanates from the stone circle at Drombeg amidst the peaceful countryside of west Cork.

BELOW This stone circle in County Wicklow got its name 'Piper's Stones' from a story that a piper and his dancers were turned into stone for having enjoyed themselves on the Sabbath.

so-called Beaker pottery, a rather finer ware found over many parts of Europe along with the early development of metal, suggesting that at least some of the wedge-tombs date from the Copper or ensuing Bronze Age. Almost five hundred of these monuments are known in Ireland, about half of them occurring between the 200- and 600-foot (60 and 180m) contour – higher than the majority of court-tombs, yet lower than most passage-tombs.

They occur predominantly in the western half of the country. Some of the best examples have massive capstones, creating an impressive visual impact as they rise in height towards the entrance. These imposing stone piles raise the question as to whether such monuments – and, indeed, all megalithic tombs – were just places in which to bury the dead or whether they may have had the added function of a ritual centre of some sort for the community which built them around four thousand years ago. Perhaps, they served many functions? Who will ever know?

STONE CIRCLES

Stone circles are examples of those gloriously mysterious prehistoric monuments where the imagination can exercise itself boundlessly as to their purpose. They tend to concentrate in particular areas such as west Cork and Kerry, and far away in Ulster. One small group in Wicklow has a tall stone standing outside the circle which, in the puritanical days of the seventeenth century, gave rise to the explanation that the Lord turned a set of circling dancers into stone because they had dared to trip the light fantastic on the sabbath, aided and abetted by a sole and standing musician who was also petrified – hence the title 'Piper's Stones'.

Other circles have one stone in the circle slightly taller than the rest and another opposite it lying flat; occasionally a line drawn between these two, when continued to the horizon, can lead the eye to some notable geographical feature where the sun may be seen to rise or set on some particularly significant day of the year (equinox, solstice or whatever). This would suggest that stone circles may have been set up to mark significant solar events.

In reality, all that would have been required to do so would have been two stones – and an eye to draw the line between them and continue it – but much more must have been involved than the recording of important events in the solar calendar. The round form must surely have been created as a place of ritual – perhaps to worship the sun, whose orb-form was imitated in the circle. The custom of building stone circles may have continued throughout the Bronze Age, while the circle at Drombeg in west Cork, when excavated by Dr Edward Fahy, provided evidence that these monuments continued to be used as late as the Iron Age, during which a burial was inserted at the centre of the circle.

STANDING STONES

Like the human figure, standing stones come in various assortments – short and dumpy, or long and lanky. You can take your pick of the many which exist in the Irish countryside. Standing upright in the middle of a field or beside a hedge, they are usually impressive while at the same time they have an aura of mystery, for – like Chesterton's donkey – they keep their secret still. One or two, on excavation, were found to have had the remains of cremated bone buried at their feet, indicating that they were probably erected as grave-markers, perhaps in the Bronze Age. The tallest and one of the most graceful of all – that at Punchestown, Co. Kildare, located close to the famous race course and reaching to a height of 19.5 feet (6m) – had the cremated remains placed in a stone cist, or box, beside the base-socket for the stone. Estyn Evans thought that some others may have been erected no more than a few centuries ago as the follies of romantic landlords or, more prosaically, as scratching posts for cattle.

CÉIDE FIELDS
Co. Mayo

During the last few centuries, the cutting away of the bog to provide turf for winter fires has revealed stone walls which had been built before the peat began to form in the wetter climate of three thousand or more years ago. By far the most extensive collection of such walls has come to light in the bog-land near the Atlantic cliffs on the north Mayo coast and close to the road from Ballycastle to Belmullet, where a pyramid-shaped Interpretative Centre has recently been erected to tell their graphic story.

Here, probably even before 3000 BC, there lived a community of farmers who buried some of their dead in a court-tomb (in Behy townland), which was discovered intact beneath the bog cover. But their most astounding achievement was the building of many rows of immensely long stone walls, running roughly inland from the cliffs, and joined at intervals by transverse walls, to create broad fields up to five acres in extent, in which the farmers kept their stock. We cannot say whether the fields were individually owned, but the walls could scarcely have been made without a tremendous co-operative effort still known in Ireland today as a *meitheal*.

Some of the walls have been laid bare in short sections by Professor Seamus Caulfield, who has been able to follow their course without expensive excavations by the simple expedient of ramming down a thin rod into the bog until the foot of the rod strikes the stones a number of feet beneath the surface. Where the rod strikes nothing, he knows that there is no more wall there. In this way, he has been able to reveal the astounding extent of these walls over 4 square miles (1,036 ha) – and there is probably more to be discovered below the blanket bog, the growth of which caused the wall-builders to abandon their settlement thousands of years ago.

BELOW Rivalling in elegance a piece of modern sculpture, the 19.5ft (6m) standing stone at Punchestown may have been erected during the Bronze Age to act as a burial marker.

RIGHT The stone walls of the Céide Fields, on the rugged Atlantic coast of County Mayo, are testimony to a co-operative agricultural effort that enclosed vast tracts of land before the time when creeping bog smothered the walls and burial place of those who built them.

DÚN AENGUS
Co. Galway

Dún Aengus is the most impressive and probably the best known of all the stone forts of Ireland. Located on Inis Mór, the largest of the three Aran Islands in Galway Bay, it is situated on the edge of a cliff which falls sheer to the turbulent Atlantic Ocean some 200 feet (60m) below. The fort consists of three stone walls, together with the remains of a fourth, the smallest being semi-circular, while the others approximate more to a D-shape. The innermost wall, though the smallest, is also the most massive and, despite reconstruction in the last century if not before, its walls – 12 feet (3.7m) high and thick – must give us a fair idea of its original appearance. The oft-posed question as to whether it originally formed a full circle is perhaps best answered by pointing out that its intentional positioning beside the cliff-face saved its builders the trouble of constructing the other half.

Outside the middle wall there is a band of stones placed upright and close together, presumably to hinder access to potential attackers. Such stones, known as *chevaux-de-frise* – from the wooden stakes placed in the way of oncoming horses by the medieval inhabitants of Frisia – occur outside one of the other forts on the same island and also at Ballykinvarga in County Clare, but whether the idea of erecting such barriers outside these forts may have originated in the Iberian Peninsula, where they occur in stone, or in central Europe, where wooden examples are known, remains a matter of some dispute.

Equally uncertain is when and by whom the fort was built. An Iron Age fibula was found in the wall in 1839, but Claire Cotter's recent excavation of part of the interior has uncovered material which may go back to the eighth or seventh century BC.

For a fort which George Petrie once described as 'the most magnificent barbaric monument in Europe', it is surprising that no reference to it is found in the earliest historic sources. Its connection with the mythical invaders known as the Fir Bolg is not recorded prior to the twelfth century. Some of the greatest brains of Irish archaeology in the nineteenth century, including George Petrie, Eugene O'Curry, John O'Donovan and Margaret Stokes, who attended a splendid evening banquet within the walls when an excursion of the Dublin meeting of the British Association for the Advancement of Science visited the site in 1857, failed to elucidate the origins of the fort. Hopefully the excavations carried out by the Discovery Programme, a modern government-funded research scheme, will uncover evidence which might help to explain some of the problems – but preferably not all of them, because a romantic place Iike Dún Aengus is much more attractive when it remains partially shrouded in mystery.

DÚN CONOR
Inis Meáin, Co. Galway

Unlike some of the other stone forts in the Aran Islands, Dún Conor (or Dún Chonchúir) on the middle island of Inis Meáin is more oval than rounded in shape. Its wall, about 18 feet (5.5m) in height and almost as much in girth, is thus more massive than the innermost wall of Dún Aengus. It has terraces on the inside, and before restoration in the last century these were linked by several flights of steps, many of which remain in their reconstructed form. It is not known whether the hut sites in the interior, also partially reconstructed, were part of the original occupation. As no excavations have taken place at Dún Conor, it cannot be established when the fort was built, but an origin in the Late Bronze Age or the Iron Age is most likely.

LEFT The stone fort of Dún Aengus, teetering on a steep Atlantic precipice on the Aran island of Inis Mór, needed only to be defended on its landward side.

RIGHT Dún Conor, on the middle island of Aran, proves that building massive forts was a great incentive to clear the neighbouring fields of stone.

DUNBEG
Co. Kerry

Promontory forts were tongues of land protected by the sea on three sides and by a man-made fortified wall on the landward side. They occur widely along various stretches of the Irish coast, and may date from anywhere between the seventh century BC and the seventeenth century AD. One of the few to have been at least partially excavated was that at Dunbeg near the southern end of the Dingle Peninsula in County Kerry, examined by Dr Terry Barry in 1977. It is defended against land-based marauders by four interrupted banks and ditches, while, close to the seaward point, there is a stone rampart enclosing a beehive hut. The rampart overlay a ditch which provided a radiocarbon date of around the the late sixth century BC. Datable finds were virtually non-existent, but the radiocarbon technique provided dates at the end of the tenth century AD for the clochán, or beehive hut. This was possibly also the period which saw the construction of similar huts on the same peninsula and on Skellig Michael, which is visible from the fort. This raises the question as to whether the stone wall at Dunbeg was built for defence, or simply as a demarcation for the (temporary?) inhabitants of the beehive hut. The bank and ditch may have been constructed a century or two earlier, but there is no evidence that the promontory fort was occupied into the second millennium AD.

ABOVE A series of earthen and stone walls protected a 'beehive hut' on the promontory of Dunbeg near the end of the Dingle Peninsula in County Kerry.

DOON FORT
Co. Donegal

Hidden away in undulating territory south of Naran-Portnoo, the small lake known as Doon Lough has an island which is almost entirely occupied by a stone fort variously known as 'The Bawn', 'Doon Fort' or 'O'Boyle's Fort'. For all that, absolutely nothing is known of its

RIGHT This imposing stone fort in Doon Lough, Co. Donegal, leaves little of its island undefended.

history – or prehistory. It closely resembles the Grianán of Aileach in the same county in having walls which narrow in thickness towards the top, but it is more oval in shape – a form partially dictated, no doubt, by the outline of the island it occupies. Its maximum internal diameter is just over 100 feet (30m) and – like most of its counterparts in the western half of Ireland – its parapet is reached by a number of internal stairways. The wall – a part of which sadly collapsed some years ago – rises to a height of almost 15 feet (4.5m), and access was gained by a single doorway, which may have been covered originally.

GRIANÁN OF AILEACH
Co. Donegal

Grianán is an old Irish word for 'sunny place', and the stone fort in County Donegal which bears the name is splendidly sited on a strategic hill-top between the valleys of the Foyle and Swilly rivers, giving fine panoramas over good parts of Counties Donegal and Londonderry. As it stands, it is almost round, with a maximum interior diameter of 76.5 feet (23.3m), and its walls – 13-14 feet (4-4.3m) thick at the base –

incline gradually to a height of about 16 feet (5m). Inside, the walls are terraced, with a series of steps leading from one level to another and giving access to the parapet. On either side of the east-facing lintelled entrance passage (not visible in the accompanying photograph), there are low chambers within the thickness of the wall.

But it was not always as neat and tidy-looking as it is today. It owes its present form to considerable rebuilding undertaken in the 1870s by Dr Bernard, the Bishop of Derry, who found the walls only 5 feet (1.5m) high and much collapsed. This dilapidation was doubtless partially the result of

LEFT Lord of all it surveys on its prominent hill-top between two estuaries, the Grianán of Aileach was the age-old seat of the O'Loughlin kings of Aileach until destroyed by Muircheartach (otherwise Murtagh) O'Brien in 1101.

ABOVE Staigue Fort stands silently mysterious in a beautiful valley in south Kerry, keeping its past history very much to itself.

what happened to the fort when it was last mentioned in the early Irish historical sources. As the *Annals of the Four Masters* put it in the entry under the year 1101:

> Murtagh O'Brien, King of Munster, at the head of the forces of Leinster, Ossory, Meath and Connaught . . . demolished the Grianán of Aileach, in revenge for the destruction of Kincora by Donnell Mac Loughlin some time before [1088] and he ordered his army to bring from Aileach to Limerick a stone of the demolished building for every such of provisions which they had with them.

What is clear from the historical sources is that Aileach was the seat of the O'Loughlin kings of the northern Ui Néill dynasty, who were distinguished from other members of the extended family by bearing the title of Aileach, which encompassed their territory in Londonderry and the peninsula of Inishowen in County Donegal. Within the walls, we have to imagine a number of houses, now long vanished, which, while probably not particularly regal in size, would have included the 'palace' of the Kings of Aileach.

Precisely when the fort was built no one knows. An eleventh-century poem in the *Book of Lecan* traces Aileach's kings back to a Niall in the fifth century, and the *Tripartite Life of St Patrick*, written around 900, speaks of Aileach as having been the seat of ancient kings before the time of St Patrick. There is even a possibility that Aileach is to be identified with the *Regia* mentioned on the second-century map of the Greek geographer Ptolemy.

It has recently been suggested that the Grianán was more of a cult centre for tribal meetings than an inhabited seat of royal power, but the remains of three further walls of earth outside the stone wall – more easily traceable from the air than on the ground – might tend to negate that suggestion and indicate a defensive use. Whatever its function may have been, the stone fort is a notable monument, described by George Petrie, its most prominent historian, as having features of the first efforts in architectural art: *les ouvrages d'un art sans art*, 'the works of an art without art'!

STAIGUE FORT
Co. Kerry

There is a distinct similarity between the Grianán of Aileach and another equally famous counterpart far to the south, Staigue Fort, lying at a height of 500 feet (150m) near the head of a valley on the Iveragh Peninsula in County Kerry commonly known as 'The Ring of Kerry'. Staigue is only marginally larger, with an interior diameter of 78 feet (23.8m), and it too has interior stairways leading to the parapet as well as two small intermural passages. But, not having been reconstructed in the last century to the same extent as the Grianán, it gives us a better idea of the original appearance of these massive stone forts and, if anything, its masonry is of superior quality. Vertical joints in the wall show that gaps were left during construction which were later filled in. It will be noted that the walls of Staigue incline markedly on the outside, giving an outline which led Estyn Evans to compare them to the squat Scottish Iron Age stone fortifications known as brochs, suggesting that this Kerry monument may have been built during the prehistoric Iron Age.

Yet, one of the most remarkable facts which Staigue shares with Dún Aengus is that, for all its imposing size, it is nowhere mentioned in the early historical sources, leaving us to speculate on both its purpose and its date. For the eighteenth-century antiquary General Charles Vallancey it was a Phoenician Amphitheatre, and his nineteenth-century engineering colleague, Alexander Nimmo, saw it as an astronomical observatory. More recently, it has even been put forward as a safe haven for pilgrims on their way to Skellig Michael, situated some 12 miles (19km) off the end of the Iveragh Peninsula.

THE ARRIVAL OF THE CELTS

It was not until after 500 BC that iron gradually came to replace bronze as the main material used for implements and weapons, thus ushering in the Iron Age which continued on into the historic period. It remains an open question as to whether the technological change was caused by, or brought with it, the arrival of new population groups, large or small. One site now demonstrating a considerable degree of continuity between the Bronze Age and the Iron Age is Navan Fort in County Armagh, where the rebuilding of a series of round houses on the same spot over a period of six hundred years, starting around 700 BC, suggests consistent, if not necessarily continuous, usage over more than half a millennium. It was possibly generations of the same group of people who utilized the site for so long, and these people introduce us to the age-old problem of when the Celts arrived in Ireland.

People known to the Greeks as *keltoi* are recognizable on the European continent by the sixth century BC. In Britain and Ireland there were those who spoke 'P-Celtic', using the letter 'p' for instance in the word *map*, meaning 'son', and those who spoke 'Q-Celtic', using the letter 'q' in their word for son, *maq*, later to become the 'Mac' well-known as the first element in many Celtic family names. Inhabitants of Britain and Gaul spoke P-Celtic, and perhaps also the Cruithní in the north-east of Ireland, who were allied to the people known as Picts in Scotland. But, with the possible exception of a few small isolated pockets, the remainder of the country presumably spoke a Q-Celtic language, the ancestor of the Irish spoken daily in parts of Ireland today. There is very little agreement among scholars as to when speakers of Celtic (or what was in the process of becoming Gaelic) first arrived in Ireland, but the general consensus would now plead for a period sometime during the last millennium before Christ. We should not necessarily envisage their arrival as a one-off event, but rather as a gradual process involving aristocratic Celtic speakers coming to Ireland in many smaller groupings over a long period. What is clear, however, is that by the time historical native records make their appearance in the sixth century AD, Irish was the dominant language of the country which, by then, had become completely celticized.

Prior to that period, we have to rely on external evidence, coming largely from Greek sources, to learn more about the names of Irish tribes and places. The whole island was called *Ierne*, a name which the Romans adapted to *Hibernia*, the Latin word for 'winter', because they had the notion that a land which seemed to lie so far north should have been in a perpetual state of winter! However, the Romans also used an alternative name *Scottia*, and *Scotti* for its inhabitants, terms transferred to what is now Scotland after the Irish gained power there in the early historic period. There the name has stuck, whereas it has gone out of use in Ireland, the original *Scottia*.

Our most detailed written knowledge of pre-Christian Ireland comes from the Alexandrian Greek geographer Ptolemy, who constructed a map of Ireland around the second century AD, giving the rough location of physical features, tribes and other interesting information. Because the sources he used may have been derived from the accounts of Roman or British sailors, it is not surprising that most of the river names he gives are locatable on the east and south coasts of Ireland – such as the Boyne, the Lee and probably the Liffey – though he also recorded the estuary of the

Like a tattooed puff-ball bursting from the ground, the erratic granite boulder at Castlestrange, Co. Roscommon, is decorated all over with swirling patterns typical of the Celtic La Tène style of art and assignable, therefore, to the last few centuries before Christ.

Shannon on the west coast. Some tribes which Ptolemy places inland from the east coast can also be tentatively identified – the *Robogdii* may be the same as the later Dál Riata in County Antrim, and his *Voluntii* are probably the Ulaid, whose cult centre was Emain Macha or Navan Fort, mentioned above, which may be what he called *Isamnion*. The *Brigantes* of Wexford are probably related to the people of the same name in northern Britain, suggesting links across the Irish Sea, while in Munster Ptolemy's *Iverni* may be identified with the Erainn, a large group of tribes who occupied considerable areas of that province, but whose name came to be associated with the country as a whole. Ptolemy's *Auteni* are probably the Uaithne, who lived around the lower Shannon.

Archaeologically, the paucity of recognizable Iron Age material in the southern half of the country, including south Leinster, makes it difficult to associate objects with the peoples who lived there. But, particularly in the north and west of Ireland, a number of bronze items decorated in the La Tène style of central European Celtic origin suggest that they were the accoutrements of a (partially P-) Celtic-speaking people in the present provinces of Ulster and Connacht. These include not only Celtic stones like those at Turoe, Co. Galway, and Castlestrange, Co. Roscommon, but also beautifully ornamented sword-scabbards and horse-bits, which give the air of having belonged to a warrior aristocracy who used horses and probably chariots as well. It is the same areas of the country and roughly the same kind of equipment which we find occurring in the great heroic epic of ancient Ireland, the *Táin Bó Cuailnge*, the 'Cattle Raid of Cooley'. This is the tale of an attempt by Medb, a warrior-queen (though more probably a goddess originally) at Cruachain in the plains of Roscommon, to capture a great bull in the County Louth peninsula which gives the epic its name. To do so, she had to fight the forces of the Ulaid in central Ulster based at Emain Macha (Navan Fort), who are led by King Conor Mac Nessa, with the able support of the youthful super-hero Cú Chulainn. The characters in the various stories associated with this so-called 'Ulster Cycle' have a life-style which shares a number of characteristics with those attributed to the continental Celts by the Greek ethnographer Posidonius. These figures belong to a heroic society which was glorified by the Christian authors who compiled the epic many centuries after its main characters are meant to have lived, in the period preceding the coming of Christianity. Nevertheless, even taking all the literary exaggerations into account, the sagas may provide us with what the late Kenneth Jackson described as a 'window on the past', letting some light into prehistoric Celtic Ireland.

The two main royal foci of the *Táin*, Cruachain and Emain Macha (Navan Fort), have a counterpart at Dún Ailinne near Kilcullen in County Kildare, which must have been an important cult centre for the Laigin, the Iron Age inhabitants of Leinster. As in the area around Navan Fort, it too produced material of La Tène type. But excavations at both of these locations produced few indications of long-term human habitation, suggesting that they were more likely to have been significant cult centres rather than permanent settlements. Judging by the importance of these places, it is reasonable to assume that they must have been associated with the activity of kings of large tribal groupings, and the same can probably be inferred from one of the best-known sites of the kind – the Hill of Tara. This low hillock was, in the subsequent historic period, seen as the symbolic seat of the High King of Ireland, though it is extremely unlikely that any of the kings who actually lived there before the site was abandoned around the sixth century AD ever had political hegemony over the whole of Ireland. Instead, it was probably the centre of a cultic kingship and one which – long after Tara had reverted to nature – was a great and much sought-after symbolic prize. In this respect one feature of Tara is significant, namely that on the hill there was a Neolithic passage-grave of about 2000 BC, which was reused during the Early Bronze Age, suggesting that the 'Kings' of Tara sought a legitimation of their title by associating themselves with the burial place of remote ancestors who, however, may have been nothing of the sort. Generally, it is remarkable how little occupation material of Iron Age date has been found at royal sites which heroic literature would associate with happenings leading up to the dawn of the historic period in the time of St Patrick during the fifth century AD.

THE TUROE STONE
Co. Galway

Totem, phallic symbol, world centre or oracle stone as at Delphi? You could speculate about all of these functions, and more, for the decorated granite 4-ton boulder at Turoe, about 4 miles (6.4km) from Loughrea in County Galway, without arriving at any satisfactory conclusion. What we can, however, say for certain is that it bears one of the most sophisticated designs in the repertoire of the Celtic La Tène art style found in Ireland, and proof positive that Celtic craftsmen had penetrated as far as the west of Ireland by around the time of Christ. Like an

ornamental egg sitting in an egg-cup having its rim decorated with a step-pattern, the upper part of the stone is covered with a variety of Celtic art motifs – whirligigs, trumpet-ends, palmettes and even something resembling a puffin-like bird beak. These are all cleverly laid out to cover the 'dome' in a never-ending, swirling, restless motion of considerable tension and in an interplay of positive and negative elements created by cutting away the background in varying depths of relief.

What only became clear when Professor Michael Duignan and Pádraig Ó hÉailidhe examined and drew out the design on paper was that it was divided into four sections – two D-shaped and two triangular, each opposite one another – which suggested that the pattern was derived from one on a four-sided object, which must have had some symbolic significance (the four corners of the earth?). It was possibly conceived originally in wood rather than stone, though designs on bronze objects in Britain may have influenced it and contributed to its complexity.

Around the turn of the century, the stone was brought to Turoe as a garden ornament from its original position close to a circular rath or ringfort which bore the name Rath of Feerwore – Rath of the Strong Men (phallic significance?). It is one of five stones in Ireland decorated in a particular variant of the La Tène style which developed among the continental Celts in the Rhineland in the fourth/third century BC, but it may have taken more than two centuries before the style was adapted by the carver of the Turoe stone. Even though we know little about the religion of the prehistoric Celts of Ireland, this stone must be seen as one of its most powerful and artistic visual expressions, which doubtless had a religious significance now long beyond our ken.

Angular and curvilinear patterns on a granite boulder at Turoe, Co. Galway, attest to the presence of Celtic craftsmen in the west of Ireland during the last few centuries before Christ.

NAVAN FORT
Co. Armagh

In the famous old Irish epic, *Táin Bó Cuailnge* – where Connacht and Ulster forces fought each other singly, collectively, heroically and, ultimately, to no real avail – Navan Fort was the eye of the storm. The modern name Navan is derived from the first of two words which described the ancient site, Emain Macha, while the second element refers to its alleged founder, the war-goddess Macha. Here, 2 miles (3.2 km) west of the modern city of Armagh, was the seat of Conor Mac Nessa, the legendary King of the Ulstermen, central figurehead of the Red Branch Knights and protector of the youthful hero Cú Chulainn, who, single-handedly, caused the retreat of the Connacht forces. Here, too, Ireland's literary heroine, Deirdre, defied the aged king to whom she was betrothed and eloped with her lover Naoise, whom she had first set eyes upon as he sang upon the ramparts – with tragic consequences for both. Those ramparts, incidentally, have the ditch inside, indicating that they were not defensive.

Archaeologically, Navan Fort has turned out to be full of Celtic surprises. The larger of the two mounds on the hill-top proved, on excavation, to overlie a number of circular structures which replaced one another, generation after generation, from about 700 BC onwards. Their most unexpected revelation was the presence among the finds of the skull of a barbary ape, which came from north Africa in the third or second century BC, thus testifying to the far-flung relationships of the owners of the site, who were presumably the Ulaid (hence the name of the province Ulster), prior to the time before the dawn of recorded history when they were pushed eastwards from the territory .

But the greatest surprise was to be unveiled when Dudley Waterman excavated the large mound between 1961 and 1972. He found that four concentric and ever-larger rings of wooden posts – thicker than telegraph poles – had been erected around a large central pole with tree-rings indicating that it had been felled in 94 BC. This structure, 125 feet (38m) in diameter, was given a conical roof of thatch supported at the top by the central pole. Then probably within a decade, the whole interior was piled up with stones to a height of about 9 feet (2.7m), and all the poles set on fire, after which the area was covered with the earthen mound which we see today in its reconstructed form. This was no ordinary structure, and the immolation no ordinary burning. Only some extraordinary communal desire on the part of the tribe and its 'druids' can have willed such a massive destruction, the intention of which can only be guessed at two thousand years on. The ultimate (fertility?) sacrifice to a tribal god, an apocalyptic Armageddon or a charring of the sacred spot to preserve it for eternity? Who knows?

One thing is sure: this was a most hallowed cult centre, one of the most sacred of ancient Ireland, and a number of unusual finds in the surrounding area, particularly in a nearby lake, can only lend support to this conclusion. It is probably more than pure coincidence, too, that wood used in the construction of an oval walled enclosure known as the Dorsey, some 15 miles (24 km) to the south-south-east, was felled in the same year as the great central post in the Navan Fort structure.

An Interpretative Centre has been set up near the main road to explain the history and prehistory of Navan Fort with the latest 'state-of-the-art' technology.

DÚN AILINNE
Co. Kildare

It was as a result of the research done by John O'Donovan, the great Celtic scholar of the nineteenth century, that the royal site Dún Ailinne mentioned in early Irish sources was identified as the rounded hill-top near Kilcullen, Co. Kildare, which now bears the name. The earliest documentary records of the site, dating from the eighth or ninth century AD, imply that it was the seat of the Kings of Leinster though, paradoxically, it had probably already been abandoned by that date. But, even if no longer in use, it was still regarded by chroniclers of the time as an active symbol of the kingship of Leinster (of which the Uí Dúnlainge tribe were then the current dynasts), possibly the location of a fair and certainly a place of great antiquity.

This latter aspect was confirmed by Bernard Wailes when he excavated parts of the hill-top from 1968 to 1975 and found traces of human occupation going back to the Stone and Bronze Ages. However, it was during the Iron Age – and most likely the few centuries before and after the time of Christ – that the greatest activity took place there. That it was much more likely to have been a ritual site rather than a permanent settlement is suggested by the round earthen wall, 1200 feet (365m) in diameter, which sits on the brow of the hill-top like a garland, and by the ditch inside the bank, a feature also found at Navan Fort; fortifications usually have the ditch outside the bank.

On the summit, three phases of round wooden constructions were unearthed. The first was a palisade or fence consisting of upright posts forming a circle about 70 feet (21m) in diameter. The second, which partially covered the first but was not concentric with it, was larger (about 100 feet/30m in diameter) and had three concentric circles of posts, growing in size as the circles expanded, suggesting to the excavator that they may have borne tiered seats, but proof for this is lacking. The circles of this second phase were approached by lines of upright posts which narrowed like a funnel as they approached the entrance. The third phase was marked by the erection of what appears to have been a tall wooden tower at the centre of the circle.

One of the most remarkable features of all three phases was that the wooden posts were removed rather than being allowed to disintegrate *in situ* – a rather different method of destruction than that found at Navan Fort. The finds included an iron spear-head, two Roman brooches and a great number of animal bones, possibly the remains of great ritual Iron Age feasts, the dominant animal consumed having been pig, which played an important symbolic role among the Celts. Whatever Dún Ailinne was built for, it seems to have largely gone out of use by the third or fourth century AD, but it continued to be venerated as a place of important tribal memory when it first came to be recorded in historical sources three or four centuries later. In the intervening years Christianity had established its alternative centre on a rival hill at Old Kilcullen only a mile or so away, as it did also when it set up the see of Armagh on a hill not far from Navan Fort in the fifth century.

Covering the gently rounded hill-top near Kilcullen, Co. Kildare, Dún Ailinne was *the* ritual centre for the early kings of the province of Leinster.

THE HILL OF TARA
Co. Meath

Long before Thomas Moore ever made it world-famous through his ballad 'The harp that once through Tara's halls', the hill of Tara in 'royal' Meath was the most historic place in Ireland. A mere 512 feet (156m) above sea-level, it was admirably suited as a centre of Irish kingship because – in good weather – hills in all four of Ireland's provinces are said to be visible from its rounded summit. Significantly, perhaps, there is no view of the sea, which is only 17 miles (27 km) away.

Its oldest monument, known as the Mound of the Hostages, proved on excavation to be a passage-grave of the late third millennium BC, which was subsequently used for Bronze Age cremation burials. That such a Stone Age tomb should stand near the Rath, or Fort, of the Synods, called after a Church synod which Adamnan, abbot of Iona and St Columba's biographer, is alleged to have held there in 695 AD, is symptomatic of the way in which myth and history are closely interlinked on this venerable hill – to such an extent that it is impossible to untangle truth from fictional fable.

Even in the early Middle Ages Tara's links went back to the prehistoric past, and the written sources of the time hint at its connection with various legendary figures of the heroic period before St Patrick's time. We get intimations that Medb 'the drunken' or 'the one who makes drunk' was the prime goddess of the royal hill, and he who would wish to establish himself as King of Tara would have to unite with her after he had drunk ale or wine as the symbol of her sovereignty of Tara. However, Lug, the good god of the pagan Celts, was also part of Tara's pagan pantheon.

Ancient lore sees its most famous king as Cormac Mac Airt, who is alleged to have lived in the early centuries after Christ. Another was Loegaire, who according to a probably apocryphal story led the losing side in the druidic contest with St Patrick over the lighting of the Easter Fire in 433 AD. Indeed, the hill was suffused with pagan druidry, doubtless a formal part of the ritual sacral kingship which the essence of Tara is likely to have been. It was certainly no normal kingship, but rather a cult distinction to be obtained only occasionally by a monarch with power and potential. As priest and king, he would watch over the circular rampart which crowns the hill and which literary sources saw as defending the site against hostile predators from the Otherworld.

Historic records suggest that the Laigin, the Leinstermen, had an early interest in the place, but that probably became a thing of the past when the Uí Néill dynasty took over the area known as Brega, in which Tara lies. It was they who fostered the legend and developed the notion of the High Kingship of Ireland associated with Tara, though the hill had probably been long abandoned when the High Kingship began to become a distinct reality in the eighth or ninth century. According to the old Irish Annals Tara's destruction was caused by a curse which St Ruadhán of Lorrha had called down on it and its king in the mid-sixth century. Whatever the historical truth of that invocation may have been, it is likely that, with the triumph of Christianity, Tara's role as a centre of pagan druidry and sacral kingship had at last outlived its usefulness. The king whom St Ruadhán had cursed was Diarmait mac Cerbaill, who was probably the last of Ireland's pagan monarchs and the one who presided over the final sovereign feast of Tara. After that, it was a question of 'The druid king is dead; long live the Christian king'. Tara was probably deserted shortly afterwards, but

its place as the evocation of Ireland's past was assured, a reputation which was to continue throughout and after the Middle Ages – to be used by Daniel O'Connell for a thronged political rally he addressed here in 1843 – and which still lasts down to our own day, evinced by the Interpretative Centre in the converted nineteenth-century church on the hill.

The rounded hump of Tara Hill is enclosed around its summit by the rampart mentioned earlier. It is known as Ráth na Ríogh, or the Rath of the Kings, and has that tell-tale sign of a ritual site, namely the ditch placed inside the bank, as at Navan Fort and Dún Ailinne. This and other monuments on the hill get their names from a description in the *Dinnshenchas*, a set of poems about place-name lore collected in the early eleventh century. While they ought to be taken with some grains of historical salt, the names are useful as tags for the various earthworks which dot the hill. These monuments are more easily distinguishable from the air, as they often fail to live up to the expectations of those walking the ground who expect something more dramatic from a site of such historic significance. To avoid disappointment, it is best to realise that all of Tara's palatial grandeur was built of wood, a material which is as ephemeral in the Irish climate as the pagan sacral kingship itself proved to be.

Given that Tara was a ritual site of surpassing importance, it is difficult to know how far the grass-grown mounds and earthworks we see today were used for permanent occupation. Many may have been utilized temporarily only when sacred functions demanded. Within Ráth na Ríogh are two conjoined rath-like smaller structures, one known as the Forradh – King's House or Royal Seat – and the other Cormac's House, where the mythical king lived, at least in the eyes of the medieval poet. Placed there now is the Stone of Destiny, the Lia Fáil, which, legend says, cried out when a proper king was inaugurated. In shape it seems like an Iron Age phallic cult stone associated with royal fertility, and it originally stood atop the Mound of the Hostages, that prehistoric passage-tomb which may have been interpreted as holding the ancestral remains of earlier prehistoric rulers of the site.

Close by is the Rath of the Synods. Between 1899 and 1902 it was the focus of rude digging activity by the British Israelites in their – need one say – fruitless search for the biblical Ark of the Covenant, the result of a 'revelation' contained in a pamphlet bought at a second-hand bookstall in London's Charing Cross Road. Just over fifty years later the rath was excavated by Seán P. Ó Ríordáin, Professor of Archaeology at University College, Dublin. While we still await the publication of the excavation report, it is known that a burial mound there was later overlain by a series of multi-period, round, wooden enclosures which, in turn, were followed by inhumation and cremation burials. These last produced Roman pottery and glass which help to date them to the early centuries AD, so that the enclosures may have been constructed at a slightly earlier date.

In line with, and to the north of, the Rath of the Synods, is a long sunken rectangular area lined on the long sides by low banks. Medieval accounts identify this as enclosing the Banqueting Hall, and the twelfth-century *Book of Leinster* even goes so far as to indicate with a diagram where the royal attendants of various grades took their festive seats in the presence of the king. Despite this imaginative interpretation, the so-called Banqueting Hall may have functioned as a ceremonial entrance to the hill, where all the roads of ancient Ireland are said to have converged. Not far away is another rath which medieval topographers associated with Gráinne,

The Hill of Tara, Co. Meath, is the most historic place in all Ireland, having played an important mythical and symbolic role in the country from the Stone Age to the nineteenth century, including that of nominal centre of the 'High Kingship' of Ireland. In the centre of the picture is the passage-grave known as the Mound of the Hostages, and to the left are the conjoint circles called the Forradh and Cormac's House. The Rath of the Synods adjoins the churchyard, and the 'Banqueting Hall' can be seen running off at an angle on the extreme right.

heroine and tragic lover, who figured in the tale of Diarmuid and Gráinne. There are many other earthworks on the hill, including probable Bronze Age ring-barrows (very low circluar mounds) discovered by the aerial photography of Leo Swan. Recent work by Conor Newman and his team, as part of the Discovery Programme, is helping to provide us with a modern computer-aided map of this venerable site, which is embedded in the Irish imagination as the centre of power of the Irish High Kingship and the visual embodiment of the glory of the Gael.

CHAPTER TWO

THE EARLY
MIDDLE AGES

THE POLITICAL SCENE

The earliest Irish historical records, dating from the sixth century AD, show that, by then, the political face of Ireland had undergone considerable changes since Ptolemy had made his map some four hundred years before. Many of the tribes he mentioned had virtually disappeared, and in Munster the Erainn were gradually being replaced by the Eóganachta (pronounced 'Owen-achta'), who made Cashel their capital. But it was the northern half of the country which experienced the greatest upheaval, with the rapid expansion of the Uí Néill (pronounced 'E-Nay-al') dynasty from their original base in the west of Ireland. One branch moved to Ulster, where they banished the Ulaid from the cult centre at Navan Fort, and set up their own northern Kingdoms of Tyrone and Tirconnell (Donegal). Another section of the family, known as the Southern Uí Néill, moved eastwards across the Shannon to capture the sacral Kingship of Tara, apparently thereby pushing back the old Leinster tribe known as the Laigin to the area south of the River Liffey.

By the sixth century the newly drawn political boundaries had stabilized, but this did not prevent the various branches of the Uí Néill dynasty squabbling for centuries among themselves in search of greater power. Their ultimate goal was domination over the whole country by making the High Kingship of Ireland a reality, a feat not actually achieved before the middle of the ninth century.

This picture of predictable internecine rivalries was soon, however, to be blasted out of its complacency by new players appearing on the scene from outside. In the last five years of the eighth century the Vikings made their first raids upon the east coast of Ireland. These were men hungry for booty, slaves, wealth, food and later land, and they came particularly from southern Norway in speedy and manoeuvrable boats powered by sail and oar, which enabled them to make lightning strikes inland and get away as quickly as they had come, before the Irish had time to organise a counterattack. The seas around Ireland, from being what the historian E.G. Bowen described as a Celtic thalassocracy, quickly became a Nordic lake. Undaunted by the Atlantic rollers, the Vikings circumnavigated the whole island, as we know from annalistic references to their descents on Inishmurray and Skellig Michael in the earlier ninth century.

Ireland must have appeared sufficiently lucrative and attractive for settlement that, from 840 onwards, the Vikings set up seaside colonies at

Silver, which the Vikings had probably brought back with them from overseas raids, became an increasingly popular material around 900 for the manufacture of brooches – some, like the bossed penannular brooch on the right, more in the Irish tradition, others, like the 'thistle' brooch on the left and the kite-shaped example in the centre, appealing more to purely Viking tastes.

Dublin, Wexford, Waterford and Cork as well as Limerick, which they soon found to be a useful springboard for making forays up the River Shannon as far as Lough Ree. Dublin, in particular, quickly developed into a mercantile depot of major international significance, a half-way house between Scandinavia and France where goods could be bartered and stored. The location of the earliest Viking settlement on the Liffey has yet to be found, but lengthy excavations have uncovered well-preserved Viking houses of the tenth and subsequent centuries in the area around Christ Church Cathedral in Dublin.

Because contemporary and slightly later chroniclers saw the Vikings as nasty marauding monk-bashers, they had a very bad press in Ireland until their vital contribution to the developing town of Dublin came to be recognized in the 1970s, and people began to appreciate that the Vikings were

Inscriptions which Liam de Paor deciphered a decade ago on this fragmentary High Cross at Castlebernard, Co. Offaly, revealed that it was erected by Maelsechlainn I, High King of Ireland between 846 and 862. This is the earliest identifiable cross erected by an Irish king, and one surely not without a hint of self-glorification.

not just battle-lusty booty-seekers, but folk who contributed to Irish life in two specific areas of activity – ship-building and trade. The Nordic inhabitants of the new maritime towns taught the Irish the advantages of commerce as well as the use of coinage, which was introduced in 997. Pagans at first, they gradually adopted Christianity and by the tenth century were happily intermarrying with the Irish. Such was their influence in the country that the element '-ster' found in the names of three of the Irish provinces is Scandinavian in origin.

At first, the Irish were incapable of mounting an effective counter-offensive, because, among other reasons, they were squabbling for power among themselves. Yet, some of the Irish were quick to realize the advantages of enlisting the help of Viking settlers in making war on their Irish royal rivals, while at the same time the Vikings were involved in internal feuds, particularly with their own people in Britain.

The years from 830 to 860 and 910 to 930 experienced the worst of the Viking attacks on Ireland, and the main efforts to curb their ferocity during these periods were undertaken by the Clann Cholmáin branch of the Southern Uí Neill. In these struggles two of its dynasts stand out as exceptional: Maelsechlainn I (846-62), who was among the first who could legitimately claim to be High King of Ireland, and his son Flann Sinna (879-916), who, for a time, halted Munster aggression against the Uí Néill by overcoming the King-Bishop of Cashel, Cormac mac Cuilleannáin, at the battle of Ballaghmoon in 908, a defeat from which the Eóganachta never really recovered.

It was not until the second half of the tenth century that the Irish began the final assault against Norse power in Ireland, and here again it is two Irish kings who can take most of the credit for it. The first of these was Maelsechlainn II (980-1002 and 1014-22), who defeated the Vikings at Tara in 980 before going on, in the following year, to take the city of Dublin and exact a heavy tribute from its inhabitants. The second was Brian Boru of the Dál Cais (1002-14), a hitherto insignificant tribe in County Clare, who started his career by filling the power vacuum in Munster after the Eóganacht decline. His meteoric rise over a few decades temporarily robbed the Uí Néill of the High Kingship of Ireland and also included a heavy defeat of the Kingdom of Leinster and the Norse of Dublin in the battle of Glenmáma in 999, after which Brian, too, sacked the city. On a visit to Armagh six years later, he could have himself described as the 'Emperor of the Irish', and it looked as if he had finally paved the way for a strong centralized Irish monarchy. Then came the Battle of Clontarf in 1014, which older history books saw as the final eclipse of Viking power in Ireland, with Brian bringing the victor's laurels with him to the grave. But, because the Norse fought on both sides, recent historians have come to regard the battle more as an effort by rival Irish kings to destroy further Dál Cais ambitions.

Clontarf took a heavy toll on Brian's family, for two of his sons fell along with him. Those who survived were not strong enough to claim the High Kingship, leaving the way open for Maelsechlainn II to reclaim his title – and to be the last of the Uí Néill kings of Tara to reign in the old style until his death in 1022. Politically, the remainder of the eleventh century was characterized by a number of provincial kings claiming the High Kingship, including O'Brien descendants of Brian Boru, but with none of them being able to maintain their claims because of the force of the opposition from rival claimants. Paradoxically, it was Dublin, the city of the defeated Ostmen (the name the Vikings gave themselves), which reaped the benefit from all this strife by becoming an increasingly important European city during the eleventh century, and the Irish kings vied for control of it, many of them becoming its king for short periods during the eleventh and twelfth centuries.

However, the native Irish were not interested in moving to the cities themselves, preferring to remain rooted in a rural society heavily stratified both socially and legally. Its simple domestic architecture has not withstood the test of time, but modern reconstructions have been created at Craggaunowen in County Clare, Gortin in County Tyrone and at the National Heritage Park near Wexford town to show what they might have looked like originally.

RATHS, OR RING FORTS

Probably the commonest field monument of early medieval Ireland is the rath, or ring fort, of which upwards of 30,000 are known to have existed. Their usually isolated location scattered in the landscape shows them to have been the homesteads of the better-off farmers – being really the forerunners of the country house or cottage of today, surrounded by its hedge. Raths normally consisted of a simple circular bank of raised earth (probably once surmounted by a wooden palisade, made more for the protection of animals than humans), though on rare occasions the addition of one or two extra earthen rings would have been perceived as adding to the status of the builder. The interiors are now invariably empty, but we have to imagine that one or more round or rectangular houses would once have stood inside. Occasionally, there is access to an underground passage known as a souterrain, which frequently had another entrance outside the bank, possibly suggesting an escape route or hiding place, though these are more likely to have been storage places for grain or other domestic produce, predecessors of the ice-house and refrigerator, rather than places of refuge.

Folklore called these raths 'Danes' Forts', suggesting that they were defences erected by the Vikings. But here folk tradition is likely to have erred, as they do not appear to have any connection with the Norsemen, nor indeed would they have been suitable to protect either man or beast against even a small marauding army. Old Irish literature suggests, rather, that they were domestic dwelling places, sometimes known by the name of *rath,* or otherwise *lios.* Occasionally, in areas where stone was more plentiful, they bear the name *cathair* (anglicized 'caher'), a word containing the element *cath* 'battle' which does, however, suggest a fortification of some sort.

While the earliest examples may have been constructed during the Iron Age, the great majority would seem to belong to the early medieval period, up to the coming of the Normans, and one example – Cahermacnaughten in the Burren region of County Clare – is known to have continued in use as a law school down to the seventeenth century.

A RECONSTRUCTED CRANNOG
Craggaunowen, Co. Clare

Crannogs were an old Irish type of settlement which is very difficult to reconstruct from the small tree-covered islet in a lake which is usually all that remains to be seen of them today. That is why the late John Hunt, the philanthropist, decided over twenty years ago to make it easier for us to

BELOW Cahermacnaughten was the centre of a famous law school as late as the seventeenth century, but the raised interior surface of this stone fort, with its accumulated debris of generations, suggests that it had been inhabited for many hundreds of years before that.

RIGHT The late John Hunt reconstructed a crannog at Craggaunowen, Co. Clare, to demonstrate what one of these artificial island settlements might have looked like in Ireland a thousand years ago.

envisage their former appearance by constructing one at Craggaunowen in County Clare. A crannog is, in effect, a man-made island, built up by laying down stones in shallow water until they rose above the surface, covering them with brush wood (hence the name 'crannog', derived from the Gaelic word *crann*, meaning a 'tree' or 'wood') and finally adding a layer of earth on which houses would have been built. The islet was finished off by being given a palisade of wood around the perimeter.

These crannogs were more like fortifications than raths, as anyone approaching by dug-out would have been vulnerable to attack. Some of them, however, may have been reachable from the land by a causeway, making them less defensive. An unexpected rise in lake level could have caused flooding, and they can scarcely have been suitable dwellings for anyone suffering from rheumatism. While some may date to the prehistoric period, the wood with which they were constructed has shown a consistent series of felling dates around the seventh century AD. One Ulster map, however, shows them to have been still in use as late as the seventeenth century.

ROMANIZATION AND THE SPREAD OF CHRISTIANITY

Tacitus, the Roman historian, quotes his father-in-law Agricola as saying often in the first century AD that 'Ireland could be reduced and held by a single legion and a few auxiliaries' but that, as far as history is concerned, was the nearest the Romans came to conquering the country. Yet, it would be wrong to conclude from this that Romans never came to Ireland or that Roman influence on Ireland was lacking. Archaeological evidence would suggest the presence of Roman immigrants, probably refugees from Britain, on the island of Lambay around the time of Agricola, and they may have crossed to the mainland and settled on the promontory of Dromanagh at Loughshinny, about 20 miles (32 km) north of Dublin.

But it is in the fourth and fifth centuries that Irish contacts with Roman Britain become noticeably closer. It is at this period that the Déise tribe from County Waterford crossed the Irish Sea to found colonies in Wales and south-western Britain; encounters there with the Roman alphabet probably served as the basis for the development of the Ogham script, which, through its use on stone monuments in the Déise homeland, provides us with the earliest written examples of the Irish language. Marginally later perhaps, the Dál Riata, who lived in the Glens of Antrim, made the much shorter sea crossing across the North Channel and occupied parts of south-western Scotland, to which they gave the name of their own country, *Scottia*. Irish mercenaries are now believed to have served in the Roman army in Britain – and beyond – and, on returning home, some of these expatriate Irish may have been involved in the setting up of the Eóganacht kingdom at Cashel in County Tipperary, the name of which is derived from a Latin word for fortress, *castellum*.

By the fourth century the power of Rome was beginning to crumble in Britain, a state of affairs not lost on the Irish, who set about plundering what they could from the collapsing empire. The Laigin in Leinster may well have been involved in these expeditions, and there are hints that the Uí Néill, too, may have been taking advantage of the situation in a similar fashion, probably in the fifth century. By far the most dramatic confirmation of this activity comes from the pen of no less a person than St Patrick himself, who describes how Irish raiders took him captive as a child from his (as yet unidentified) home, probably in northern Britain, and brought him back to Ireland as a slave. He later escaped, only to hear in a dream the voice of the Irish calling on him to return. He had himself ordained a priest, and came back to Ireland to start his successful campaign to evangelize the Irish.

But he was, almost certainly, not the first to have done so. Disputed accounts of the existence of missionaries before St Patrick, including St Declan of Ardmore, tell of their activities in the south-east of Ireland, which would suggest that Christianity was first introduced into Ireland from south-western Britain, if not directly from late Roman Gaul. Indeed, the very first reference we have to Christianity in Ireland occurs in the works of the Gaulish chronicler, Prosper of Aquitaine, who tells us that in AD 431 Pope Celestine sent Palladius (probably a deacon at Auxerre in central France) as the first bishop to the Irish believing in Christ. Prosper's announcement confirms that there were already Christians in Ireland at the time and it may well have been they who requested the presence of a bishop. Muirchú, one of St Patrick's earliest biographers in the seventh century, claimed a link between St Patrick and Germanus of Auxerre, but it seems likely that later Irish sources confused and conflated Palladius and Patrick, melting them into one and the same person. For more than fifty years scholars have hotly debated the problems of St Patrick's life and mission, leaving, as one commentator put it, no stone unthrown. One of the difficult questions is whether he died in 461 or 493, but the tide now seems to be turning in favour of the latter year, though this would cast some doubt on the date of 444/5 as the foundation year of his principal bishopric in Armagh. What we can say, however, is that Patrick was a humble yet obviously forceful personality who, during the course of the fifth century, carried out a successful christianizing mission in the northern half of Ireland and apparently as far west as Mayo.

It has been widely assumed that St Patrick founded a number of bishoprics and that his church was organized on a diocesan basis. Such an assumption would be quite plausible, as this was the kind of church which he would have known when growing up in Britain, where the Roman towns would have provided both base and congregation for a bishopric. But, as the Ireland of the time was a country of isolated homesteads without the advantages of towns to provide support for a bishop, it has been thought that this nascent diocesan organization withered and died within a generation of St Patrick's death, and that the ensuing vacuum was, almost of necessity, filled by the creation of monasteries which sprang up like mushrooms in the green fields of Ireland during the course of the sixth century. St Patrick himself does not say that he founded any dioceses, and the sources which credit him with the creation of bishoprics date from almost two centuries after his death, when they were probably used for propaganda purposes. It is, therefore, not unreasonable to query whether St Patrick really did set up a network of dioceses in Ireland and to ask whether the 'Church' which he helped to found was properly organized at all, as the national apostle may have had to put more energy into conversion than organization. Nevertheless, it must be said that, while monasteries certainly became the dominant Church leaders in the second half of the sixth century, bishops who had been properly ordained, but did not have dioceses, continued to play an important role in the seventh and subsequent centuries, as it was their duty to see to the administration of the sacraments, even in the smaller parish churches.

ABOVE St Patrick's Cathedral in Dublin proudly displays this statue as a figure of St Patrick, the national apostle to whom the cathedral is dedicated, but the identification may be taken with some grains of salt, as head and body originally belonged to totally separate monuments.

RIGHT The Rock of Cashel has been linked with the name of St Patrick since the seventh century. Legend says that, while baptising the local king Oengus there, the saint accidentally thrust the pointed end of his crozier through the foot of the monarch who, thinking it was all part of the ceremony, suffered the incident in silence.

St Patrick was, seemingly, well disposed towards monasticism, and a number of his converts are thought to have become monks and nuns. He wanted to visit Gaul, presumably because he saw it as the home of Western monasticism, but there is no reason to believe that he ever got there. It was, however, to the leading churchmen in the neighbouring island of Britain that the Irish monastic founders of the sixth century looked for inspiration and guidance – St Ninian of Candida Casa (Whithorn) in Galloway in

south-western Scotland, St David in Wales and Gildas in Britain. One of the earliest Irish monastic founders is thought to have been St Enda of Aran, who died around 530. He is said to have studied in Whithorn, but we know insufficient about him to evaluate his role properly in the development of Irish monasticism. Slightly later, and considerably more important, was St Finnian of Clonard in County Meath, a monastery which was to be very significant in the centuries to come, but of which nothing remains today. He is said to have had twelve outstanding disciples, including Columba of Durrow and Derry, Ciarán of Clonmacnoise, Brendan the Navigator – born near Ardfert Co. Kerry and buried at Clonfert, Co. Galway – as well as St Molaise of Devenish, Co. Fermanagh.

Saints Finnian and Ciarán both fell victims to the disastrous plague which had been spreading throughout Europe during the 540s, and it is noticeable that the numbers who joined monasteries swelled considerably in

its wake. While the plague, and famine associated with poor crop growth, may have been factors which contributed to the popularity of monasticism at the time, another probable reason which attracted the Irish to this ascetic life-style was the desire to renounce the world, not so much to get away from its evil ways, as had been the case with the early desert fathers in Egypt, but to leave behind the good in search of something better, a higher spiritual goal. There were, however, other monasteries which developed independently of the influence of Clonard, and these included Bangor in County Down, founded by St Comgall, Glendalough in County Wicklow where St Kevin came to pray among the mountains, and Cork, founded by St Fionnbar, to name only some of the most important.

From this list of early monasteries, one might get the impression that there were no convents for nuns. That this was not in fact the case is shown by St Brigit's monastery (for both nuns and monks) at Kildare, St Ita's at Killeedy in County Limerick, where St Brendan the Navigator was fostered, and St Moninne's at Killevy in Co. Armagh. We know that women were equally, if not indeed more, attracted to the religious way of life than men, but the comparative paucity of convents was probably due to the fact that, by old Irish law, women were only allowed a life interest in land, which would have to be returned to their kin on their death, so that the chances of a convent having a long life were thereby considerably reduced.

For the male monasteries, the land on which they stood was granted by the more affluent and important families, and it was they who usually provided the abbots over a number of generations. Thus, the founders tended to have an aristocratic background. One of the rare exceptions was St Ciarán of Clonmacnoise, and many of his successors were drawn from lesser tribes and doubtless chosen more for their qualities than their blood. The aristocratic background of the abbots of most monasteries led to their being, in terms of status, the equivalents of local kings, thereby helping to integrate church and lay society. That this tendency went even beyond the bounds of the country itself is shown by the case of Iona, that beatific monastery on an island in the western Hebrides founded in 563 by St Columba, ten of whose twelve successors as abbot belonged to the same family as himself, the Cenél Conaill in County Donegal.

St Columba, or Colm Cille (pronounced 'Cullum-kill-yeh') to give him his Irish name, was undoubtedly one of the most remarkable churchmen in early medieval Ireland. For many, he is remembered today for the (possibly apocryphal) tale of having surreptitiously copied a manuscript of the Gospels without permission, and being forced to return it to its owner by the king of the time who settled the matter by pronouncing the world's first copyright judgment with the words, 'To every cow its calf, to every book its copy'. The tale further relates that he went to war because he considered the judgment to have been unfair and that 2000 people lost their lives in the ensuing battle. Thereupon, the saint is said to have decided to leave the country and go overseas to found his monastery on Iona. We have no way of knowing whether this voyage was entirely of his own volition or not, but he himself saw his voluntary exile as a form of self-penance, renouncing his native heath to go on pilgrimage for the sake of God and to evangelize the heathen, thereby starting a trend which many others were to follow.

We know something of the appearance of these early monasteries through the saint's *Life* written by St Adamnan, a late seventh-century abbot of Iona, who provides us with a valuable contemporary insight into

RIGHT One of the few surviving architectural remnants of an early Irish convent is the cyclopean lintelled doorway at Killevy in County Armagh, where a community of nuns was established by St Moninne, who died in 517 or 519. Dating perhaps from the tenth or eleventh century, the doorway was retained to serve as the entrance for a later medieval church on the same site.

LEFT A cross-carved stone beckons pilgrims to stop and pray in the remote west Donegal valley of Glencolmcille, which bears the name of St Columba – in Irish, *Colmcille* – though no early record exists of his ever having visited this beguiling glen.

ABOVE St Columba was born in Donegal and in 563 set out on pilgrimage for Scotland, where he founded the monastery of Iona in the Outer Hebrides. Certain sites in his native county suggest Scottish links, including Carndonagh, where this pillar bears a figure with bell, book and staff – possibly representing a pilgrim coming to venerate some relic of the saint there.

the physical make-up of the monastery. It was enclosed within a *vallum*, a wall of earth, and its main centre was a wooden church. In front of this was a *platea*, or open courtyard, around which other buildings of the monastery were grouped – a refectory and a scriptorium for writing, as well as the monks' domestic quarters, though the abbot's house was probably larger and set somewhat apart from them. In addition, there would also have been the community's cemetery.

From Iona St Columba's monks, after his death, were to penetrate through Scotland as far as northern England, where Lindisfarne became the most important foundation. But in the course of the following centuries many others were to follow the footsteps of St Columba in leaving their country to go overseas, not only on pilgrimage, or *peregrinatio* as it was known, but also to spread the word of God to areas which had been devastated earlier by the wandering Germanic tribes. Prime among these was St Columbanus who set out from Bangor, on the shores of Belfast Lough, and went to France where, although running foul of the local monarch for his outspoken remarks about the king's extramarital affairs, he was very influential in setting up important Merovingian monasteries. But he continued from there across the Alps to found his last monastery at Bobbio in northern Italy, where he died around 613. He was something of a mystic in his writings and was bold enough to query even the pope himself on the thorny question of the date of Easter, when he maintained that the Irish celebrated Easter on the day determined by the true tradition of the apostles, rather than that worked out by new-fangled computations introduced on the continent in the fifth century. One of his disciples was St Gall, whom he left behind in Switzerland at the place where the modern town bearing his name now stands and where the old monastic library preserves important manuscripts brought there by Irish monks more than a thousand years ago.

49

Returning once again to St Columba (not to be confused with St Columbanus), it may be said that, according to tradition, he managed to prevent the poets of Ireland from being banished from their country because of their avarice and arrogance, and thereby preserved the literary tradition which has continued to make Ireland famous down to our own century. Columba himself had the reputation of having loved books, and the earliest surviving manuscript, the so-called *Cathach* (battle talisman) preserved in the Royal Irish Academy in Dublin, could conceivably have even been written by the hand of St Columba himself. It may be noted, too, that the monasteries which he and his successors founded have produced the most famous codices to survive in Britain and Ireland from the first millennium – the Books of Durrow, Lindisfarne and Kells – which would never have been created without the activities and, one might almost say, the prescience of St Columba.

By the time St Columba died in 597, Ireland had become unique in Europe in having most of its churches ruled by a monastic hierarchy, and their libraries contained works descended from classical antiquity, not just the writings of the Church Fathers but of classical Latin authors as well, a number of which the Irish can claim to have preserved for posterity. In that sense, there is much wisdom in Cardinal John Henry Newman's description of these monasteries as 'the storehouse of the past and the birthplace of the future'. The fifth-century Church had introduced Latin script as well as a knowledge of Latin, and this heritage stood the monasteries in good stead, for the Irish monks learned to write a fluent Latin, as witnessed by the works of Columbanus and the commentaries which the monks wrote on the Bible and the Church Fathers.

It would be wrong to think that the activities of St Patrick and his fellow-missionaries in the fifth century succeeded in converting the Irish to instant Christianity. This was a much more long-drawn-out process, but it would seem to have been completed by the end of the sixth century, aided by the first flush of monastic foundations. Yet a great change was to come over these monasteries in the course of the next hundred years, in that many of them became secularized as they integrated into the social hierarchy of the time, even becoming, in the case of Kildare, the seat of kings. Indeed, in some cases one may well ask whether they should be described as monasteries at all, because many are unlikely to have had ordained clergy among their community, and probably rarely even saw a priest. Pastoral care receded; priests became a rare commodity and – like clergy today – frequently had to service a number of isolated churches. Within their own *tuath* (petty kingdom) these priests were entitled to a house and rations, including a milch cow four times a year and food on feast days.

Bishops, meanwhile, continued to play an important role, and the celibate bishops were the most respected of clerics. Their function, in addition to that of adminstering the sacraments, was the care of churches and liturgical furnishings, and they lived, among other things, from burial fees. But in the larger monasteries, where many of the bishops would have resided, the people who really mattered were the abbot and his prior. The former was the one who had temporal control, and dynastically minded abbots had the status of local kings. Their honourable position ensured, too, that they were influential in the making of laws. As the Christian Church and what had formerly been a pagan society came closer by the seventh century, a potential collision between ecclesiastical and secular law was avoided by the Church taking the leading role. Through the laws which were codified

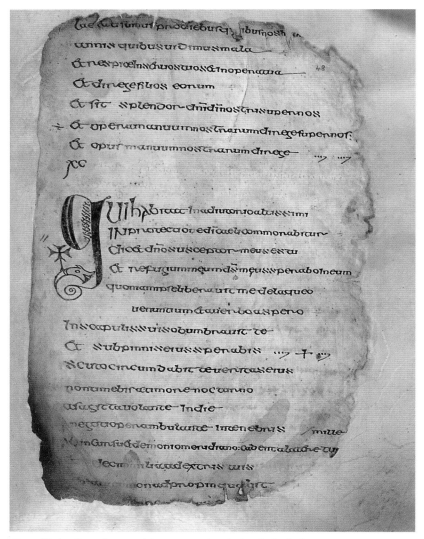

One of Ireland's earliest surviving manuscripts is the *Cathach*, the greatest treasure now housed in the Royal Irish Academy in Dublin. Its Irish name indicates that it was formerly brought into battle as a talisman by the O'Donnells, St Columba's own family. It is a copy of the Psalms, written in black ink and with the initials decorated with trumpet and spiral patterns and, in one instance, a fish and a cross. These first letters of each psalm are also enlarged, and the succeeding letters get gradually smaller until they are of the same size as the remainder of the text – a trait continued and embellished later in the *Book of Durrow*. The *Cathach* is usually dated to the period around 600, so that there could be some truth in the age-old tradition that the manuscript may have been written by 'the man who loved books', St Columba himself, who died in 597.

at this time, the laity came to provide a certain amount of upkeep for the clergy in return for religious services – preaching, baptism and burial. Those churchmen known as *Romani,* who unsuccessfully tried to win over the Irish to the values of Roman law, did at least triumph in finally convincing the Irish to adopt the celebration of Easter on the day computed by Rome, though this did not happen without a struggle.

The Church establishments varied in size and kind – some were free, others unfree, but the major change visible in the seventh and eighth centuries was the development of the larger 'monasteries' into what were really small towns of a secular nature. They fulfilled the role of landlords, were purveyors of social services, patrons of the arts, fosterers of the sons of the nobility, and storehouses for grain and regal valuables. Around the central church, the area of sanctuary and the community cemetery, there grew on the periphery of the monasteries whole quarters where craftsmen lived and also lay tenants who, though called *manaig* (Irish for 'monks'), were in fact married – even if they were not permitted the luxury of polygamy allowed by secular law. They were expected to attend certain church services and, in return, got free education for their children, the first-born of whom normally had to be offered to the church. The *manaig* must have spent much of their day working in the fields, and they almost certainly made up the majority of people associated with these monastic 'proto-towns'. This work-force ensured that the monastic land was extensively worked, aided by the recently introduced heavy plough, which could not only break the ground but turn the sod as well. Another innovation for which the monasteries were probably responsible was the watermill – both horizontal and vertical – which was used to grind the grain that belonged to the monastery or that the monastery stored for local potentates.

Slowly but surely, these monasteries were developing into market centres important for the regional economy, and the expanding population in the monastic towns must have required a greater degree of physical planning, in the laying out of and cobbling of streets, for instance, and in the preparation of cemetery land. Gradually evolving an urban status, the monasteries busied themselves with building up the portfolio of their church properties often well beyond the bounds of the monastery, and sometimes even beyond the provincial boundary. None was more assiduous in building an ecclesiastical empire than Armagh itself, which changed from an episcopal to an abbatial regime in the course of building up its jurisdictional claims. Though Armagh could not boast possession of St Patrick's relics (for no one knew any longer where he had been buried), it sought primacy over the whole of Ireland because of the bishopric which it claimed the national apostle had founded there in the fifth century. From the seventh century onwards Armagh created a whole cult for St Patrick in order to further its own proprietorial ends. The *Book of Armagh*, now in the Library of Trinity College, Dublin, and written around 807, contains many important documents about the saint, including biographical sketches by Tirechán and Muirchú, whose purpose was to aggrandize Armagh through publicizing the glorious activities of St Patrick. But this was done at the expense of the other fifth-century missionaries, particularly Palladius, whose work was apparently swept under the carpet and credited instead to St Patrick himself (though an Easter table compiled by Palladius survived into the seventh century).

But while it claimed supremacy, Armagh was by no means alone in expanding its sphere of influence in the seventh century. Clonmacnoise, in the midlands, was seen as one of its rivals, and this we know because Tirechán railed against the claims that Clonmacnoise was making to certain churches, which Armagh felt were its preserve. The other two important centres during the seventh and eighth centuries were Kildare and Iona. Though overseas, in the Scottish Kingdom of Dál Riata, the latter had built up a monastic federation, or *paruchia*, a family of monasteries which were affiliated with one another and shared a common monastic founder in St Columba. Kildare countered the territorial encroachments of Armagh and tried to add to its own importance by writing three separate lives of St Brigid, one of which, by Cogitosus, gives a famous descrip-

tion of the double church in Kildare. It might be remarked in passing that it was the desire to increase power among these monastic towns that spawned the early saints' 'Lives' dating from the seventh century – Tirechán on St Patrick, Cogitosus on St Brigid and Adamnan on St Columba – which must be counted amongst the earliest specimens of hagiography in these islands.

St Columba was also the inspiration for some of the earliest extant specimens of literature in the Irish language, which were written shortly after his death in 597. It was the combination of, and the interaction between, Latin and Irish that encouraged literature and the arts to flourish from the seventh century onwards in both large and small monastic complexes, and this at a time when the monasteries were becoming more and more secularized. The monks, of whichever kind, had the monopoly of education, encouraged scholarship and quickly developed important schools to which pupils came from England and the continent of Europe (including the later King Dagobert of Austrasia) to learn the best of what scripture and the classical authors could offer. The native teachers wrote their own exegetical commentaries on the Bible, usually in Latin, but also – hesitantly at first, and then increasingly – in Irish too. They became adept in Latin grammar, furthered the science of astronomical and calendrical calculations known as computistics, and Iona started a chronicle of contemporary affairs which Irish centres such as Bangor and Clonmacnoise expanded after 740, providing us with the very valuable Annals that flesh out our framework of early Irish history. This activity also prompted the compilation of genealogies which give us a tremendous insight into the history of various ruling dynasties, and particularly those associated with the monasteries.

Not unnaturally, the scriptorium must have been a very active building in the monastic complex. The Irish scribes developed their own particular form of script, which in the course of time influenced that of Anglo-Saxon England. From the period of St Columba onwards, the monks must have devoted considerable attention to the writing – and also to the decoration – of manuscripts which reproduced the sacred texts. Mention has already been made of the *Cathach* of *c*.600, which shows the tentative beginnings of the elaboration of the initial letters of paragraphs. During the following century this tendency increased, as we can see in the *Book of Durrow*, which was kept for centuries in the midlands monastery of the *paruchia Columbae* whose name it bears, before being presented to the Library of Trinity College, Dublin, where it is now preserved. Even if we cannot say for certain where this manuscript was written, it represents one of the most important artistic documents of seventh-century Europe, and a significant development in brilliant manuscript illumination which was to reach its apogee in the *Book of Kells* of *c*.800, also preserved in the Library of Trinity College. The origin of *Kells* is equally unknown, though Iona is currently considered to be the most likely candidate. The *Book of Kells*, with its intricate, brilliantly colourful and sometimes witty ornament, executed by a number of different hands, can probably be claimed to be the most richly decorative manuscript to survive from the whole of the first millennium. When its theft from Kells in 1007, and subsequent rediscovery shortly afterwards, were recorded in the Annals, it was described as the great 'halidom', or precious relic, of St Columba. The *Book of Lindisfarne* of *c*.700, now in the British Library, can also be placed on the same exalted plane, but there are other manuscripts of probably Irish origin or written under Irish influence which can be

LEFT St John, with the eagle evangelist symbol above his head and the gospel clasped in his elegant hands, decorates folio 11v of the later eighth-century bound manuscript known as the Stowe Missal in the Royal Irish Academy in Dublin – a pocket-sized volume small enough to have been carried around on the person.

BELOW During the early Middle Ages high-ranking personalities (including ecclesiastics) wore decorative brooches, probably at special ceremonies. One fine example, possibly of Irish origin and now in the British Museum, is the so-called Londesborough brooch, dating from *c.* 800. Of silver gilt, it is beautifully ornamented with birds, animals and interlace, as well as amber and glass.

placed not many steps beneath it, including some which were brought to St Gall in Switzerland and preserved there in the old monastic library.

In addition to manuscript production, the monasteries would have had workshops producing valuable metalwork, often decorated with coloured effects created by the use of enamel and amber, for instance. Such workshops were, however, known from non-monastic contexts, such as the crannog at Moynagh Lough, Co. Meath, excavated by John Bradley. The tradition of metalworking was one that reached back into the mists of pre-history, but it was given a new impetus with the production of pinned brooches, which were inspired by those used in Roman Britain during the fourth and fifth centuries and which were then followed by many elaborate pieces of jewellery such as the 'Londesborough' Brooch, now in the British Museum, London. Liturgical vessels, such as hanging bowls and chalices, can also be classed among the consummate achievements of the age. The two most superb examples are the Ardagh Chalice from County Limerick and that discovered along with an excellent paten and stand at Derrynaflan, Co. Tipperary, in 1980.

Among the most important possessions of any monastery were the relics of the founding saint, and any others which it may have been able to lay its hands on by fair means or foul. These were taken on tour to gather church dues and also to help in the promulgation of special laws known as *Cána*, which were designed to ensure that clerics did not have to go to war, for instance, or to protect innocent women and children. At the end of the eighth century some of these relics were enshrined in house-shaped caskets, and later the abbatial staffs of the founding fathers were also

encased in reliquaries having the form of a crozier. Many of these reliquaries, and other pieces of metalwork mentioned above, are now preserved in the National Museum in Dublin. Paradoxically, the preservation of others we owe to the Vikings, who carried them off back to Norway where they were buried with the dead and brought to light during the last hundred years. So extensive was the Viking booty that the Norwegian museums have – after the National Museum in Dublin – the best collection of such decorative Irish metalwork of the eighth and ninth centuries. It was no wonder that the Vikings found the Irish monasteries so attractive, because they were centres of such wealth and a store-house of both royal and ecclesiastical treasures.

By the time the Vikings first descended upon Ireland in the last decade of the eighth century, religious discipline had become so slack that a new reform movement was instigated in an effort to encourage devotional practices. This was the *Céli Dé*, the servants of God, whose centres were the two Dublin monasteries of Tallaght and Finglas, though it also encompassed other foundations such as Terryglass in County Tipperary and Castledermot in County Kildare. The Irish name for this last was Dísert Díarmata, the place-name *Dísert* coming from the word for a desert. Its use indicates a remote place like those chosen by the early hermits Paul and Anthony in the Egyptian desert, whither those who wanted to live an eremitical existence could retire to a life of prayer and peace. There, too, on the margins of their manuscripts, they wrote some beautiful, short lyric poems which are among the earliest of their genre to survive in a European vernacular language, of which the following

LEFT One of the greatest masterpieces of the Irish gold- and silversmiths' art, the twin-handled Ardagh Chalice was discovered by a boy out looking for rabbits in 1868. The vessel is made of silver, richly decorated with gold and glass, and enlivened by a complex filigree ornament that has few rivals. The chalice, indeed, is one of the peak European achievements in the field of ecclesiastical metalwork to survive from the period around the later eighth century.

BELOW An eighth- or ninth-century copper-alloy strainer, found in the excavation of Moylarg crannog, Co. Antrim, in 1893, bears a whirligig design and may have been used for liturgical purposes, like a similar example found with church vessels at Derrynaflan, Co. Tipperary.

example is preserved in one of those manuscripts in the St Gall library referred to above:

> Over me green branches hang
> A blackbird leads the loud song;
> Above my pen-lined booklet I hear a fluting bird-throng.
>
> The cuckoo pipes a clear call
> Its dun cloak hid in deep dell:
> Praise to God for this goodness
> That in woodland I write well.

TRANSLATED BY THE LATE MÁIRE MACNEILL

But, even before the Vikings arrived, there had been a number of ascetics who had withdrawn from the world, doubtless in rebellion against the laxity of life which had developed in the secularized monastic towns of the seventh and eighth centuries. Many went to islands: some inland, such as Iniscealtra, Co. Clare, Monaincha, Co. Tipperary, or Church Island on

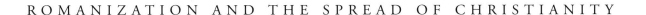

LEFT Church Island, Lough Currane – near Waterville in County Kerry – is one of many islands near Ireland's Atlantic seaboard to which holy men retired, singly or in groups, there to commune with their maker 'far from the madding crowd's ignoble strife'.

ABOVE The Ogham stone in Ardmore Cathedral, Co. Waterford, bears two separate inscriptions, one going up one edge and down the next, while the other is on a third angle. Though not easy to decipher, the latter may refer to a bishop of some sort, though it sadly provides no basis for dating the stone.

Lough Currane, Co. Kerry; others off the Atlantic coast of Ireland, such as Inishmurray, Co. Sligo, or Skellig Michael, Co. Kerry. On other smaller islands we sometimes find small corbelled huts and oratories of stone, frequently surrounded by a stone wall which also enclosed a cross or stele presumably marking the grave of the hermit, which later generations were to come and visit on pilgrimage.

Many of the cleverer minds – men like Johannes Scottus and Sedulius Scottus – chose another direction and left Ireland to seek a market for their considerable learning on the European continent, penetrating such exalted circles as the culture-hungry court of the Carolingian emperors. But it was not so much their departure as the consistent Viking raids which affected the vitality of craftsmanship and cultural life of the monasteries. Due to these constant and demoralizing depredations, the quality of monastic metalwork and manuscript illumination declined, and the scriptoria grew fewer in number. However, on the positive side, it was probably the fear of the swords and hordes from Scandinavia which encouraged the change from bronze to stone in the housing of saintly relics in immovable stone shrines, the erection of stone churches which could not be burned, and the creation of crosses in the same material, which, unlike those made of bronze, could not be hauled away for barter and burial in Norway. What the Vikings could not break was the spiritual life of devotion, as witnessed by the religious literature of the ninth century, while among the laity the practice of pilgrimage began to take on a new lease of life in the tenth century, once the worst of the Viking excesses had passed.

A further advantage of the Norse incursions was that the squabbles between monasteries over property and power, which had reached their height in the eighth century, came to an end as the individual monasteries concentrated on fighting for their own survival. In the process, many of the smaller establishments probably sank without trace, but the larger monasteries managed to revive by allying themselves with the secular powers. During the ninth century the links with ruling families increased, culminating in the monarch of Cashel, Cormac mac Cuileannáin, combining the offices of king and bishop. In the course of their continuing recovery during the tenth century the successful monasteries experienced increased prosperity and, by the eleventh, became increasingly involved in the affairs of government. By the turn of the millennium, the spiritual and literary heritage of the Céli Dé had virtually disappeared and, with the growing worldliness of the monasteries in the eleventh century, it was time for Ireland to come under the influence of the new Church reform movement which had begun to take the European continent by storm.

OGHAM

Ogham – or Ogam – derived from the name of Ogmios, the classical god of eloquence, is a script which preserves the earliest known form of the Irish language. Usually found on stones, though occasionally also in manuscripts, it consists of groupings of between one and five notches on either side of, on or diagonally across a central line, which, in the case of the stones, is an angular corner. Each of the notch groupings represents a letter of the alphabet, plus one diphthong (NG). The script is derived from an alphabet, probably the Latin, but was developed independently for use with the Irish language, some time no later than the fifth century AD. Mostly, Ogham survives in the form of lapidary inscriptions usually giving the name of a person (in the genitive case) together with his relationship to another, such as 'of A son of B' or 'of X descendant of Y'. The archaic form of the language used in these inscriptions has led scholars to date them to the period between the fifth and the seventh century, but they continued in use for hundreds of years – the key to their transcription (Ogham's Rosetta stone, as it were) being found in the *Book of Ballymote* of *c*.1400. Ogham was still being used in inscriptions in Kilkenny and Tipperary in the nineteenth century. In those days it was incumbent upon the owner of a horse and cart to have his name written on the shaft of the cart. One Cork owner was prosecuted for not having his name on his cart. His profusive objections to the contrary were not believed until a priest was brought as a witness from the far end of the county, who testified that the owner's name was indeed written on the cart – but in Ogham.

IRISH MANUSCRIPTS AT ST GALL
Switzerland

The Stiftsbibliothek, or monastery library, in the Swiss town of St Gall(en) contains perhaps the most important collection of Irish or Irish-influenced illuminated manuscripts outside Ireland. The saint, Gall, from whom the town gets its name, was a disciple of St Columbanus, who left him behind in Switzerland before crossing the Alps to make his last foundation in Bobbio, northern Italy, during the second decade of the seventh century. While Irishmen may have visited Gall's tomb and erected cells in the vicinity, St Gall was never an Irish monastery as such. Nevertheless, there must have been some Irish participation in the monastery which was founded there in the eighth century, as its rule seems to have broadly followed that of St Columbanus. It certainly was an important centre of Irish influence in continental Europe, and some of its manuscripts must have been brought there by Irishmen, as they were described in a library catalogue of the third quarter of the ninth century as *scottice scripti* – written by the Scotti (Irishmen). Two of these fine manuscripts now preserved in the library but

The monastic library in St Gall, Switzerland, preserves colourful Irish, or Irish-inspired, manuscripts of the eighth or ninth centuries. The most important one is catalogued as No. 51 and is richly illuminated: there are pages of pure decoration (below left) and texts with elaborately decorated initials (right) as well as illuminations of the evangelist St John, the Crucifixion and the Second Coming of Christ (below).

XPI autem
generatio
SIC ERAT

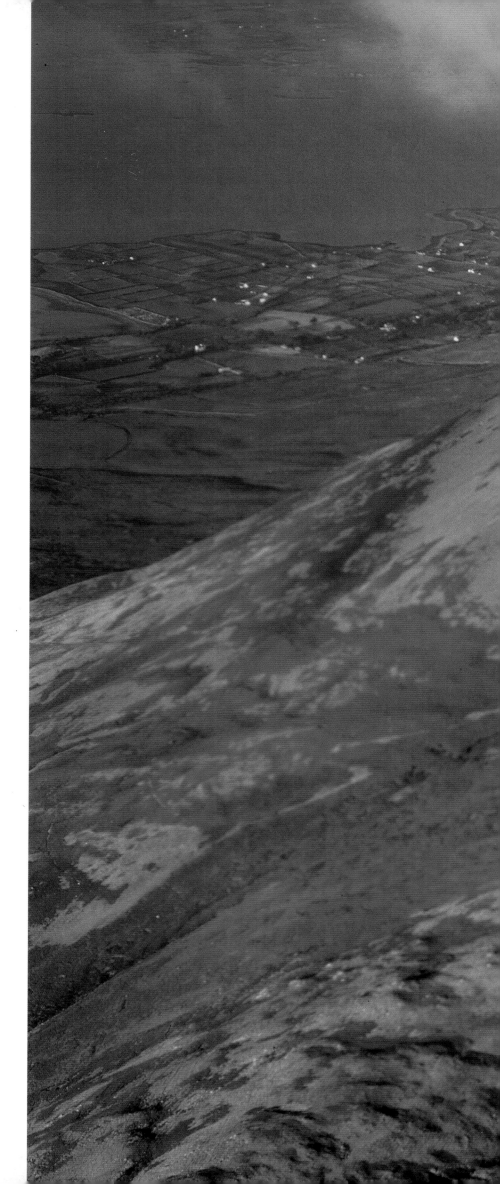

not listed in that catalogue were either written by Irishmen or under Irish influence and deserve special mention here. One is Manuscript 51, which is a Gospel Book including illustrations of the Crucifixion and the Second Coming of Christ as well as of the Evangelists. Dating from around the late eighth century, its ornament could be claimed to herald that of the *Book of Kells*. The second is Codex 904, a copy of Priscian's Grammar in Latin, dating from the middle of the ninth century. It has, unexpectedly, some inscriptions in the Ogham script, and contains a number of glosses in Old Irish which are very important for our knowledge of the Irish language in the ninth century. But some of the glosses are written in Latin, including one with the very human sentiment, 'This page is difficult. The third hour. Time for dinner.'!

CROAGH PATRICK
Co. Mayo

Clew Bay on the Atlantic coast of Mayo is dominated by the bald and brooding peak of Croagh Patrick, whose cone shape – so easily recognizable from many miles distant – makes it an obvious candidate for being Ireland's holiest mountain, a Fujiyama of the Western world. Following the pattern of Moses, his mountaineering Bible forebear, St Patrick is traditionally reputed to have spent forty days and nights fasting on the summit, pleading – with some success it is claimed! – that the Irish should be given special concessions to get them into heaven. But tradition may have erred slightly, as there is a considerable possibility that the saint may never have actually made it to the summit. Today, however, thousands do so on the last Sunday in July, though the practice of making the pilgrimage up the rocky scree-slopes barefoot and partially in the dark is gradually disappearing in favour of easier methods. The prayers of the often youthful pilgrims are interspersed with laughter and good-humoured chat, for this is a happy event and one with a long tradition stretching back into the mists of prehistory. Máire Mac Neill, in her enchanting book *The Festival of Lughnasa* (1962), pointed out that the last Sunday in July is the modern equivalent of the pagan festival held in honour of Lug, the good god of the Celts, when people gathered from miles around once a year to meet friends, match-make, settle disputes and do heaven knows what else. So, today's Christian pilgrimage in honour of Ireland's patron saint is the continuation of a practice which forms a direct link with the country's pagan past two thousand years ago. Excavations by Gerry Walsh and a team of helpers, as recently as 1994, uncovered the remains of an oratory on the summit (2500ft/750m), which bears a remarkable similarity to Gallarus oratory (see p. 76-7) and has recently provided a likely calibrated radiocarbon date of between 568 and 770.

Croagh Patrick in County Mayo – Ireland's Holy Mountain *par excellence* – is climbed annually by thousands of Christian pilgrims on the last Sunday in July, just as their prehistoric predecessors did before them to honour the pagan, Celtic, good god Lug.

EARLY CHURCHES OF WOOD AND STONE

Tara's mighty burgh perished at the death of her princes: with a multitude of venerable champions the great Height of Machae [Armagh] abides.

Rathcroghan, it has vanished with Ailill, offspring of victory: fair the sovranty over princes that there is in the monastery of Clonmacnoise.

Aillenn's proud burgh has perished with its warlike host: great is victorious Brigit: fair is her multitudinous cemetery.

Emain's burgh it hath vanished, save that its stones remain: the cemtery of the western world is multitudinous Glendalough.

These verses come from the Prologue of the *Martyrology of Oengus*, written by a monk around 800, and they hammer home the message that the old pagan ritual sites of Navan Fort, Rathcroghan (Cruachain), Dun Ailinne and Tara were dead and gone, replaced by the great centres of Christianity – Armagh, Clonmacnoise, Kildare and Glendalough. By the seventh and eighth centuries, these foundations of Saints Patrick, Ciarán, Brigit and Kevin, respectively, were becoming the most important religious settlements in the country, and it is here that we find some of the earliest monumental examples of Irish ecclesiastical architecture in stone.

What we must realize, however, is that the monuments which greet us today on these and many other smaller sites – be it churches, Round Towers or High Crosses – are not the products of the era of their monastic founders, but of many centuries later. It comes almost as a surprise to learn that wood was the main material for constructing churches and other domestic buildings during the first four or more centuries of the monasteries' existence and that, even as late as the twelfth century, St Malachy was still using smoothed planks to build an oratory at Bangor in County Down – 'an Irish work of sufficient beauty' in the words of his biographer, St Bernard of Clairvaux. Nothing remains of them above ground today, but traces of such wooden churches, or what may have been such, have come to light in about eight different locations throughout the country during excavations over the last forty years or so. Yet none of these suffices to give us any real idea of their original appearance. But here literary references in law tracts and saints' Lives do assist us in reconstructing some of their features.

One law tract, preserved in the sixteenth-century Manuscript H.3.17 in Trinity College, Dublin, tells us that artificers of a much earlier date were paid a differing number of cows or heifers for building wooden churches, depending on whether the structures were 15 feet (4.5m) or more long, and whether they were roofed with thatch or shingles. The Irish name for these edifices, *dairthech*, indicates that oak was used in their construction, and some of these must have been of considerable size if we can judge by one annalistic reference to a church at Trevet in County Meath, in which 260 people died in the year 850.

One large wooden church at Kildare was described in the seventh century by St Brigit's biographer, Cogitosus, but it was unusual in that it served the combined forces of monks and nuns in a double monastery. It was probably rectangular in shape, tall, and contained three chapels (*oratoria*) separated by walls of planking, which were painted with images (probably in the form of panels rather than frescoes) and hung with curtains. A cross-wall separated the altar from the rest of the church, and on either side of it lay the shrines of St Brigit, the founding abbess, and her bishop, Conlaed. Another seventh-century text, the *Hisperica Famina*, describes in rather convoluted language a wooden church of massive timbers which, unexpectedly, had a central altar, a western *porticus*, or porch, and four steeples, as well as a small chamber above the ceiling. One text in the fifteenth-century *Leabhar Breac*, in describing the consecration of what is likely to have been a much earlier church, tells of five crosses being marked on the altar with a knife, and further ones inscribed on a *tel* column (whatever that may have been) on the eastern exterior of the church, as well as on the corner pinnacles (*benn cobar*), perhaps identical with the 'steeples' on the *Hisperica Famina* structure.

Apart from Cogitosus, these texts give us little information about church furnishings, but we may assume that the altar and the Kildare wall-partitions were of wood, and a beautifully decorated eighth-century bronze door-handle recently discovered at Donore in County Meath was probably removed from a church door and buried to prevent it falling into Viking hands. The famous depiction of the Temple at Jerusalem in the *Book of Kells* and the equally shingle-roofed capstones of High Crosses, such as that of Muiredach at Monasterboice, have been used to further elaborate on the appearance of wooden churches, but, even if they were to have copied elements they found on contemporary Irish structures, they do not really extend our picture materially. Saints' Lives, most of them scarcely earlier than the twelfth century, cannot be relied upon to provide us with further descriptive detail, such as the church of St Maedoc of Ferns, which had 'wondrous carvings and brave ornaments'.

Early churches were also built of materials other than wood. At Iniscealtra, Co. Clare, Liam de Paor discovered the remains of a church (25 x 15 feet/7.5 x 4.5m) built of wattle and clay. In the seventh century Tirechán tells us that St Patrick built a church of earth because there was no wood nearby and it is interesting to note that, in an excavation carried out in 1994 on the islet of Illaunloughan near Portmagee in County Kerry, Jenny White Marshall and Claire Walsh uncovered trenches of two sod-built oratories beneath another of stone. These sod-built structures may date from the seventh or eighth century and suggest that the proliferation of churches, later to become such a feature of sites such as Clonmacnoise and Glendalough, had already become a reality at that time. Each church may have been designed for different classes of congregation, as the eighth-century *Liber Angeli* informs us that bishops, priests and anchorites worshipped in the south church at Armagh, whereas the north church was reserved for 'virgins, penitents and those serving the church in legitimate matrimony'.

The stone oratory at Illaunloughan produced a radiocarbon date ranging between 640 and 790, the earliest date so far recorded for a stone oratory. It was probably a dry-stone building constructed without the use of mortar, like its larger, more famous and better-constructed counterpart at Gallarus, near the end of the Dingle Peninsula in the same county. The early date for the Illaunloughan structure does not necessarily imply that Gallarus is equally early, but warns us against automatically presuming a date as late as the twelfth century for it. Boat-shaped oratories such as Gallarus, where the side-walls curve inwards to merge imperceptibly into the stone roof, were considered by earlier authorities such as H.G. Leask as having contributed to the development of the later churches in stone, where there is a clear distinction between the upright side-walls and the slanting roof. But

The peaceful island of Iniscealtra in Lough Derg on the lower Shannon has a notable Round Tower and a number of stone churches, but excavations in the 1970s revealed a small church of wattle and clay older than any of them.

the west-coast distribution, which the mortarless oratories shared with the 'beehive huts' found on Skellig Michael, would suggest that the Gallarus-type oratory was the result of local experimentation in adapting the corbel construction method of the round dry-stone huts to the rectangular shape of the oratories.

The exciting new technique of obtaining radiocarbon dates from mortar, which Rainer Berger of the University of California has recently used successfully for the first time in Ireland, now gives us reason to believe that it was around the eighth century that the Irish began to build in earnest with mortar. Significantly, some of the earliest identifiable buildings to have used this substance were not churches in the strict sense, but stone reliquary shrines such as St Molaise's House on the island of Inishmurray off the Sligo coast, the burial shrine of St Ciarán (*Teampull Chiaráin*) at Clon-

macnoise and, probably somewhat later, the lowest part of St Columba's House at Kells, all perhaps constructed to cater for an increase in pilgrimage traffic and/or the desire to ensure that the sacred relics could not easily be destroyed or removed in times of trouble.

At around the same time, however, the Irish also began to utilize mortar in church buildings. This was apparently the case in the first phase of St Michael's Church on Skellig Michael, which provided a radiocarbon date between the years 688 and 777, and it is more than likely that the first annalistic entry to mention a stone church – at Armagh in 789 – referred to

a mortar church, but it has not survived for us to be able to check. By the ninth century the Irish had come to realize the monumental power of stone, as the great Scripture Crosses amply demonstrate, and early in the following century they were already at work building the largest surviving early medieval church in Ireland – the cathedral at Clonmacnoise.

The Irish word to describe these stone churches was *damliac,* from which is derived the place-name Duleek in County Meath, where St Patrick is said to have built one. Typically, these churches were rectangular in plan, and were entered through a west doorway described as trabeate, because its gently inclining jambs were covered by a gigantic stone lintel across the top. These lintels are occasionally decorated with a simple cross – the only ornament which these churches normally bear. Light was admitted by a simple inward-splaying window in the east gable, and sometimes through another in one of the long walls of the church. But their most characteristic feature was the extension of the north and south walls beyond the gable ends. Known as *antae*, these extensions presumably bore wooden bargeboards, which ran up the gable and helped to keep the rainwater from dripping on to the masonry. These *antae* are probably skeumorphs, that is, they copied the projecting frames of wooden and bronze reliquary shrines or the stout corner posts presumably used in the wooden churches, where they may have been surmounted by the pinnacles (*pinnas*) mentioned in the *Hisperica Famina* or those referred to as *benn cobar* in the *Leabhar Breac.* In the stonier parts of the west of Ireland, in the Burren of northern County Clare and on the Aran Islands, for instance, these *antae* may have continued in use as late as 1200, if not slightly later. The (twelfth-century?) stone-roofed church on St Macdara's Island off the coast of Connemara seems to have imitations of wooden shingles carved into its roof stones, suggesting that this would have been one method of roofing a wooden church which would have preceded it on the site, but thatch was another material which would also have been used to roof these early stone churches. In comparison to the much larger contemporary edifices on the continent, these early Irish stone churches, though 'widowed now without their furnishings' as the architectural historian Conant said, are small yet beautiful. They exude a classic and serene simplicity, their monumentally large stones – used particularly in the lower courses – having the agelessness of a fairy-tale giant, and their solid, reassuring doorways are perhaps, in Maurice Craig's phrase, 'the most distinctive and the most perennially satisfying features to be found in the whole course of Irish architecture'.

CLONMACNOISE
Co. Offaly

When entering the precincts of Clonmacnoise today, and encountering the restfulness broken only by the sound of birds and small groups of admiring visitors, it is hard to imagine that this was once a thriving town and one of Ireland's most prolific artistic and literary centres. What must have helped it to become so was its nodal position at the point where ancient Ireland's main east–west roadway – the Eiscir Riada – intersects with the north–south-flowing Shannon traffic artery, thus making it the central crossroads of Ireland. This strategic location preordained its fame, and there may already have been some form of settlement at the river crossing when St Ciarán decided to found his monastery here around 545, as the Gaulish wine-merchants whom he encountered there would scarcely have been offering their wares to empty fields. But St Ciarán, a Connacht man, only enjoyed the fruits of his foundation for a mere nine months before being struck down by the plague, yet that must have still been enough time for him to have cast the mantle of his charisma over the place. The death of Ireland's very first recorded pilgrim (of whom a wooden statue stands near the entrance to the new Interpretative Centre) occurred in the first decade of the following century, suggesting that people were already coming here to venerate the saint's tomb little more than half a century after his death.

That tomb is now housed in the smallest and what may seem to be the most unprepossessing building at Clonmacnoise, the stone oratory known as *Teampull Chiaráin*, or St Ciarán's Church. A recent radiocarbon date for its mortar suggests a construction date somewhere between 681 and 881, making it one of the oldest-known mortared buildings in Ireland, though it was doubtless preceded by some wooden shrine now long since vanished.

Despite its rather battered-looking condition – the result of many partial rebuildings down the years to hold the sacred reliquary together – it still retains its original rectangular shape with *antae* at the exterior corners.

But even before the construction of the *Teampull,* St Ciarán's foundation had been expanding, and Adamnan tells us that it had around it a *vallum,* or wall and ditch, when St Columba paid a visit there late in the sixth century. By the time another hundred years had passed, it was probably already the second most important church in the country after Armagh, and possibly with paved streets laid out within the compound. At this stage of its development, the monastery was becoming increasingly secularized and politicized; that we know because the men of Munster were obviously being denied the opportunity of joining the roll of office holders, including the abbacy. In the eighth century the Leinstermen too were being increasingly excluded, and the power – as exercised by the abbot and by the prior – was coming more and more into the hands of the men from Connacht, the birth-province of the founder. The Kings of Connacht were probably giving royal patronage to the monastery in return for rights of burial, and a cross-decorated stone found at Athlone, but possibly originally from Clonmacnoise, records the name of a King of Connacht, Ailill aue Dunchatho, who died in 764 and who may well have been buried in the monastery. It is the earliest documented date for the many hundreds of such 'grave-slabs' found on the site, of which some representative examples are on display in the foyer of the Interpretative Centre.

In its efforts to expand its power, the monastery went to war on various occasions in the second half of the eighth century in order to keep rivals such as Birr and Durrow at bay. During the course of the following century Clonmacnoise seems to have become embroiled in a north–south struggle, with the ascetic Munster King Feidlimid mac Crimthainn devastating the monastery in the 830s in an attempt to curb the expansionist tendencies of the Clann Cholmáin, Uí Néill Kings of Meath. But, at the same time, the ever-growing monastic town became a prey to invasion from a totally different quarter – the Vikings, who came up the Shannon from Limerick.

The inhabitants must have been incensed when, according to the story, Ota, wife of the Norse leader Turgesius, pronounced oracles from the high altar of their church.

There is some evidence that by the second half of the ninth century the Uí Néill kings were beginning to take an even greater interest in Clonmacnoise. The extremely fragmentary inscription on the South Cross (now in the Interpretative Centre) could be seen as suggesting that the cross was erected by Maelsechlainn I (846-62), and it was his son Flann Sinna, king from 879 to 916, who seems to have been responsible for commissioning the Cross of the Scriptures, which has also been moved to the Interpretative Centre to protect it from the elements. Both crosses have been replaced *in situ* by casts.

It was the same Flann Sinna who helped the abbot of the time to build the earliest part of the stone cathedral in 908. Conleth Manning has convincingly demonstrated recently that the original south wall of this cathedral lay about 6 feet (1.8m) further south than at present, which helps to explain why the west doorway is off-centre in the gable wall. This reconstruction brings the original dimensions of the cathedral to about 58 x 32 feet (17.7 x 9.8m), which makes it the largest-known ecclesiastical structure to survive from pre-Romanesque Ireland – yet still very small in comparison to the large continental churches of the period. These latter, however, contained the founder's tomb in the crypt, while here it is housed in the diminutive Teampull Chiaráin nearby. When contrasted with the complexities of its continental counterparts, Clonmacnoise Cathedral is a simple church, rectangular in shape and with *antae*, and we can be fairly certain that it was preceded by one or more wooden churches. The stone cathedral underwent many subsequent changes. The width of the interior may have been reduced at the same time that the original west doorway – doubtless trabeate – was replaced by one in the Romanesque style around 1200. During the fifteenth century the eastern end of the church had internal Gothic vaulting added, perhaps when the decorative north doorway was inserted by Dean Odo around 1459. The present sacristy may be no earlier than the sixteenth century.

From the tenth to the twelfth centuries the burial rights accorded to Kings of the Southern Uí Néill, of Connacht and of other lesser kingdoms, must have brought considerable patronage with it, as the number of structures surviving from this period testify. Fergal Ua Ruairc, King of Connacht from 956 to 966/7, is credited with the building of the Round Tower, though its upper portions are the result of a rebuild after it was struck by lightning in 1135. The same king is said to have built a roadway leading to the site, and others within the town were laid down during the course of the eleventh century. The apogee of Clonmacnoise as a rich monastic town can be said to have been the twelfth century, when it may even have minted its own coinage. Another Round Tower was part of the original design of St Finghin's Church, which was fashioned in the Romanesque style down near the river in the second half of the century. A better-preserved Romanesque church is the Nuns' Church (see p. 122), built almost a quarter of a mile (400m) to the east of the settlement by Dervorgilla in 1167 for the Arrouaisian Augustinian nuns, whose male brethren had been installed at Clonmacnoise in 1142. This attractive ruined nave-and-chancel church is well worth a visit not only for its peaceful surroundings but also for the quality of its carving on the chancel arch and west doorway (both restored in 1865). Other churches, Temple Conor to the north and Temple

of Clonmacnoise, found in Teampull Chiaráin and now in the National Museum in Dublin.

Clonmacnoise was also a great literary centre, with a scriptorium recorded as early as 730. But it was most active around 1100 when it produced not only the oldest and most important collection of secular texts known as the *Book of the Dun Cow* (*Lebor na hUidre*) but also a series of most valuable annals – those of Tigernach, of Clonmacnoise and the compilation known as the *Chronicon Scotorum* – which shows a very considerable interest in the recording of Irish history.

The coming of the Normans began to toll the knell of Clonmacnoise's decline. Already during the last quarter of the twelfth century, the Bishopric of Clonmacnoise was reduced in size and status, and the building of an impressive, if now ruined, Norman castle in a field to the west around 1216 must have had a stultifying effect on the life of the monastic town. The foundation of a secular college for four local priests in 1459 was unable to stem the rot which had set in during the late Middle Ages, and the final blow came in 1552 when the English of Athlone plundered and devastated the place, leaving not a bell, an image or an altar, a book or a gem, or even glass in the church window.

Gone was the world conjured up in the fifteenth-century Irish poem of Enóg Ó Gilláin, translated by T.W. Rolleston as follows:

In a quiet water'd land, a land of roses,
Stands Saint Ciaran's city fair;
And the warriors of Erin in their famous generations
Slumber there.

There beneath the dewy hillside sleep the noblest
Of the clan of Conn,
Each below his stone with name in branching Ogham
And the sacred knot thereon.

There they laid to rest the seven Kings of Tara,
There the sons of Cairbre sleep
Battle-banners of the Gael, that in Ciaran's plain of crosses
Now their final hosting keep.

LEFT A Round Tower was incorporated into the design of the twelfth-century St Finghin's Church at Clonmacnoise, Co. Offaly, and placed close to the chancel arch.

ABOVE This small bronze Crucifixion plaque from Clonmacnoise may have been connected with pilgrimage around 1100, an activity that greatly enriched the monastery, but also Church life in general, throughout the twelfth century.

But even if the place was deserted in the Elizabethan period, Clonmacnoise has continued to our own day to be one of the most important and oldest places of pilgrimage in the country – its most famous pilgrim being Pope John Paul II in 1979. By the time of his visit, the clutter of nineteenth-century tombstones, which created such a desolate picture for the novelist Frank O'Connor in the 1950s, had largely been laid down flat by the Office of Public Works. This beneficial act left Clonmacnoise as one of the most beautiful ancient monastic sites in Ireland, a magnet to draw us back again and again to enjoy the peace and calm of the place beside the majestically flowing Shannon, which provides the most dramatic approach to this monastery of ancient glory.

Rí to the south of the cathedral, were both built around 1200. These extensive building projects in the twelfth century were doubtless due to the great influx of pilgrims who must have been crowding to Clonmacnoise during a period when going on pilgrimage was the most popular activity in Europe. We get a glimpse of the size of the town at the time when we read in the Annals that 105 houses were burned in 1179.

The richness of the cathedral is indicated by the annalistic account telling how, fifty years earlier, the treasures carried off from it included a chalice, cups and what may have been a model or reliquary in the form of Solomon's Temple. Some of these items may well have been fabricated by workshops in the town, for Clonmacnoise is likely to have been a centre not only for the stonemason's craft, but also for the metalsmith's as well. Products of this Clonmacnoise workshop probably include the eighth- or ninth-century 'Athlone' Crucifixion plaque and others of a different type dating from around 1100, a period which also saw the creation of a beautiful silver inlaid bronze crozier-shrine, known as the Crozier of the Abbots

LEFT St Kevin's Church in Glendalough has the unique combination of a Round Tower and a stone roof, both typical features of Irish architecture.

GLENDALOUGH
Co. Wicklow

In the poetic prologue to Oengus's *Martyrology* of *c.*800 Glendalough is mentioned along with Armagh, Clonmacnoise and Kildare as one of the thriving Christian centres which had triumphantly taken over from the deserted pagan sanctuaries. Hidden away like an Aladdin's Cave in the Wicklow Hills, Glendalough is never likely to have been as large a monastic city as the other three, but its inclusion in the quartet is a sure sign of its importance in the earlier medieval period, something which was scarcely intended or envisaged by its founder, St Kevin. He came to this secluded valley around the sixth century to commune in peaceful prayer with his maker and to get away from the pressures of the world by practising the ascetic life of a hermit, before dying around 618 at – it is alleged – the biblical age of 120. He may have been attracted by the occasionally melancholic mood of the valley of the two lakes – as the name Glendalough may be translated – and tradition points out a man-made cave on the rock-face above the Upper Lake as his penitential bed.

> By that lake whose gloomy shore
> Sky-lark never warbles o'er,
> Where the cliff hangs high and steep,
> Young Saint Kevin stole to sleep . . .

according to Tom Moore's ballad, which goes on to tell how he was followed thither by a luckless love-struck maiden:

> Fearless she had tracked his feet,
> To this rocky wild retreat!
> And when morning met his view,
> Her mild glances met it too.
> Ah! You saints have cruel hearts!
> Sternly from his bed he starts,
> And with rude repulsive shock,
> Hurls her from the beetling rock.
> Glendalough! thy gloomy wave
> Soon was gentle Cathleen's grave.

RIGHT In Glendalough – literally, the 'Valley of the Two Lakes' seen in the background – the centre of the ancient monastery probably focused around the area between the two Round Towers, that on the left rising above the roof of the church dedicated to the founder, St Kevin, who sought peace here in the sixth century.

Whatever the origin of that unlikely tale, the area around the Upper Lake, with 'St Kevin's Bed' and 'Cell', is one possible focus for the original site of St Kevin's hermitage. But if that was where he settled, the monastic town which gradually developed after his death appears to have favoured a location farther down the valley where the main buildings are now clustered. It was less the fresh air and the scenery, and more the relics of the saint, which attracted people to come to Glendalough along the stone-paved road across the Wicklow Gap from west Wicklow and the midland plains. Having got there, it was regarded as an honour to be buried in Glendalough, for the same poem by Oengus, mentioned above, states that it was the cemetery of the western world. Significantly, the word the poet uses for 'cemetery' was *rúam*, derived from the name of the Eternal City, and it is likely that the Seven Churches of Rome to which people went on pilgrimage provided the title 'Glendalough of the Seven Churches', by

which it has come to be known by tradition, even though Glendalough has more than seven churches to its credit.

Two of these are close to the Upper Lake – the rather inaccessible Temple-na-Skellig, a simple rectangular structure of *c.*1200, and the somewhat earlier Reefert Church, around whose walls sleep many Leinster kings. A most romantic ruin when seen among the leaves of summer, it is one of the many Glendalough granite churches with a contemporary nave and chancel – a very characteristic feature of the churches here and one rarely found elsewhere in the country.

The main monastic town was situated on a ridge farther down the valley near the confluence of two small streams, and it is here that we find the major concentration of ecclesiastical buildings. The oldest of these is probably the cathedral, which, however, underwent many changes in the course of its history. Its earliest parts are the large and well-cut ashlar stones form-

ing the lower courses of the rectangular nave and its *antae*. Some time later, perhaps when the church was extended by the addition of a chancel and its Romanesque arch in the later twelfth century, the upper courses of the nave were completed in much smaller rubble masonry. At the same time, the original west doorway with inclining jambs was given a new lintel with a relieving arch over it to prevent it being broken by the pressure of the stonework above. The simple plan of the nave has only slightly smaller dimensions than the cathedral at Clonmacnoise which may have acted as a model, suggesting a possible date in the first half of the tenth century for the earliest part of the cathedral here. One of the intriguing questions posed by this structure is the presence in the interior of large column- or pilaster-like stones, which were laid flat in the second-phase rough masonry but belonged to the first-phase ashlar beneath them. Could these have formed a portico outside the west doorway of the first stone church of

the kind described in the much older *Hisperica Famina*, or have been the curious and unexplained *tel* column referred to in the Church Consecration tract from the *Leabhar Breac* mentioned earlier (p. 60)?

In addition to the Round Tower which lies to the north-west of the cathedral, there are other ecclesiastical structures in the vicinity which are noteworthy. One of these is the small Romanesque building known as the Priest's House, whose interior dimensions are only 14ft 8in by 7ft 9in (4.5 x 2.4m). Its eastern end has a Romanesque arch only visible from the outside, and with a small (partially restored) slit in the blocking wall. This building has long been mooted as the tomb-shrine of St Kevin, and the slit, if original, could be explained as a 'peep hole' for pilgrims to view the grave of the founding saint and enable them to lower their pieces of cloth to touch the earth in which he lay interred, without allowing them access to the interior. The only entrance is a narrow doorway in the south wall, over which is a lintel carved with three figures. An upper stone, now missing but extant in the nineteenth century, showed the lintel to have had the shape of a pedimented gable, and one possible interpretation of the three figures is that they represent the seated St Kevin, flanked by two bowing pilgrims, one bearing a staff and the other a bell. If the Priest's House were St Kevin's tomb-shrine, it raises the question as to whether the present concentration of buildings represents the original area of St Kevin's hermitage or whether the saint's relics were translated here from the Upper Lake when the monastic town developed and needed a focal point for an increasing amount of pilgrimage traffic? The house lay within a trapezoidal enclosure surrounded by a now scarcely recognizable earthen wall which takes cognizance of the presence of the cathedral and is, therefore, likely to be later than it. Its entrance was marked by a granite ringed cross, which still stands on its original site.

RIGHT The diminutive Priest's House in Glendalough may have been built in the twelfth century to house the relics of St Kevin, the founder of the monastery who had died five centuries earlier.

LEFT Reefert Church, located in sylvan surroundings overlooking the Upper Lake at Glendalough, has a cyclopean doorway of well-dressed granite stones, which look as if they had been previously used in an earlier church on the same site.

The first church today's visitor to Glendalough usually sees is Trinity Church, which lies beside the approach road to the ancient monastery. It was scarcely earlier than the eleventh century, with a contemporary nave and chancel seen here, and its western end once boasted a Round Tower, which was blown down in 1818.

On a slightly lower terrace nearby is Glendalough's most famous building, St Kevin's Church. It gets its alternative folk-name, St Kevin's Kitchen, from the fact that a Round Tower projects upwards like a chimney from the stone roof above the west doorway, which also has a relieving arch in the style of the doorway of the cathedral's second phase. This feature, and the vaulted roof within, which is a simpler version of that found in Cormac's Chapel at Cashel of 1127–34, suggests a twelfth-century date for the building. A chancel was added subsequently, but the sacristy is a much later addition. The likelihood that three of these buildings – the cathedral, the Priest's House and St Kevin's Church – were either built or added to in the twelfth century, suggests that the monastery (like Clonmacnoise) was quite extensive at this period, and a report from the year 1177 tells of a flash flood which broke down a bridge and mills, and left fish strewn around the town's streets. Where that bridge stood we do not know, but it was not necessarily where the present road-bridge leads the visitor through the arched (originally two-storey) entrance building to the main enclosure because, as late as the nineteenth century, the stream there was crossed by a series of stepping stones, some of which can still be seen beneath the modern bridge.

Four further churches deserve mention. One is the nave-and-chancel church just on the other side of the modern wall from St Kevin's Church. It was dedicated to St Ciarán, probably the founder of Clonmacnoise, with which Glendalough apparently had some links, possibly part of a 'pilgrimage network'. A second church, St Mary's, lies in a field to the west of the cathedral. The lintel of its simple doorway is decorated on the underside with a saltire or St Andrew's cross, which was doubtless why it was singled out for special praise by the Scottish novelist, Sir Walter Scott, when he visited the site in 1825. Beside the road leading to Glendalough today is Trinity Church, consisting of a contemporary nave and chancel, but formerly distinguished by having yet another Round Tower rising above a square base outside the west doorway until it fell in a storm in 1818. The round-headed south doorway was rebuilt in 1875, but a stone cross embedded in the bottom of the north wall seems to be in its original position.

The final church to be mentioned here lies three-quarters of a mile (1.2 km) further down the valley floor from the cathedral. St Saviour's Priory, a nave-and-chancel church with chancel arch and wrongly assembled stones around the east window, all finely ornamented in the Romanesque style, is unusual in having domestic buildings of stone attached to it. This church is normally, and probably correctly, associated with the name of St Laurence O'Toole, the second great saint of the valley of the two lakes. He was a scion of the local Uí Muiredaig dynasty which had taken control of Glendalough before the twelfth century, and he was elected abbot of the monastery before being raised to the dignity of Archbishop of Dublin in 1162. He died at Eu in Normandy while on his way to Rome in 1180, and was canonized in 1226. In addition to having probably founded St Saviour's for the Augustinian Canons, he is also likely to have been responsible for the twelfth-century buildings in the monastic town – the Priest's House, St Kevin's Church and the chancel of the cathedral. The other churches may have been erected before his time, but how much earlier it is difficult to say.

In its hey-day the monastery must have been a centre of considerable learning, as we know that law was studied there and, in addition to a mathematical tract and a school-book which have survived, some of the material contained in the twelfth-century compilation known nowadays as the *Book of Leinster* may have originated from Glendalough. Being in the mountainous territory which the Normans found difficult to penetrate, the monastic town survived until 1398, when the English forces finally succeeded in destroying it. Since then it has remained the cluster of picturesque ruins which led the nineteenth-century scholar John O'Donovan to describe it as 'the Palmyra of Ireland'. But one feature lived on, and that was pilgrimage, for which Glendalough was famous as far back as the ninth century. However, by the time Joseph Peacock's oil-painting (preserved in the Ulster Museum and Art Gallery in Belfast) came to depict the pilgrimage in 1813, it had become an annual fair, with visitors dressed up in all their finery, and being entertained at stalls by the usual three-card-trick merchants and much else besides. Just under fifty years later the saint's annual 'pattern', or pilgrimage, had become so full of 'drink and debauchery' that the Catholic Church decided to abolish it. A sad and sorry end to a long tradition, perhaps, but not one which nowadays prevents thousands of visitors from enjoying the site throughout the year.

KELLS
Co. Meath

The County Meath town of Kells, anciently called Cenannus, may well have developed from a defensive Iron Age *dún*, whose round shape stamped itself on the outlines of the ninth-century monastery and the fortified Norman town, and is still traceable in the street pattern today. Around 804 it was granted to the Columban community of Iona, who probably sought a safe inland haven in Ireland where they could store their monastic treasures after their Hebridean island foundation had been ravaged by the Vikings. Three years later a *civitas* (monastery) was established, which was incorporated into the family of churches associated with the foundations of St Columba, with its headquarters at Iona. At the end of a further seven years, a church – possibly of stone – had been completed, and this was probably located where Thomas Cooley's Protestant church of 1778 stands today. It was presumably this long vanished church that housed the famous *Book of Kells*, which was stolen from the western sacristy in 1007 and, thankfully for the world, recovered less than a year later before being deposited more than three centuries ago in the Library of Trinity College, Dublin.

Other than a Round Tower, the only building to survive from the early monastery is a curiously tall, stone-roofed structure known today as St Columb's House. Two mortar specimens removed from the lower part of the structure provided calibrated dates ranging between 650 and 890, and 654 and 786, respectively, making it possible that the bottom section of St Columb's House may have been built not long after the foundation of the monastery in the early ninth century, possibly to house the relics which the monks had brought with them from Iona. It could thus be seen to conform to the pattern at Clonmacnoise, Glendalough and Inishmurray, where the relics were preserved in a shrine separated from, and at a diagonal to, the main church – though, in the case of Kells it cannot have been the saint's body which was interred there, as St Columba was buried at Iona.

Such relics, if they existed, may well have been kept in a crypt, now accessible through a not very ancient-looking doorway low down in the south wall. Between this basement level and the lofty stone vault there is likely to have been an intermediate floor, accessible through a doorway in the west wall which no longer exists. Comparison with St Kevin's Church at Glendalough prompts the suggestion that the upper part of the structure, including the stone roof, may represent a second building stage, dating perhaps from as late as the twelfth century

Monks who moved to the greater inland safety of Kells in County Meath, in order to escape further Viking raids on their island monastery on Iona in the Hebrides, may have begun construction of St Columb's House shortly after their arrival in Kells early in the ninth century to protect the relics of the founder, though the stone roof is probably later.

SKELLIG MICHAEL
Co. Kerry

The most dramatic visualization of the ascetic religious life of Early Christian Ireland is undoubtedly to be found on the island of Skellig Michael, or Sceilg Mhichíl, which lies 8 miles (13 km) off the western end of the Iveragh Peninsula in County Kerry and is occasionally reachable by boat from Portmagee. Rising steeply out of the Atlantic to a peak 714 feet (218m) above sea level, it forms a triangular silhouette, a shape and setting that predestined it to be a holy place, and a height that suggested a dedication to St Michael the Archangel, the patron saint of high places, though the dedication is not recorded until after the year 1000. Who its patron saint was before that no one knows – perhaps the local saint Finian, much venerated on the nearby mainland? One of its monks was carried off by the Vikings in 823, and an abbot is recorded as having died there later in the same century.

Its main focus is a cluster of buildings on a terrace 550 feet (170m) above the sea in the western half of the island, reached by an open stone stairs – not as old as it looks – which seems to reach towards heaven like a Jacob's ladder. The buildings include a series of five complete beehive huts, and a sixth fragmentary example, which are domed on the outside but square in plan within. While we know that they were not all built at the same time, they cannot be dated satisfactorily, though the eighth and subsequent centuries is the most likely period of their construction. A very simple rectangular church in front of them has recently provided a likely date in the eighth century for its earliest phase on the basis of its mortar, and its second phase belongs somewhere in the years between 985 and 1160. In addition there are two small undatable oratories of the Gallarus type (see pp. 76-7). The location of these buildings high up on a lonely island prompted Sir Kenneth Clark to consider that Early Western Christianity survived for a century or more by clinging to places like the Skelligs.

The terraces which provided these buildings with a foothold on the steep slopes of the island must have required considerable community effort, which could scarcely have been achieved by a single hermit or even a few of them. The thought that even the hardiest hermits would have found it a struggle to survive the many winter months when the island was cut off by bad weather prompts the question as to whether this fascinating settlement may not at least in part have been a summer pilgrimage centre built by the church, with the beehive huts providing a shelter for stranded pilgrims. Skellig Michael was certainly on the itinerary of one rather later pilgrim, Heneas MacNichaill, who had to do a tour of a number of Irish pilgrimage sites in 1543 to obtain forgiveness for the sin of having murdered his son. Nevertheless, the presence of an abbot in the ninth century does suggest some form of monastic foundation on the island.

One of the most astounding features of the island is a small hermitage near the peak, difficult to reach even for the nimble, where there is also a third small oratory, for which a date around 800 has recently been suggested. It must be one of the eeriest locations for a hermitage known to man, more lonesome and dramatic than anything at Meteora or on Mount Athos in Greece.

For those not able to get to the island, a taste of what it offers can be experienced at the Skellig Centre near Portmagee, which organizes a sea-trip around, but not to, the island.

Nowhere is the asceticism of the old Irish monastery brought to life more vividly than on the island of Skellig Michael, where beehive huts (right-hand peak) and small oratories perch on perilous ledges 550ft (170m) above the Atlantic waves, which must have frequently made the island virtually inaccessible during the winter months.

INISHMURRAY
Co. Sligo

Along with Skellig Michael, the island of Inishmurray off the Sligo coast – reachable by boat from Mullaghmore – preserves the most striking early medieval complex anywhere in Ireland. Long and low when seen from the mainland, the island is 223 acres (90ha) in extent, tricky to land on, yet well worth a visit because of its fascinating collection of stone monuments unique in the country. The main feature is the *caiseal*, or stone-walled enclosure, not far from the southern shore. Comparable in construction to the stone forts of the Aran Islands, it contains a church, an oratory, a beehive hut and cross-inscribed slabs. Its oval shape raises the old chicken or egg problem: which came first, the wall or the buildings within? The question has never been solved satisfactorily, though the balance of probability would probably favour the *caiseal* being older.

The interior of the *caiseal* is divided into sections of differing sizes by stone walls of varying heights. Probably the oldest building within is *Teach Molaise* – St Molaise's House – an almost square building with a low, lintelled doorway, a round-headed east window, and an internal ledge which supported the thirteenth-century(?) wooden statue of the founding saint Molaise, before it was moved for safety to the National Museum in Dublin. But the saint's house itself is very much older – its mortar having recently provided a likely eighth-century date for the structure. The rather larger St Molaise's Church (otherwise known as the Men's Church) may be about two centuries later. Also within the enclosure are a domestic building with a central hearth, a beehive hut (perhaps once bearing the name of St Brendan the Navigator?) and the famous cursing stones. These are a group of rounded beach stones on a raised 'altar' which a person is said to be able to turn with advantage against an adversary who has wronged the turner; but, if the cause be unjust, the curse turns back on the originator of the scheme. During the Second World War, it is alleged, the stones were turned against Hitler – and we know what happened to him.

Near the shore is the late medieval Nuns' Church, and dotted around the island's perimeter are numerous 'stations', piles of stones, often surmounted by a cross-decorated slab, at which pilgrims did the rounds up to our own century. In his book *Inishmurray* (1982), Dr Paddy Heraughty, a native of the island, was able to recall details of the complicated succession of prayers which had to be said at each of these individual stations.

The founding patron, Molaise, lived in the sixth century, and is reputed to have been the one who pronounced banishment on St Columba in 563. But the island itself is not mentioned in historic documents until 747, when an abbot died, and the death of a learned man of the island is recorded in 798. The only other appearance of the island in historical sources occurs just four years later when the Vikings burned the island. Thereafter, history is silent for more than 800 years. What happened in the meantime? Did a small monastic community live in the *caiseal*, was it just a place of pilgrimage, or a combination of both, leading in time to the lay community of islanders who were finally forced to abandon their ancestral home in 1948?

TUAMGRANEY
Co. Clare

Tuamgraney, near the western shore of Lough Derg in County Clare, has what is probably the oldest church still in use in Ireland. The nave of the existing Protestant church can reasonably be identified with that mentioned under the year 964 in the *Chronicon Scotorum*: 'Cormac Ua Cillín, of the Uí Fiachrach Aidhne, comarb (abbot) of Tuaim-gréine, by whom the great church of Tuaim-greine and its Round Tower were constructed, died.' That brief obituary was probably written at Clonmacnoise, where Cormac was also abbot, and he may have modelled the Tuamgraney church on the rather larger cathedral there. Until the 1980s the Church of Ireland used the church for divine service, but this is now conducted only in the chancel, which was added in the Romanesque style in the twelfth century (possibly after a fire in 1164). The nave at the western end now functions as the East Clare Interpretative Centre, housing many interesting Romanesque fragments. Brian Boru is said to have repaired the Round Tower – but obviously not well enough, for no trace of it survives.

LEFT The cluster of buildings on the uninhabited island of Inishmurray off the coast of Sligo is one of the most intact examples of an early Irish monastery.

RIGHT The typically Irish form of upwardly narrowing doorway is subtly emphasized by the carving of a gently raised architrave around the deep entrance to the church at Tuamgraney in County Clare – probably the oldest surviving building in the whole of Ireland still used for divine service.

LABBAMOLAGA
Co. Cork

The ruined and much reconstructed church at Labbamolaga in north Cork has as its most distinguishing feature a lintelled west doorway constructed of only three stones – a single jamb-stone on each side supporting a lintel on top. For all its primeval, almost megalithic appearance, the doorway has an architrave on the lintel which might suggest a date no earlier than the eleventh century. St Molaga himself lived in the fifth century and is alleged to have been a disciple of St David of Wales. A stone on the south side of the floor is said to mark the saint's *leaba*, or bed (hence the name of the place – the 'bed of Molaga'); local tradition avers that rheumatism can be cured if the sufferer spends a night under the stone – though a nasty cold would seem to be a more likely outcome!

GALLARUS ORATORY
Co. Kerry

Because of its excellent state of preservation, Gallarus is probably the best-known of the early Irish boat-shaped oratories, so-called because their shape resembles that of an upturned boat. Rectangular in ground-plan with an external plinth, it is built by the corbel principle, whereby each layer of stones of the long walls juts slightly further inwards than the layer below until the two sides meet together at the top, thus creating side-walls which form a continuous curve with the roof. This principle, devised for use in round buildings like the beehive huts on Skellig Michael, has one weak-point when adapted to rectangular buildings, and this is that the long sides have a tendency to fall inwards in the centre and collapse. But while a sag is noticeable at Gallarus, the walls remain

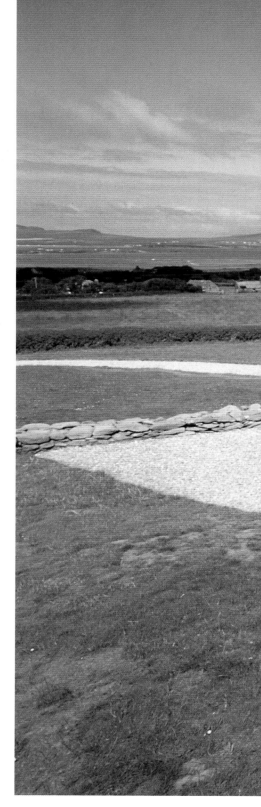

RIGHT Gallarus Oratory on the Dingle Peninsula successfully translated the corbel technique of round (beehive) huts to the rectangular shape of a church, although it would have collapsed where it sags slightly in the middle had it not been built by a consummate master highly skilled in the art of dry-stone masonry.

LEFT The simple construction of the church doorway at Labbamolaga, using no more than three large stones – two uprights and a lintel – creates an air of cyclopean monumentality that contrasts with the smaller stones used elsewhere in the fabric of this small County Cork church.

intact because of the splendid quality of the dry-stone masonry used, whereby each stone is carefully hewn to fit into the bed provided by the stones in the layer beneath. The similar oratories on Skellig Michael have also survived intact, but the walls have collapsed in the other known examples, all of which are located along the western seaboard of Ireland. They are similar in structure to the *bories* found in Provence or the *trulli* in the heel of Italy, some of which may be as late as the eighteenth century, but it is unlikely that there is any direct connection between them.

The doorway of Gallarus has jambs which incline in the way that the lintelled doorways of other Irish churches do, but it has one interesting feature not found on the other examples. This is the horizontal perforated stones projecting from the interior wall just above the lintel. They would only make sense if the door is understood as having hung on a horizontal hinge attached to a peg placed in the perforated stones, so that the doorway opened upwards from below.

Because the oratory is nowhere mentioned in historical sources, its date has been a matter of dispute, with suggestions varying from the seventh to the twelfth centuries. The recent calibrated radiocarbon date of roughly 568–770 for a similar version on the summit of Croagh Patrick (p. 58) and the mortar date of around the eighth century for a more primitive and less well-built version at Illaunloughan, on the Iveragh peninsula to the south, would now argue for not too late a date within this timespan, but it is best left an open question.

The oratory is located a few hundred yards from the Saint's Road which led sea-borne pilgrims landing at Ventry harbour past Kilmalkedar church on their way to the top of Mount Brandon, where St Brendan the Navigator was honoured. Its location somewhat off the pilgrim road may possibly have been chosen so as to provide the pilgrim with a view of the summit of the 3027-foot (923m)-high mountain, which would not have been possible from the nearest part of the pilgrims' road only a few hundred yards away.

HIGH CROSSES

High Crosses may be considered as Ireland's greatest contribution to the monumental art of medieval Europe. They are not confined to Ireland, and get their alternative name 'Celtic Crosses' from the fact that they are also frequently found in parts of Britain where Celtic languages are still spoken – Scotland and Wales – though they are also found in the north of England as well. Ireland, however, has the finest and most varied selection of such crosses anywhere in these islands.

The adjective 'high' seems very suitable to describe monuments which, on occasions, can be as tall as 20 feet (6m) – but it is also appropriate because this is precisely the term used when the old Irish Annals refer to a cross. Indeed, only a single example – the so-called Cross of the Scriptures at Clonmacnoise – can, in all likelihood, be identified with one mentioned in the Annals. Nowhere does early Irish literature give us any description of the crosses, so that it is left entirely up to us to work out why and when the crosses were erected.

The differing views on the why and the when are both numerous and contradictory, and – like the world view of Heraclitus – they are currently in a state of flux. Even when they were erected about a thousand years ago, there was perhaps no one single reason as to why they were created; enough of them survive to make us realize the possibility that they may have fulfilled a multiplicity of functions: boundary crosses, demarcators of sacred areas, recorders of happenings or agreements, teachers of the Bible's message, evokers of pious prayers and, as we shall see, monuments to political power and its co-operation with the Church.

One of the most frequent questions asked about the crosses is the purpose of the ring around the junction of the arm and shaft of the cross. One answer must surely be structural, namely the desire to ensure that the heavy stone cross-arms stayed in place and did not snap off, which they occasionally did at the point where there is a narrow constriction in the arm. But as the sculptor Imogen Stuart has pointed out, no self-respecting stone carver would have invented the shape of the perforated ring cross because of the danger of cracking the stone when breaking through the holes between arm and ring. Because there is a strong possibility, however, that the ring-form may have developed in some other artistic medium, such as wood, textiles or metalwork, we need not envisage the structural function of the ring as having been the primary one. Instead, it should also be seen as having been combined with a symbolic purpose, though scholars are divided as to what that purpose may have been – a garland of victory for the Christ figure at the focal point of the cross, an echo of the pagan sun god or a cosmic symbol, at the centre of which is represented the Christ whose Crucifixion early Christians saw as the most important event in the whole history of the universe. Again, perhaps, no one explanation by itself may have been accepted as satisfactory – the cross would have meant all things to all people.

As the symbol of Christianity, the cross in Ireland must be as old as the arrival of its religion in the country, and we do know of wooden crosses

Reaching a height of 21.5ft (6.5m), the West Cross at Monasterboice, Co. Louth, is the tallest of Ireland's High Crosses. It probably dates from the second half of the ninth century, its west face is sculpted with panels illustrating the life and death of Christ.

which were erected in the monastic foundations, but what they looked like is nowhere explained in the historical sources. The Irish were erecting cross-decorated pillars of stone at places such as Kilnasaggart, Co. Armagh, in the early eighth century, and the English were erecting crosses in stone at roughly the same period, if not before, but it must have taken the Irish some time before they began to adapt the idea and make it their own.

At present, we have no reliable basis for dating the Irish crosses before 800 with any degree of certainty, but it cannot be ruled out that some of the surviving examples may have been erected during the preceding century. Nevertheless, it is around the beginning of the ninth century that we can begin to trace a 'school' of cross carving based probably in Clonmacnoise, though some of its best products may have been prepared for other sites (see Banagher on p. 82). The High Cross at Bealin in County Westmeath is the only monument from this workshop which can be proved to have been a cross as opposed to a pillar and, in addition to its geometrical decoration, it has only a single human figure (on horseback). What may be the product of another, more isolated, school of masons, related more closely to Scotland than to Ireland, is the stone slab at Fahan Mura in County Donegal, which bears just two human figures, neither of which can be identified. Both Bealin and Fahan bear inscriptions, but none of the personal names recognizable in them can be identified with historically known persons.

It is not until the middle of the ninth century that we can finally document the erection of crosses on the basis of (newly deciphered) inscriptions which identify a king who is encountered in the old Irish Annals – Maelsechlainn I (846-82). He and his son Flann Sinna (879-916), both of the Clann Cholmáin branch of the Southern Uí Néill dynasty, would appear to have been patrons of crosses in the midlands, where we see the flowering of those great Scripture Crosses at centres such as Clonmacnoise and Durrow. Other important groups of crosses are found nearer the east coast at monasteries such as Kells and Monasterboice.

These great crosses are remarkable in having panels illustrating a series of biblical scenes on the surfaces of the cross – a feature rare in Christian art, but one which is known on an enamel cross from Rome in the early ninth century. The scenes span the whole of the Bible from Adam and Eve to the Last Judgment. Sequences from the Old Testament, including the story of the Creation, Exodus, David and Daniel, were chosen partly as examples of God helping those who were faithful to him in their time of peril, but partly also as prefigurations of events in the New Testament illustrated often on the other face of the crosses, such as the Childhood, Miracles, Passion, Death and Resurrection of Christ. Even a scene or two from the apocryphal parts of the Bible make their appearance as do the desert hermits Paul and Anthony, who could be claimed to have been the founders of monasticism and, thus, suitable for portrayal on crosses which may well have been carved by monks.

The selection of Bible scenes varies, of course, from cross to cross, so that each one is unique. But the choice was obviously well thought-out in each case in order to put across a particular idea or message. Some, as far as we can see, present a series of scenes from the Old and New Testaments like a film strip, simply to elucidate the Bible in visual form for those who were probably illiterate, but other selections were intentionally made to impress upon the populace certain tenets of Church dogma, such as the sacraments or the idea of Christ as King.

ABOVE Clonmacnoise may have started the vogue for High Crosses with examples that are more ornamental than scriptural, such as the North Cross, now moved inside into the Interpretative Centre.

RIGHT Granite crosses in the Barrow valley use deceptively naive methods to provide wonderfully graphic illustrations of bible stories, such as the Miracle of the Loaves and Fish seen here on the North Cross at Castledermot.

There is a remarkable concordance between the composition and choice of biblical scenes on the crosses and what we know of frescoes in the continental churches dating from the time of Charlemagne and his sons, suggesting that the High Crosses may have formed a substitute for frescoes, which would have been difficult to paint on to the darkened interior walls of the much smaller Irish wooden churches of the period. It also suggests that the High Cross carvers may ultimately have been drawing on the same iconographical sources as the fresco painters, whose inspiration – as far as Europe was concerned – was ultimately coming from the church interiors in the eternal city of Rome. But the comparison with continental church frescoes also raises the possibility, indeed almost the probability, that the High Crosses were originally painted with the same kind of colours (browns and whites) which we find surviving in Carolingian frescoes on the European continent, though not a trace of colour has ever been discovered on any of the Irish crosses. Exposure to the Irish elements for over a thousand years would have put paid to that, and the Office of Public Works must be praised for its recent activities in bringing some of the crosses (e.g. Clonmacnoise) inside to prevent further deterioration from acid rain, etc. There must have been considerable variety in the sources available to the sculptors for the compositions of their biblical scenes on the crosses, as some of the scenes – Adam and Eve and the Adoration of the Magi, for instance – occur in a range of forms on the different crosses.

There are certain hints to suggest that the High Crosses in stone may have been copied from models in other materials, including wood, which may have been considerably smaller – probably small enough to have been accommodated inside churches. Why it was felt necessary to start carving the crosses in stone is uncertain, but one possible explanation is that it was to prevent their being damaged or removed by marauding Vikings, in the same way that some geometrically decorated bronze crosses had been plundered by the Norsemen and brought back to Norway. Whatever the reason may have been for the sudden popularity of stone crosses in the ninth century, it is likely that many people would have prayed on their knees in front of them – the reason ingeniously put forward by the epigraphist John Higgitt as to why the inscriptions are all on the bottom of the shaft, where they could most easily be seen by those kneeling in front of them. Sometimes, too, the most important of the bible scenes – other than the Crucifixion – are placed in the lowermost panel on the shaft, and probably for exactly the same reason.

Many of the 'big' crosses are carved in one or more pieces from fine-grained sandstone, while granite was used for those at Moone, Castledermot and elsewhere in the Barrow valley. With the possible exception of the Drumbane grit used in St Patrick's Cross on the Rock of Cashel, it has not yet proved feasible to pinpoint the quarries which provided the stone for the crosses.

The distribution of crosses of ninth- or tenth-century date is spread over many parts of Leinster and Ulster, with correspondingly few in Munster and Connacht. The stimulus of political patronage may have been partially responsible for this, while the availability of trained carvers is another consideration. However, it has never been established where the stonemasons may have got their initial training, particularly to execute the naturalistic figure carving of classical inspiration which is alien to the Celtic tradition of stylizing the human figure so evident in contemporary manuscripts. Perhaps some influences from outside the country may have been at work.

RIGHT Fragments of two different crosses mounted together at Clones in the province of Ulster, where the same Old and New Testament events frequently recur on a number of other crosses.

The 'Unfinished' Cross at Kells shows that carving took place when the unhewn blocks had already been placed in position, but we cannot say whether 'workshops' of stonemasons were locally based or moved from one area to another in search of work, like the masons who worked on the great Gothic cathedrals of Europe.

Production of the great series of Scripture Crosses seems to have been scaled down during the course of the tenth century, but two hundred years later a new series was initiated, often without the ring so prevalent in the earlier group. The biblical scenes had largely – though not entirely – given way to high relief carvings of Christ (sometimes crucified, at other times triumphant) and a bishop or abbot figure, presumably the local church founder, was chosen to impress those who would have been coming on pilgrimage to the site in order to venerate his relics. Here, Munster (e.g. Cashel and Dysert O'Dea) and Connacht (Tuam) come into their own, using not only sandstone but the much harder limestone as a material, though some examples do occur also in Ulster (Downpatrick) and Leinster (Glendalough). The Tuam crosses are noteworthy because of the inscriptions they bear, demonstrating the patronage of the O Conor High Kings who may have used them as a symbol of the revival of an earlier Golden Age to further their political aims.

The Normans were instrumental in bringing to an end the creation of High Crosses which had spanned four or more centuries. Later medieval and seventeenth-century crosses are of a different kind, and are usually less impressive, but it is interesting to note that the Celtic ringed cross experienced another revival in the mid-nineteenth century, this time also for political reasons, as an expression of the Celtic resurgence and increased economic prosperity among the Irish middle classes.

BANAGHER
Co. Offaly

A decorated stone shaft about 4ft 6in (1.4m) high, which came originally from Banagher in County Offaly but now in the National Museum in Dublin, is one of half a dozen monuments likely to have emanated from a workshop which was active probably in Clonmacnoise around 800 and was among the earliest to have produced High Crosses in Ireland. The socket holes at the top of the narrow sides of the stone were presumably designed to receive the lower segments of a cross ring, but because these cut into the decoration they are clearly secondary, so that there is no certainty, therefore, that this shaft originally formed part of a cross. It may, simply, have been a free-standing pillar. The narrow sides are decorated with interlace and animal ornament, but the main faces bear a horseman with staff (or crozier), a deer caught in a trap and lions, as well as human interlace – all neatly framed and carved in false relief. The symbolic significance which they must once have had is now, sadly, lost to us.

FAHAN MURA
Co. Donegal

The stele at Fahan Mura has played an important part in academic discussions about the development of the Irish High Cross because its arm-stumps were seen to represent the breaking out of the cross from the upright decorated slabs which were thought to have preceded them in the seventh century. But it is probably preferable to see this slab as being more closely associated with the sculptural development of Pictish slabs in Scotland, which share the pointed pediment with it. The Fahan monument is best known for the Greek inscription on the north side, translatable as 'Glory and honour to the Father, Son and Holy Spirit', a formula which was accepted by the Council of Toledo in 633 but one which cannot be used to date the slab to the seventh century because it is also found in a penitential tract of c.800 and is still used in the Irish of Munster today. Even if we cannot establish a date for this unique stone (seventh, eighth or ninth century?), it is a remarkable piece of carving, with an intricately woven cross on each face. That on the west face has figures (bearing indecipherable inscriptions) standing at the foot of the cross, which expand on either side at the bottom of the shaft, now beneath ground level.

Fahan usually has the name Mura attached to it, in honour of the abbot Mura who founded the monastery here in the early seventh century, and whose crozier-shrine and bell are preserved in the National Museum in Dublin. His name is associated with a metrical Life of St Columba, which could help to explain the possible connection with Scotland. A later abbot, Fothad (819), was responsible for having all monks and clerics exonerated from war service, and another, Mael Mura, who died in 887, was a well-known poet.

CLONMACNOISE
Co. Offaly

Bealin, Banagher and their siblings were like the early buds of spring when Clonmacnoise was making its first efforts to create stone crosses around 800, after which there is a long and rather inexplicable

LEFT Animals – a lion, a horse (with crook-bearing rider) and a deer caught in a trap – dominate the cross-shaft or pillar from Banagher, Co. Offaly, perhaps one of the earliest surviving High Crosses in Ireland, preserved in the National Museum of Ireland.

BELOW Intricate ribbon interlace – a design well known among the Picts in Scotland – weaves a cross pattern on the face of the pedimented slab at Fahan, Co. Donegal.

RIGHT Placed formerly in front of the door of Clonmacnoise Cathedral, but now removed to the shelter of the Interpretative Centre, the Cross of the Scriptures, with its pre-eminent ring and tilted arms, is one of the most gracefully proportioned of all the Irish crosses. At the head of the east face, shown here, is the Last Judgment.

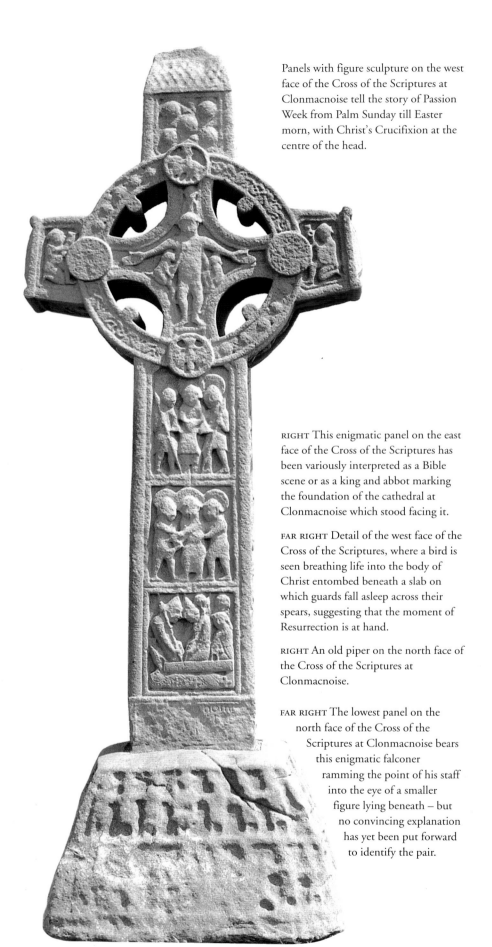

Panels with figure sculpture on the west face of the Cross of the Scriptures at Clonmacnoise tell the story of Passion Week from Palm Sunday till Easter morn, with Christ's Crucifixion at the centre of the head.

RIGHT This enigmatic panel on the east face of the Cross of the Scriptures has been variously interpreted as a Bible scene or as a king and abbot marking the foundation of the cathedral at Clonmacnoise which stood facing it.

FAR RIGHT Detail of the west face of the Cross of the Scriptures, where a bird is seen breathing life into the body of Christ entombed beneath a slab on which guards fall asleep across their spears, suggesting that the moment of Resurrection is at hand.

RIGHT An old piper on the north face of the Cross of the Scriptures at Clonmacnoise.

FAR RIGHT The lowest panel on the north face of the Cross of the Scriptures at Clonmacnoise bears this enigmatic falconer ramming the point of his staff into the eye of a smaller figure lying beneath – but no convincing explanation has yet been put forward to identify the pair.

gap of at least fifty years before the full flowering represented by the matured South Cross and the high sophistication of the Cross of the Scriptures, both produced around the second half of the ninth century and now moved for protection into the Interpretative Centre.

The South Cross, which stood close to the south-western corner of the church known as Temple Hurpan, is mounted on a base which appears to bear an Adam and Eve scene on the south side. The only New Testament sculpture on the cross is a Crucifixion, which, unusually, is carved on the shaft of the west face rather than at the centre of the head, possibly because it copied carefully an upright rectangular model which could not have been comfortably accommodated on the head of the cross. An inscription was discovered on the bottom of the west face of the shaft, but it is so badly weathered that it is very difficult to decipher. However, one interpretation of the defaced letters between those which can just be made out would allow it to be reconstructed as asking a prayer for Maelsechlainn, son of Maelruanaidh – the same monarch whose patronage enabled the erection of the Castlebernard cross, thus providing a probable date for this cross around the middle of the ninth century.

Maelsechlainn's name may also have been present among the somewhat better preserved inscriptions on the two faces of the Cross of the Scriptures, so-called because it is probably correctly identified with the cross of

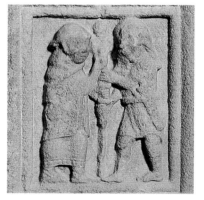

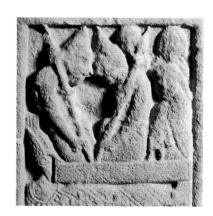

that name mentioned in the *Annals of the Four Masters*. But here his name would have appeared merely as the father of the man who commissioned the cross, Fland, better known as Flann Sinna, who was King of Ireland from 879 to 916. We may, therefore, have here a cross of a generation later than the South Cross mentioned above.

The proportions and the unusual uptilting arms of the Cross of the Scriptures make it one of the most graceful of all the Irish crosses. It is also the first of the crosses presented here which illustrates an extensive series of biblical events, though their interpretations have proved to be very controversial – particularly those on the north side for which no coherent story has yet been elicited. Those on the other side and on the two faces do, however, provide us with a programme which does make sense even if some of the panels still present difficulties. The main theme represented is the Passion, Death and Resurrection of Christ, with the Crucifixion on the head of the west face forming the central focus. Immediately beneath it is a scene of the Soldiers deciding not to part Christ's Garment – an event sometimes forming part of the Crucifixion representation in early medieval art and symbolizing the indivisibility of the Church. Beneath it are a Mocking scene and Christ in the Tomb, with a bird breathing life into the mouth of the Saviour, suggesting that the moment of Resurrection is at hand. The same theme is continued on the base, where on the bottom register we find rather worn carvings of Christ entering Jerusalem, the Resurrection and the Holy Women coming to the Tomb. Above that is Christ with Six Apostles, and the Passion is continued around the corner on the south side of the base with the Arrest of Christ.

The head of the east face of the Cross of the Scriptures is occupied by the Last Judgment, with Christ in Majesty above, and Jesus handing the Key to Peter and the Gospel to Paul immediately beneath it. The two panels lower down the shaft have proved much more difficult to interpret. The bottom panel has been the subject of various suggestions involving local events. It shows two differently clad men holding an upright staff between them, evincing interpretations including King Diarmait mac Cerbaill, perhaps the last of the pagan High Kings, helping St Ciarán set up the corner post of his church, or Abbot Colman and Flann Sinna, who built the cathedral in front of which the cross stands. Both of these local scenes might be seen as somewhat out of place on a cross described as being 'of the Scriptures'. The only biblical interpretations offered for the two lower panels on the east face, even though they do have their problems, are that the lower one represents Joseph interpreting the Dream of Pharaoh's Butler and the upper one the fulfilment of that dream, when the butler was reinstalled in his post three days later. This interpretation has the attraction that it could be taken as an Old Testament prefiguration of Christ rising from the Tomb three days after his death, as he himself had foretold – the scene which is shown back to back with the lowest panel on the west face of the cross. The correct evaluation of all the scenes on this cross, taken together, will surely provide ample scope for discussion in the years to come, as they have already done for centuries past.

St Columba's important foundation at Durrow in County Offaly has bequeathed to us this fine High Cross of around the ninth/tenth century and the seventh-century *Book of Durrow* now in the Library of Trinity College, Dublin.

DURROW
Co. Offaly

Durrow was one of those monasteries founded by St Columba before he left Ireland in 563, and is best known for its famous seventh-century Book removed a thousand years later to Dublin, where, along with that other Columban marvel, the *Book of Kells*, it forms one of the great treasures of Trinity College Library. The most important of the monastery's monuments to have remained *in situ* is the High Cross, which has both contrasts and similarities with the Cross of the Scriptures at Clonmacnoise. Unlike the latter, its base bears no figure sculpture, and the Old Testament is better represented, with various panels illustrating the Book of Genesis and two of David; there are two unusual scenes on the north side apparently of St John the Baptist, and one of the panels on

the east face of the shaft has knots of interlacing. These contrasts are balanced by the similarities, including the decoration of the ring and the details of both sides of the head, the snakes intertwining with human heads on the underside of the ring, the tronco-pyramidal arm-ends imitating metalwork bosses of the kind found in the Oseberg ship in Norway and, above all, the Passion iconography on the west face of the shaft. The details of this last feature are not quite close enough to suggest that the same hand was at work on both crosses but they at least entitle us to think in terms of a single 'workshop' being involved.

One of the surviving inscriptions on the Durrow cross surprises us by intimating that it could be a generation earlier than the Cross of the Scriptures. The inscription on the west face has too few letters intact to be intelligible, but that on the bottom of the north side of the shaft could once more suggest that the same team which erected the Castlebernard cross was at work here too, as a likely reconstruction reads in translation as: 'Pray for Maelsechlainn King of Ireland, pray for Colman who made the cross'. The appearance of Colman's name on the cross strengthens the case for seeing him as the king's stonemason-carver, but making this cross date to the reign of Maelsechlainn (846-62) in contrast to the Cross of the Scriptures, apparently erected by his son Fland (879-916).

KELLS
Co. Meath

The monastery of Kells, as already noted, was founded by Columban monks early in the ninth century, presumably to provide a safe haven for the relics of St Columba brought from Iona in the western Hebrides. Iona is considered an important centre in the development of the ringed cross, and its monks may have brought new ideas with them for the erection of High Crosses in Kells during the ninth century. But the dearth of scriptural scenes on the Iona crosses when compared with

the rich selection found on the Kells crosses suggests rather that Kells may have looked more to the European continent for inspiration in the choice of biblical material, and a case can be made for seeing Kells as one of the, if not *the*, most important centre for the dissemination of biblical iconography on the great series of Irish Scripture Crosses.

There are four crosses, as well as a separate round base, surviving in Kells. The one first seen by most travellers is that in the Market Place, dating from the ninth century. The other three are all in the churchyard surrounding the Protestant church where the original stone church of the monastery presumably once stood. One of the three (p. 81) is unfinished, and shows that the final carving of the crosses took place after they were

LEFT AND RIGHT Since 1688, and probably long before, the Market Cross has stood at what was probably once the entrance to the Columban monastery at Kells in County Meath, founded early in the ninth century.

erected. It may be later than the rest, perhaps no earlier than the tenth century, whereas the other two probably both belong to the ninth century, though one of them, which stands close to the Round Tower, may not, according to Roger Stalley, have been erected much before the year 900. Its lack of compartmentalization of the biblical scenes, and the lower relief of its carving, could well support the notion of such a date.

Originally the more important of the two was what is now known as the Broken Cross but, because it has lost its head, it is regrettably all too often overlooked by the visitor. As its massive stump still stands to a height of about 8 feet (2.4m), it must have presented an impressive, even awesome, appearance of monumentality when still surmounted by its now lost head.

It may, however, not stand in its original position because the placing of the Old Testament material on the west face – as opposed to its normal positioning on the east face – suggests that it has been re-erected at some stage in its history.

What is so fascinating about this cross is its unusual selection of biblical scenes, of which seven out of a total of twelve are found on no other Irish cross. While the sides are largely decorated only with geometrical, interlaced and bossed patterns, the two faces are filled with scriptural panels, with the Old and New Testament being allotted to different faces. The west face shows, in ascending order, Adam and Eve, Noah's Ark, followed by three scenes from the Book of Exodus: probably the Turning of the Waters of Egypt into Blood, the Pillar of Fire in the Desert, and a fragment of the Passage of the Israelites through the Red Sea. On the east face illustrated here we find the Baptism of Christ, the Marriage Feast of Cana, then a panel probably combining The Healing of the Lame Man at the Pool of Bethesda with Christ and the Samaritan Woman, followed by the apocryphal Washing of the Christ Child, surmounted by the Three Magi questioning Herod and, finally, Christ's Entry into Jerusalem.

There is a neat correlation between the two faces in the choice of some of the panels, as instanced by quadrupeds being the common denominator in the Red Sea and Entry into Jerusalem scenes at the top, and the supernatural light shared by the Pillar of Fire and the star which led the Magi to question Herod. Water can be seen to form a vital component in the stories of eight of the panels represented, suggesting that the scenes were carefully chosen to demonstrate the cleansing power of water. The purpose of this was to stress the importance of Baptism as a sacrament, a point further

RIGHT When originally standing to its full height, complete with its now lost head, the Broken Cross at Kells in County Meath must have struck awe into the beholders who came to 'read' the Bible story in pictures. The high relief panels on the east face, shown here, illustrate events in the New Testament including the Baptism of Christ on the bottom and the Miracle at Cana above it.

emphasized by placing Christ's Baptism in the Jordan out of its proper chronological order on the bottom of the shaft where those kneeling in front of the cross could see it at eye level. Baptism was seen as providing a regeneration for mankind, and back to back with it at the bottom of the west face are Adam and Eve, who represent the first generation in the Book of Genesis. The iconography of this cross demonstrates the care taken to choose scenes that illustrate an important message, in this instance, the sacrament of baptism, which was only one of two recognized by the Church at the time – the other being the Eucharist. One could well imagine that this once massive cross, with its well-thought-out biblical material, might well have been a seminal influence on the development of Scriptural Crosses in Ireland, and it may well date to around, if not before, the middle of the ninth century.

MONASTERBOICE
Co. Louth

Monasterboice was founded by St Buite, about whom little is known, though tradition says that he died on the same day that St Columba was born in 521. This may indicate some connection between the crosses at Kells and those at Monasterboice, which must date from around the same period in the ninth century as some of the Kells crosses. Of the two complete High Crosses at Monasterboice, the one nearest the Round Tower (p. 78) is over 21 feet (6.4m) tall. The other, illustrated here, is more squat and solid in its proportions, and is one of the most impressive and best-preserved crosses in the country. The quality and inventiveness of the carving puts to shame all of those poor nineteenth-century imitations which hedge it in, and emphasizes how much better it would look if the example of Clonmacnoise were followed and the tombstones of the graveyard were laid flat.

Muiredach's Cross, as it is known, gets its name from an inscription at the bottom of the west face of the shaft which asks a prayer for Muiredach who made the cross. We are given no clue as to who this Muiredach was – king, abbot or even carver – but it was probably some time during the course of the ninth or even as late as the early tenth century that he added this great cross to the treasury of early medieval Irish art. Its biblical figures are carved in a remarkably high relief, creating shadows which help the figures to jump out at us from their background. Its east face manages to pack in an unusually large number of individual figures, culminating in the thronged Last Judgment scene at the head, which is one of the earliest grandiose representations of this subject to survive anywhere in Europe.

The focal point of the west face is the Crucifixion at the centre of the head, flanked not only by the usual sponge- and lance-bearers, but also by the sun and moon, as well as other figures which may represent earth and ocean. These may refer to the four elements, with the ring encircling them symbolizing the cosmos. The four Magi in the Adoration scene on the other face may denote the four corners of the earth from which the Magi are traditionally said to have come and the panels on the shaft beneath the Crucifixion seem to continue the same earth and heaven theme. The lowermost panel (above the inscription, which is fitted in between cats) shows Christ being mocked as the earthly King of the Jews; above it comes the Raised Christ, showing Christ as King of the Heavens, and beneath the Crucifixion Christ handing to St Paul the Gospels of the Church on Earth

Muiredach's Cross at Monasterboice, Co. Louth, the best preserved of all the Irish High Crosses, dates from around the second half of the ninth century. Its west face is richly carved with New Testament scenes, the figures on the shaft panels being noticeably larger than those on the head, where the Crucifixion is the focus of attention.

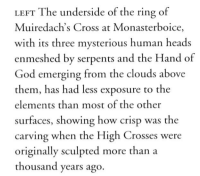

LEFT The underside of the ring of Muiredach's Cross at Monasterboice, with its three mysterious human heads enmeshed by serpents and the Hand of God emerging from the clouds above them, has had less exposure to the elements than most of the other surfaces, showing how crisp was the carving when the High Crosses were originally sculpted more than a thousand years ago.

LEFT Two back-to-back, tail-biting animals of indeterminate species at the bottom of Muiredach's Cross at Monasterboice share the same frolicsome appearance with the capricious creatures who enliven the lines of the *Book of Kells.*

and to Peter the Keys of the Kingdom of Heaven. Taken together, these subjects would appear to have been chosen to illustrate the theme of Christ as King of Heaven and Earth. On top, Christ can be seen ascending to heaven, while on the south arm is shown the first stage of that celestial journey – Christ's Resurrection.

MOONE
Co. Kildare

Moone is a monastery which has been associated with the Columban family of churches from at least the tenth century, yet its unusual High Crosses (of which only one is complete) bear no stylistic affinities to those on other sites which we have seen to be associated with St Columba, such as Durrow and Kells. The Moone cross is unique in its tall slender form and its beguilingly schematic carvings which make it into one of the most appealing of all the Irish High Crosses. The only recognizably biblical figure on the cross itself is the figure of Christ at the centre of the east face, most of the remainder of the cross being taken up by curious birds and animals.

But the real fascination of Moone lies in the base, all four faces of which are carved with figures, mostly with bodies so flat that they must have been coloured originally. The base consists of two trapeze-shaped stages, with the upper part narrowing more noticeably than that beneath it. On the east face the scenes, in ascending order, are Daniel in the Lion Pit (its seven lions demonstrating that it is illustrating an apocryphal book of the Old Testament), the Sacrifice of Isaac and, on top, Adam and Eve (the only panel on the cross with rounded relief). The reason for making the chronological order read downwards rather than upwards was, presumably, so that

RIGHT The tall base is the main bearer of the biblical message on the unusually slender High Cross at Moone, Co. Kildare, which has now been moved to a recently re-roofed church nearby to protect it from the elements.

Adam and Eve, perpetrators of the original sin which ultimately led Christ to give his life on the cross, could be placed back to back with the Crucifixion above a jovial set of twelve apostles on the west face.

Two of the subjects on the east face – Isaac and Daniel – serve to illustrate the theme that God helps the faithful who are in danger, and the same theme infuses all three subjects on the south face. The scheme is continued here with the chronologically earliest scene on the top – the Three Hebrew Children, saved from a fiery death in the furnace by an angel that spreads its wings to protect them. One of those winged agents of God also appeared to Joseph to tell him to take the Holy Family with him into Egypt, a scene of God's help which fills the middle panel in the form of the Flight into Egypt. The Virgin rides side-saddle, and only Christ's head appears diagonally beside hers. His body must surely have been painted on her rather unflatteringly square torso. It was God's aid, too, which helped Christ perform the Miracle of the Loaves and Fishes and feed the five thousand faithful listening to the word of God on the mount, an event brilliantly portrayed in the lowest panel by five flat loaves and four fish, without the figure of Christ being portrayed at all, surely one of the most graphically ingenious representations on any Irish High Cross.

The granite crosses of south Leinster lack any inscriptions to help us date them, but we would probably not go far wrong in envisaging the Moone cross as a wonderful work of the ninth century.

CASTLEDERMOT
Co. Kildare

Castledermot – in Irish, *Dísert Díarmata* – was founded around 812 as a hermitage by a man named Diarmait, under the auspices of the reforming Céli Dé movement. Its two crosses bear figure sculpture which seems stiff and stylized because it is carved from granite, a rather intractable stone, but their Apostles and Loaves and Fishes share something of the attractiveness of the same subjects on the cross at Moone. The back-to-back placing of Our First Parents and The Crucifixion at Moone is here raised to a statement of greater import by allotting them a whole face each on the head of the North Cross. Around Adam and Eve on the west face are clustered the harp-playing David (left arm), Abraham and Isaac (right arm) and Daniel in the Lions' Den (below). The central figures on the two lowermost panels of the shaft are each surrounded by animals, perhaps tempting St Anthony, the model hermit in the desert, and possibly alluding thereby to the Irish name of the place.

On the base are high-relief S-spirals looking as if they had been squeezed from a tube of toothpaste. But in the interstices there are round and diamond-shaped bosses, which must surely be copies in stone of the heads of metal rivets used to hammer a bronze spiral-decorated plate onto the base of a wooden cross which acted as a model – a neat demonstration that Irish stone crosses must first have been worked out in wood and bronze, and perhaps other materials as well, before being carved in stone.

Castledermot has a second cross, placed to the south of the church, which is unusual in having biblical scenes on only one of the faces, whereas the other face is entirely devoted to geometrical ornament. Standing isolated between the two crosses is the surviving Romanesque doorway of a twelfth-century church, demolished in the thirteenth century to make way for a larger Gothic parish church.

TOP Father Abraham sacrificing his son Isaac was most expressively rendered by a master carver on the Moone Cross.

ABOVE The graphic representation of the Miracle of the Loaves and Fishes on the base of the cross at Moone, Co. Kildare, succeeds in putting its message across, even though Christ as the wonder worker is omitted.

RIGHT AND FAR RIGHT Obdurate granite yielded to the carver's chisel in producing charming crosses at Castledermot, Co. Kildare, with Adam and Eve unusually occupying centre stage on the North Cross (far right) and the more usual Crucifixion in the same position on the South Cross (right).

AHENNY
Co. Tipperary

Historical sources may be silent about Ahenny, but the site has two of the most sensitively chiselled High Crosses in the country. Instead of biblical sculpture standing out in relief, patterns are carved with gossamer delicacy into the flat surface of the stone, including spirals wound up like the spring of one of those old-fashioned watches. Ruffling their calm swell is an unexpected human interlace at the centre of the shaft – its symbolism lost to us, like the rest of the decoration. While the five bosses could symbolize the five wounds of Christ upon the cross, they may have been modelled on ornamental rivet-heads copied in stone from the bronze original.

Analogous to Moone, the base is the main bearer of the human figure sculpture, the side shown here representing Christ and six of his staff-bearing apostles. The same scene appears in a similar position on the Cross of the Scriptures at Clonmacnoise, so that Ahenny may represent a regional school of quality sculptors in contact with Clonmacnoise and possibly roughly contemporary with the Scripture Crosses there, rather than being seen as among the earliest of Ireland's fully developed High Crosses, dating from the eighth century, as some have suggested.

DYSERT O'DEA
Co. Clare

One of the local O'Dea family, who attached their name to the *Dísert*, or hermitage, where St Tola established himself in the eighth century, 'repaired' this twelfth-century cross in 1683. But while Michael O'Dea doubtless went to work with the best of intentions, he may have inadvertently mounted together a shaft and a head of two different crosses, in the same way that stones from two separate portals were compressed into one famous Romanesque doorway (p. 120) in the nearby church – probably at the same time and by the same hand. The Viking-inspired animal interlacings characteristic of the lower shaft of the cross certainly differ markedly from the geometrical decoration on the head fragment.

On the east face the long-robed Christ in high relief, akin to the much-venerated statue of Christ known as the Volto Santo in the Italian city of Lucca, occupies the upper fragment. Beneath him stands the mitred figure of a bishop or abbot, presumably St Tola, who was, doubtless, portrayed to impress pilgrims who would have come here to venerate his relics, including the bell and enshrined crozier now preserved in the National Museum in Dublin. The pyramidal base of the cross, which stands on decorated stones originally part of the nearby church, is one of the few twelfth-century examples where the earlier fashion of illustrating bible scenes is continued with the representation of Adam and Eve among the spreading branches of the apple tree on one face, and what may be Daniel in the Lions' Den on the side.

GLENDALOUGH
Co. Wicklow

The so-called 'Market Cross' now preserved in the Interpretative Centre at Glendalough shows that twelfth-century crosses are not the exclusive preserve of the western half of the country. Though smaller in stature, it shares many of their features, such as the small figures on the base, as at Tuam, and the animal ornament on the sides which is derived from a Viking style of decoration known as 'Urnes'. In addition, it also bears the figure of Christ wearing a loin-cloth, as found on many of the small bronze crucifixes of the period, and beneath it an abbot or bishop, who most likely represents St Kevin, the founder of Glendalough.

LEFT Christ Triumphant and the figure of the local saint Tola beneath stand out in very high relief on the east face of the twelfth-century cross at Dysert O'Dea, Co. Clare.

RIGHT Possibly of ninth-century date, the North Cross at Ahenny is exquisitely carved with decorative motifs in shallow relief on shaft and head, while reserving the biblical figures for the base.

RIGHT St Kevin is probably the ecclesiastic portrayed on the shaft of the Market Cross at Glendalough, now housed in the Interpretative Centre there.

MEMORIALS AND
MYSTERY SCULPTURES

While the High Crosses are certainly Ireland's most memorable and noticeable contribution to the treasury of early medieval figure sculpture in Europe, the country preserves, in addition, a considerable number of other witnesses to the contemporary stonemason's talents. Some of these may be simple crosses, free-standing or carved on pillars, still giving silent testimony to the strength of Christian faith in medieval Ireland as they languish in some corner of a half-forgotten field. On other memorials lying flat in a once-important monastic site of pilgrimage the cross may be accompanied by the name of an individual past recall, whose lapidary request for a prayer still reverberates across the intervening centuries. Human figures, in high or false relief, also make their appearance in stone but, uttering no words and with penetrating gaze, they call upon our imagination to interpret their message and their meaning to the best of our abilities.

REASK
Co. Kerry

Reask is a roughly circular enclosure near Ballyferriter, well known for its collection of cross-decorated slabs, some of which are now on display in the Heritage Centre in Ballyferriter. The most famous one still *in situ* has an encircled cross of arcs standing on a base of ornamental spirals and bears the simple inscription DNE – an abbreviation presumably of the Latin word *domine*, meaning 'Lord'. Its date is unknown, but it may be ascribed to the period between the seventh and the tenth century. Like so many other sites near the western end of the Dingle Peninsula, Reask has no history attached to it. Much of what can be learned about it had to be gleaned from the excavating spade of the late Tom Fanning, who uncovered the remains between 1972 and 1975.

KILNASAGGART
Co. Armagh

The earliest Irish stone monument datable by inscription is a pillar standing to a height of 7ft 4in (2.2m) in a field at Kilnasaggart ('The Church of the Priest'), Co. Armagh. One face of the stone bears an old Irish inscription which, in translation, reads: 'This place, Ternóc, son of Ciarán the Little, bequeathed it under the protection of Apostle Peter'. As the death of Ternóc is recorded in the *Annals of Tigernach* under the year 716, the stone is likely to date from around the first quarter of the eighth century, and probably some considerable time before the Irish began to erect stone crosses. Above the inscription is a Latin cross and, beneath it, an encircled equal-armed cross with curling terminals. On the

LEFT On the pillar-stone at Reask, Co. Kerry, the encircled cross on top adds force to the three vertical letters DNE beneath, standing for DOMINE, an invocation of the Lord.

RIGHT The inscription on the pillar at Kilnasaggart, Co. Armagh, recording a gift by a man named Ternoc who died in 716, makes it the earliest reliably datable stone in Early Christian Ireland.

other face ten further equal-armed crosses are incised and surrounded by a circle in relief. Excavations by Ann Hamlin in 1966 and 1968 uncovered stone graves around the foot of the stone, some stone-built, others dug, but no trace of a church from which the place gets its name.

CLONMACNOISE
Co. Offaly

Clonmacnoise has the largest collection in the country of those flat cross-inscribed slabs which are generally taken to have been grave-markers, but which the cautious Macalister described simply as 'memorial slabs'. More than six hundred survive, most of them fragmentary, and they range in date from perhaps as early as the seventh century up to the twelfth. The crosses are of various kinds, most typically equal-armed in a square frame (mainly eighth and ninth centuries) or unframed Latin crosses with decorated arm-ends expanding into a semi-circle (probably ninth to eleventh centuries). Frequently, they bear inscriptions starting with the formula $\overline{\text{OR}}$ DO (a prayer for) followed by the name of the individual commemorated. Only in rare instances can the person named be identified in historical sources. One of the finest of these stones is that of Tuathal Saer, a wright (*saer* in Irish), who sadly cannot be identified, but its style suggests a date in the ninth or tenth centuries, when the

LEFT Clonmacnoise houses the greatest Irish collection of cross-decorated slabs, the products of a workshop active from about AD 700 to 1200. Over the centuries, the designs varied considerably; this example, with an inscription asking a prayer for Tuathal the wright, probably dates from around the ninth or tenth century.

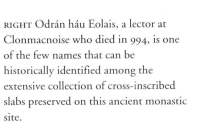

RIGHT Odrán háu Eolais, a lector at Clonmacnoise who died in 994, is one of the few names that can be historically identified among the extensive collection of cross-inscribed slabs preserved on this ancient monastic site.

95

Clonmacnoise workshop was producing not only stones like this but High Crosses as well. One rather degenerate example, on display with a selection of others in the foyer of the new Interpretative Centre, commemorates Odrán háu Eolais, a scribe or lector of Clonmacnoise, whose death is recorded in the *Annals of the Four Masters* under the year 994.

TULLYLEASE
Co. Cork

Even if the collection of cross-decorated memorial slabs at Tullylease in north Cork is numerically far smaller than that from Clonmacnoise, at least one of the stones there is its equal in quality. This is the one requesting in Latin that whoever reads the inscription should pray for Berechtuine. Within a frame it has a Greek cross with chalice-like terminals and a shaft which expands to a hemisphere below. A circle of interlace dominates the centre of the cross, the remainder of which is decorated with a fretwork pattern. In addition, there are four spiral circles in the interstices and Christ's monogram XPS in the upper right-hand corner.

Tullylease is a site with Anglo-Saxon connections. The Berechtuine of the inscription is the Anglo-Saxon name Beorhtwine, but it cannot be associated historically with either of the two slightly similar-sounding names referred to in early sources – an early eighth-century Bercert or a Berichter who died in 839 – so that the date of the slab must remain in the realms of speculation (eighth or possibly ninth century?). The cross bears a resemblance to one in the *Book of Lindisfarne* of *c.*700, but this is probably best explained by both being derived from a common source rather than one being derived directly from the other.

BOA ISLAND
Co. Fermanagh

At the northern edge of Lower Lough Erne the small graveyard of Caldragh on Boa Island, which is joined to the mainland by road at both ends, contains two remarkable pieces of stone sculpture, of unsettling and almost menacing appearance. The smaller of the two comes from an even smaller island off-shore known as Lustymore, while the larger one always seems to have been associated with Boa Island itself. The larger piece is the upper part of an almost square block of stone out of which two figures are carved, back to back. The two heads are triangular, almost pear-shaped, their prominent eyes with countersunk irises outlined by a ridge above and below. One has a curling moustache, and both have beards cradled in the arms which cross the body beneath them. A belt at the waist binds both figures together, and their hair is interlaced, falling down on the sides between the heads. The pair of figures have been compared to the back-to-back Roman Janus idols, thus suggesting to many that the Boa Island statue represents some dual Celtic god. If so, it would obviously be prehistoric in date, but the presence of the curious medieval figures on White Island further up the lake has recently given rise to increasing suspicions that the Boa Island figures are more Christian in date, whatever their inspiration. But, no matter what their age, they remain perplexing and mysterious in any context.

ABOVE Berechtuine, whose name appears on this fine cross-inscribed slab at Tullylease, Co. Cork, cannot be positively identified, but his memorial is likely to have been carved in the eighth or ninth century.

RIGHT Like Easter Island in the Pacific, Boa Island in County Fermanagh's Lower Lough Erne has its mysterious and perplexing statues. We cannot even be sure whether this one, representing two figures back-to-back, is pagan or Christian.

WHITE ISLAND
Co. Fermanagh

Lough Erne was doubtless a busy waterway in the early medieval period, and its islands were favoured as sites for churches. Devenish, near the upper end of Lower Lough Erne, was the most impressive of these, but further downstream and close to the wooded eastern shore, there is a smaller but no less fascinating island, reachable from the marina at Castle Archdale. This is White Island, where a modern wall encloses a medieval church of *c.*1200, with the only complete rounded Romanesque doorway surviving in northern Ireland.

Since the beginning of the nineteenth century, a variety of curious carvings have been extracted from its walls, and these have now been attached to the interior north wall. Apart from two showing mainly heads, they are grouped in three sets of two full figures, each varying in size from the other, and all strongly modelled in high relief with penetrating forward-facing gazes. One of the smallest sits cross-legged, while another has its hands in a muffler. One of the figures in the largest group holds a staff or crozier in one hand and a bell in the other, while the second figure of the group puts one hand up to its mouth and has a pouch-like object at the waist. The medium-sized grouping with curly hair comprises one holding two animals (with bird-head, but four legs) face to face, while the other holds a sword and miniscule shield in front of him. This last figure also wears a penannular brooch on the breast, which suggests a date in the eighth or ninth century for the whole group.

Both individually and collectively, these figures present problems of identification and function. The group comprising the pouch-bearing figure and the warrior have tentatively been interpreted as David and Goliath, another suggestion being that they should be seen in conjunction with pilgrimage activity on the site. Being unique in the canon of Irish medieval stone sculpture, it is difficult to know what purpose the figures may have served. Here, too, theories abound – paired supports for the steps of a pulpit or a reliquary shrine of less permanent materials, now long perished. Suggestions there are many, but the mystery of the figures will remain.

KILLADEAS
Co. Fermanagh

One of the links in the little circle of curious figure carving in and around Lower Lough Erne in County Fermanagh is the small upright slab in Killadeas churchyard, between Enniskillen and Castle Archdale. Known as 'The Bishop's Stone' and dating probably from around the eighth or ninth century, it is just over 3 feet (0.9m) high and is carved on the narrow side with a head featuring a raised rectangular mouth, relating it to the White Island figures, and with an interlace beneath it. On one of the broad faces of the stone, and fitting in with the curving outline of the upper surface of the pillar, is the profile of an almost caricature-like figure carved in false relief with a noticeably projecting chin. In one hand he bears a staff or crozier, giving rise to the name locals give the stone, and in the other a bell. On his feet he wears shoes with a high back and front. Does he really represent a bishop or could his staff, bell and shoes suggest that we may have here a realistic representation of an early Christian pilgrim on his way to make the rounds of nearby islands, particularly Devenish, where the relics of St Molaise were venerated? We shall never know, but, whoever he was, he is a charming piece of stylized carving, done by a craftsman with a feel for caricature, one suspects.

ABOVE Differing sizes, tonsures, expressions and attributes make the enigmatic ninth-century(?) figures on White Island, Co. Fermanagh, very difficult to interpret.

RIGHT Hunched to fit the shape of the stone, the figure at Killadeas, near Lower Lough Erne in County Fermanagh, has attributes which could well have been those of a pilgrim to nearby Devenish – a staff, a bell and a stout pair of shoes.

ROUND TOWERS

Round Towers stand along with High Crosses (not to mention wolfhounds and shamrocks) as one of the great archetypal symbols of Ireland, because they are found almost exclusively in Ireland; elsewhere only three examples are known, two in Scotland and one on the Isle of Man. Intact specimens stand to a height varying between 70 to just over 100 feet (20-30m), their gracefully tapering shape being usually topped by a neat conical cap. However, some (e.g. Kildare) have crenellated tops, not all of which need be later than medieval in date. Their entrance doorways, normally about 10 feet (3m) above ground level, faced roughly in the direction of the major church on the sites where they stand. Both doorways and window-openings vary in shape, some round, others flat-headed and occasionally even pointed. Except for the four top windows, symmetrically arranged around the circumference, the smaller windows on the way up point in different directions, suggesting that the interior stair-cases did not ascend in a straight line. Instead, they probably alternated in direction as they went up level by level, of which there may have been as many as seven, the floor levels being indicated by offsets or corbels in the interior walls. Both floors and stairs were of wood, and while no original examples have survived, modern replacements have been inserted in some instances (e.g. Kildare, Devenish, Kilkenny and Clondalkin, Co. Dublin) to provide visitors with access to the top, where the panorama makes the climb worthwhile.

Bells may have been rung from the top windows, as suggested by the old Irish word for these towers, *cloicthech,* meaning a 'bell house' or 'tower'. This indicates that they shared the function of the Italian *campanile* and were used like their modern Islamic counterparts, the minarets, to call the faithful to prayer. But that was probably not their only purpose. During the nineteenth century they were claimed to have been Phoenician fire-towers, stylite columns and even phallic symbols. It was not until 1845, when George Petrie published his findings on what could be gleaned about these towers from old Irish literary sources, that it became clear that they were not only bell-towers but also places of refuge and storehouses of monastic treasures such as bells, croziers and even books. These items may have been looked upon, too, as reliquary shrines, and one possible explanation as to why the doors were generally placed so high above the ground is that these shrines may have been placed in the doorways where they could have been seen and venerated by pilgrims, but sufficiently far out of reach so that they could not be touched. To serve this purpose, the towers, of course, need not have been as tall as they are, and it is likely that they were built to such a height so that they could be seen by monk or pilgrim from a great distance, to indicate to the traveller where the monastery lay. Indeed, the first indication of the approach to a site like Clonmacnoise or Glendalough today is the upper part of the Round Tower, in the latter case looking like a rocket about to be launched heaven-wards – and a celestial symbolism might even have been intended originally.

About sixty-five towers survive in Ireland today, some virtually intact, others little more than stumps. The old Irish Annals record that a number fell because of wind or as a result of being struck by lightning, while others were burned. If the wooden interiors were set on fire, the air going up the chimney-like towers would have quickly fanned the flames into a raging inferno, reducing everything inside to ashes in a very short time, including laymen, monks and even kings, who are recorded as having been burned inside them.

LEFT With merely the peak of its conical cap missing 85ft (26m) above the ground, the Round Tower at Donaghmore, Co. Meath, stands out in the landscape as one of the most impressive and complete in the country.

RIGHT Today, as of yore, the 100ft(30m)-high Round Tower appearing above the trees at Glendalough, Co. Wicklow, gives visitors the first visual confirmation of their approach to the sacred ground where the remains of St Kevin lie buried.

Popular tradition sees the towers as having been erected to provide protection from the monk-bashing Vikings, though it was as much the Irish themselves as the Norsemen who attacked the Irish monasteries. But the worst of the Viking raids were already over by the time the old Irish Annals record the existence of an Irish Round Tower for the first time in 950. From then on until 1238, various references are found to Round Towers, suggesting that the majority may have been the product of the eleventh and twelfth centuries. It may be more than mere coincidence that the first record of a tower in 950 (that at Slane in County Meath, one of those which has since disappeared) coincides almost to the year with renewed pilgrimage activity after an interruption of more than a century, probably the result of the unsettled conditions caused by the first phase of the Viking wars.

However, towers were probably built some years or decades before 950, but how long before we cannot say, and they may well have been preceded by some form of wooden tower of a kind built at York around 800. Yet, although Ireland has an almost complete monopoly in such towers, the idea is probably not Irish in origin. Free-standing round towers, with crenellated tops though with doors at ground level, are thought to have existed in Rome perhaps as early as 700, and Carolingian churches of the late eighth, ninth and tenth centuries on the European continent had round towers (with spiral staircases) incorporated into the western corners of the structure. Furthermore, an idealized plan of the monastery of St Gall in Switzerland, of about 820, also shows similar towers. It is from some such continental source that the idea of the round towers may well have found its way to Ireland, perhaps by way of Anglo-Saxon England.

KILMACDUAGH
Co. Galway

One of the tallest of the Irish Round Towers is that at Kilmacduagh in County Galway, reaching a height of just over 100 feet (30m). It is also one of the best preserved, though its conical cap was largely rebuilt in 1878-9. The round-headed doorway is unusually high off the ground, at a height of about 24 feet (7m). Probably because the tower stands on some burials (discovered beneath the foundations during the rebuilding works), it leans to the south by about 2 feet (60cm), but it cannot of course be said to have provided a model for its infinitely more famous counterpart at Pisa! The date of the tower cannot be ascertained, but it was probably built around the eleventh or twelfth century.

The monastery at Kilmacduagh was founded by St Colman in the early seventh century on land donated by his brother Guaire, a king celebrated for his hospitality. The saint's grave, appropriated by Bishop French for his tomb in 1852, lies not far from the Round Tower. Some time around 1200, Kilmacduagh became a bishopric, and the cathedral is the largest of a number of churches surviving from the early monastery. The elevation to the status of bishopric may have provided the occasion to enlarge the earlier church, whose gable – with finely worked lintelled doorway – can be seen as part of the west wall, but the cathedral only reached its present extent in the late medieval period. Four other churches survive at Kilmacduagh, one – on the other side of the road – was dedicated to the Virgin, and another is the attractive 'School of the West' church, a few hundred yards west of the cathedral, dating from the early thirteenth century and

having traces of a small cloister. An unusual structure to the north of the cathedral is the 'Bishop's House', a two-storey building of around the thirteenth century. The complex of buildings at Kilmacduagh make it one of the most interesting monastic sites in the west of Ireland, placed in a lovely setting with the limestone hills of the Burren forming a highly scenic backdrop.

LUSK
Co. Dublin

Lusk, in the north County Dublin area known as Fingal, is one of those early monasteries best seen from the air because the round wall or bank which originally surrounded it can be seen reflected in the modern pattern of curved streets. The monastery is said to have been founded by St Mac Cuillinn, or Lochan, details of whose *Life* were borrowed in their entirety from that of St Finnbarr of Cork – for some inexplicable reason. The monastery throve for centuries, but not without its share of misfortunes: the Vikings raided it twice in the ninth century; prisoners were taken from its stone church in 1053; nine score people perished in the same church at the hands of the men of Munster in 1089; and the Meath men burned the church full of people and relics in 1133. This all helps to explain why the only remnant of the early monastery is not a church but a Round Tower.

In the later medieval period a square tower was built beside it, incorporating the old Round Tower at one corner and with a new rounded tower at each of the other three corners to harmonize with it. The medieval church adjoining it to the west houses some fine tombs, including the Elizabethan effigies of Sir Christopher Barnewall and his wife, of 1586, while the modern church of 1847, to the east, acts as the Willie Monks Memorial Museum, containing local folklore and historical material.

LEFT Despite having been constructed with well-hewn ashlar masonry, the 100ft (30m) Round Tower at Kilmacduagh, Co. Galway, leans some 2ft (60cm) out of the perpendicular. It was built some centuries before its more famous Italian counterpart at Pisa.

RIGHT The builders of the medieval rectangular belfry at Lusk in Co. Dublin added a rounded tower at three corners to keep up with the Early Christian Round Tower seen separately on the left.

DEVENISH
Co. Fermanagh

Devenish, on an island in Lower Lough Erne, is the only Irish monastery known to have had two separate free-standing Round Towers, one probably built to replace another which had fallen, leaving only the foundation courses discovered by Dudley Waterman in 1972-3. The intact tower has a door 9 feet (2.75m) above the ground, and through it the visitor can now go inside and climb to the topmost windows. The conical cap peaks at 81 feet (25m) above ground, and immediately beneath it is a frieze running around the whole circumference and bearing four human masks, all but one with a luxuriant growth of moustache and beard. Their style would indicate that this Devenish tower was built around the second half of the twelfth century – probably one of the latest of these great towers. But it is also one of the best, for the quality of the stonework is excellent, a feature shared by another remarkable building on the site – St Molaise's House, a Romanesque church originally with a stone roof, which fell some two hundred years ago.

St Molaise, who founded the monastery here, died in 564. By the tenth century, it belonged to the ascetic Culdee community, which continued to exist after the Augustinian canons founded their own priory in the twelfth century and built St Mary's church near the top of the hill.

SCATTERY ISLAND
Co. Clare

Lying off Kilrush in the estuary of the River Shannon, from where it is reachable by boat, Scattery Island was known in Irish as Inis Chathaigh, called after a horrible monster, Cata, defeated by St Senan, who founded a monastery here some time before his death in 544. It was twice ravaged by the Vikings – once in 816 and again in 835 – and they may have occupied it briefly from 972 to 975, but it was recaptured from them by the great Munster King Brian Boru. The island is dominated by the Round Tower, which is 120 feet (37m) high and the only one of its kind in the country to have its doorway at ground level. The reason why it differs from all the others in this respect is unknown. Nearby is the cathedral, a church with *antae* and lintelled doorway, much altered in the thirteenth or fourteenth century, and there are also other churches on the island, including one on what is known as the Hill of the Angel, where St Senan is said to have overcome the monster. One of the churches was built in the Romanesque style of the twelfth century, perhaps associated with the brief period when Scattery was the seat of a diocese. The monastery apparently survived until the sixteenth century. The sanctity of the island was held in such great respect by sailors that they sailed their craft sun-wise around the island, a custom smacking somewhat of prehistoric origins, and pebbles from the island were popular as talisman protectors against shipwreck.

LEFT Devenish, the pride of Lough Erne and the finest monastic site in Northern Ireland, has one of the few complete Round Towers where you can climb to the top and enjoy the kind of spectacular scenic panorama they offer.

LEFT The Round Tower on Scattery Island in the Shannon estuary, off Kilrush in County Clare, is the only one in Ireland to have its door at ground level.

BELOW The Round Tower at Kildare stands sentinel over St Brigid's Cathedral and is one of the rare surviving vestiges of the great double monastery which existed there from at least as early as the seventh century.

KILDARE

In the prologue to the *Martyrology of Oengus* (*c.*800) the destruction of the pagan Dún Ailinne (p. 39) is contrasted with the victory of Brigit: 'fair is her multitudinous cemetery'. What is being referred to here is the monastery of Kildare, associated with a sixth-century saint, Brigit (normally spelt 'Brigid'), whose veneration – by a curious irony – may go back to the cult of a pagan goddess, for the saint's feast (1 February) happens to fall on the same day as the old pagan festival *Imbolc*, which heralded the beginning of spring. An eternal fire, mentioned by the twelfth-century Welsh historian Giraldus Cambrensis as being looked after by nuns, also sounds like the continuation of some pre-Christian vestal cult. Giraldus further described an illuminated manuscript in Kildare with such glowing words of praise that some have thought that he must have been describing the *Book of Kells*, but it is almost certain that Kildare had its own counterpart to the Kells codex, and one sadly lost since.

This manuscript certainly underscores the importance of Kildare, which can be followed back to the seventh century when Cogitosus wrote his *Life of St Brigid*, best known for its description of the wooden church of the double monastery for monks and nuns. In the following century Kildare, as the most important church in the whole of Leinster, and in close alliance with the Uí Dúnlainge kings of the province, competed for the primacy of Ireland. But, though Brigit is counted among the three national apostles of Ireland, she lost the contest with Armagh, as a result of which Kildare declined thereafter.

It was presumably some time during the second half of the twelfth century that the Romanesque door was carved for the Round Tower, which, with the possible exception of what has been taken to be the 'Fire House' (of very uncertain date), is surprisingly the only pre-Norman building surviving from the old monastic town. With the battlements on top apparently an addition of 1730, the tower stands to a height of about 105 feet (32m), the second tallest in Ireland. The masonry changes from regular granite ashlar to rough limestone rubble about 9 feet (2.75m) above ground level, but it is difficult to say whether this was the result of a change in building plan or indicates a difference in time between the two. The doorway's sandstone contrasts with the colour of the limestone; it has a pointed gable above and is recessed in four orders – the three inner ones being original, if not entirely well preserved. In recent years laudable local initiative has provided a ladder up to the door, from which one can now climb to the top and obtain a good view of the adjacent cathedral (p. 157), the town and the flat-lands to the east known as the Curragh, famous for its horses and race-course.

TIMAHOE
Co. Laois

The Round Tower at Timahoe is the only building of the early Middle Ages to survive from a monastery founded by St Mochua mac Lonan, who died in 654. The nearby church, later transformed into a castle, is probably no earlier than the fifteenth century. The Round Tower, about 96 feet (29m) high and – as is so often the case – with its conical cap rebuilt in the last century, is one of the thickest examples known. It is most renowned for its splendid Romanesque doorway, starting about 15 feet (4.5m) above the ground. With the most elegant entrance to any of the Round Towers, it is like two doorways each of two orders, one behind the other, with the ground stepped up as the sides recede towards the interior. Bearded faces with intertwining hair feature on the capitals but also on the bases, some of which, however, are barrel-shaped. Unusually, a window on the third floor has a pointed architrave and is decorated with heads similar to those of the doorway. Because it is sheltered from the elements, the inner part of the doorway is well preserved, but its carving is not quite of the same quality as that of its nearest analogue, the doorway of Killeshin church in the same county, built – like the tower – around the third quarter of the twelfth century.

ARDMORE
Co. Waterford

Ardmore in County Waterford will claim our attention further below (p. 126) when discussing the cathedral. Here it is just necessary to draw attention to the gracefully tall, slender Round Tower dominating the skyline of the old monastery of St Declan and looking out over the Celtic Sea. The tower is unique in having three string-courses distributed over its tapering 90 feet (27m). The round-headed doorway has a simple rolled moulding encasing it, and both the human and animal-headed corbels in the interior walls suggest a twelfth-century date. As the tower may have been erected when Ardmore briefly became the seat of a bishop around 1170, it may have been one of the latest to have been built in the country.

RIGHT Three string-courses create a horizontal contrast to the vertical elegance of the twelfth-century Round Tower at Ardmore, Co. Waterford.

LEFT AND BELOW LEFT (detail) The twelfth-century Round Tower at Timahoe, Co. Laois, has its doorway finely ornamented in the Romanesque style, with chevron decoration and mask-head capitals.

CHAPTER THREE

THE ELEVENTH AND TWELFTH CENTURIES

THE POLITICAL SCENE

The eleventh and, more particularly, the twelfth century was to prove to be an important turning point for Ireland in a number of ways, tearing the country out of its centuries-old Celtic way of life and bringing it face to face with new political and religious developments in an increasingly feudal Europe.

At the beginning of the new millennium Brian Boru had finally achieved a true High Kingship, and used the Church for his own political ends. But his fall at the Battle of Clontarf in 1014 anticipated developments during the next two centuries in showing how the struggle for High Kingship depended not on the old-fashioned precepts of the Brehon Laws but the power of the individual's sword. Clontarf precipitated an end to the Dál Cais pretensions to a hereditary High Kingship but was not, as is so often thought, an end to Viking power in Ireland – for that was already a thing of the past. Instead, it opened the way for Dublin and other Viking towns to become valuable pawns in the political power-struggle and, through Dublin's workshops, to play a new role in providing artistic stimulus to the rest of Ireland. Bereft of power, its people turned to peaceful pursuits and concentrated on their trading interests.

The death of Brian Boru left the prize of High Kingship open to a number of different dynasts who fought their way to the top during the following century and a half with a ferocity hitherto unknown, blinding, maiming and killing their opponents, and trying to carve out for themselves kingdoms which were becoming increasingly feudal in character. These provincial kings came to wield growing power over local kings, acting as owners and bestowers of land which did not belong to them by heredity, in order to gain homage and military service from their vassal kings. The more lengthy and frequent wars which they waged gradually necessitated the development of an administration in their own home kingdom in order to deal with the day-to-day problems which arose in their absence on long campaigns.

F.X. Martin likened these wars to a game of musical chairs, played to discordant military tunes, whereby, if you lost your chair, you were likely to lose your life as well. In these struggles the petty kingdoms, or *túatha*, of preceding centuries were gradually edged out one by one so as to become virtual vassals of the provincial kings, but the latters' efforts to obtain the elusive High Kingship were often so inadequate that contemporary annalists dubbed them 'High Kings with opposition', as they failed one by one

to achieve their goal. A twelfth-century poet could justifiedly speak of the 'arrogance of kings'.

After Brian Boru's death, his Dalcassian tribe was no longer strong enough to continue his claim to High Kingship, and the going was once more taken up – for a mere eight years – by the Uí Néill, whose leader, Maelsechlainn II, was able to buy an altar-front for the cathedral at Clonmacnoise but taxed his people to pay for it. When he died in 1022, Brian's family again made a bid, but were outdone by a King of Leinster, Diarmaid mac Mael na mBó, who came to the fore in the middle of the eleventh century. He it was who realized the key position of Dublin and captured it. For the next seventy years Dublin became such an important prize that during this period it was occupied by two Leinster kings, two from Munster and another from Connacht. Its importance lay in its trade potential and its overseas contacts – a lively and dynamic town which, as recent excavations have shown, expanded considerably during the eleventh century. It was full of small wattle houses end-on to the street, some of them shops and workshops which could produce goods seen as valuable and attractive by the Irish in the hinterland.

After the death of Diarmuid mac Mael na mBó, power passed once again to Brian Boru's descendants, the O'Briens as they were now called, for this was an age when Irish kings were adopting surnames of the kind we all use today to help distinguish themselves from their subject kings. Turlough O'Brien, though in Irish eyes only a King of Munster, had sufficient power to be addressed by Lanfranc, Archbishop of Canterbury, as King of Ireland. He was able to pass on his power to his son Muircheartach, who was to be one of the most significant rulers between Clontarf and the arrival of the Normans, reigning from 1086 until his death in 1119, though weakened by illness for the last five years of his life. Like his father, he too was greeted by an Archbishop of Canterbury as King of Ireland and, more than any other king of the period, he kept abreast of affairs outside the country, marrying one daughter off to a King of Norway, and another to the brother of the Earl of Shrewsbury, who was attempting to oust Henry I from the English throne. He was noted for making a circuit of parts of the north of Ireland, destroying the hill-top fortress of the Grianán of Aileach (p. 34-5) along the way. But he is most remembered for having handed over the Rock of Cashel to the Church, thereby showing himself to be a benefactor of the Church while at the same time putting Cashel nearly beyond the reach of the Mac-Carthys, whose ancestral stronghold it had been before the O'Briens seized it in the previous century. It is, however, ironical that the MacCarthys got

The gift of the Rock of Cashel to the Church in 1101 by Muircheartach, King of Munster, was an important symbolic gesture in getting the twelfth-century Church reform off to a good start in Ireland.

their own back when Cormac, a subsequent MacCarthy King of Munster, who reigned with O'Brien support, built the country's first great Romanesque church on the Rock – Cormac's Chapel – between 1127 and 1134. By that time, the power of Munster was on the wane, for Muircheartach, despite all his political achievements and innovative contributions to Church reform, had proved to be a failure. Nevertheless, in the century between Brian Boru's death in 1014 and Muircheartach's illness exactly 100 years later, the O'Briens had made Munster the most progressive province of all and one which was in closest contact with the outside world.

His death opened the way for power to pass to the O Conor dynasty in Connacht, who were to provide Ireland with her last two High Kings, Turlough (1106-56) and his son Rory, who was in power when the Normans landed in 1169. Turlough may have opened up the way to France, but he also encouraged Clonmacnoise to become the rival of the Ostman towns around the coast. Ruthless in dividing the territory of his enemies, he destroyed the power of Munster between 1115 and 1131. From 1140 onwards he concentrated on consolidating his position as High King, and succeeded in removing the centre of power from the southern to the northern half of Ireland. As part of his campaign, he became the first to construct strategic bridges across the River Shannon and to build a number of castles – at places like Galway and his own power-base at Tuam – but these can no longer be identified. He was also one of the first Irish kings to realize the power of a navy, and came to build up one of considerable size himself.

When he died in 1156, power shifted even further north, this time to Muircheartach MacLochlainn of Aileach, who during his ten-year struggle allied himself to, among others, the rising star of Diarmuid (Dermot) Mac-Murrough, King of Leinster. But in 1166 Rory O Conor took the reins back again to Connacht and he, together with his ally Tighernán O'Rourke of Breifne, moved against MacMurrough, who had abducted O'Rourke's wife, Dervorgilla, some years earlier. Deserted now by his allies, MacMurrough went overseas and sought help from Henry II, King of England, who responded in 1169 by sending Norman barons to Ireland. They landed in Wexford, took Waterford and then Dublin. Fearful of losing control of his vassals, Henry came to Dublin in 1171 to curb their power. In return for help, MacMurrough had promised his kingdom to his son-in-law Richard, Earl of Striguil, better known as Strongbow, who on MacMurrough's death in 1170 took over the Kingdom of Leinster. The Normans had superior armour and horses and, by using a system of warfare to which the Irish were not accustomed and were ill-accoutred to combat, they took control also of the east midlands and parts of Ulster within a decade of their arrival. Their subsequent story, however, belongs to the later Middle Ages.

CHURCH REFORM

With the dawn of the new millennium the monasteries – widely laicized since the seventh century – continued in their accustomed way to be the Church leaders in Ireland. Although obviously in need of reform, the Church nevertheless had its good sides. It had saintly churchmen and – despite the Viking attacks – its schools had been able to keep up the tradition of Irish learning, for which the monasteries had been famous centuries before. The flow of Irish scholars to the continent, which had picked up again in the tenth century after the passing of the worst of the Norse raids, continued unabated in the eleventh century, when people like Marianus Scottus went to Germany and compiled a valuable world chronicle, while another Marianus moved to Regensburg. It was there that the first of the Irish monasteries in Germany known as the *Schottenklöster* was founded, only to be followed by a number of others in the following centuries. Contact with the European continent at the highest level was to be maintained through kings going on pilgrimage to Rome, though this seems to have largely come to an end after 1066 when the Norman conquest curtailed the overland route through England. We also know of a small foundation of Irish clerics in Rome in the eleventh century, and they – together with the royal pilgrims – must have been keeping Ireland informed of the efforts at Church reform on the continent associated with Popes Gregory VII and Urban II, who were determined to strengthen the power of the papacy in both the political and ecclesiastical spheres.

The Irish monks and monasteries were not exactly enamoured by the new Benedictine reforms spearheaded by the great monastery of Cluny, but as the years of the new millennium ticked by, they were to find it more and more difficult to take shelter from the winds of change.

By a curious paradox the recently Christianized Ostman town of Dublin cast the first stone into the pond which set the waves of reform in motion. In 1038 Sitric, the Norse king of the ever-expanding town, founded a new church, now known as Christ Church, which in due course set itself up as a cathedral with the consequent necessity of requiring a bishop. The town did not want to be associated too closely with the Irish monastic system and so, through contacts with territories overseas, it decided to send its newly elected Bishop Dunan to be consecrated by the Archbishop of Can-

At some time between 1001 and 1025 the eighth-century box known as the Soiscel Molaise (probably originally containing a gospel book associated with St Molaise of Devenish) was given a 'face-lift' with the addition of evangelist symbols, which must have indicated hope for the future after the turn of the millennium had proved not to be the end of the world, as some had feared. This book-shrine is now preserved in the National Museum of Ireland in Dublin.

terbury. This placed the fledgling diocese of Dublin in the position of being a suffragan of Canterbury, and two later Italian archbishops of Canterbury – Lanfranc (1070-89) and St Anselm (1093-1109) – determined to use this foothold in the Irish scene to press for the reform of the Irish Church. Shortly after he had consecrated Dunan's successor, Patrick of Winchester, Lanfranc took the opportunity of writing to Turlough O'Brien, whom he described as 'noble king of Ireland' and admonished him to abandon the Irish practice of divorce – the first official clash between the Gregorian reform and the ingrained Irish system enshrined in the local law. He also recommended him to abolish the custom among Irish bishops of bestowing holy orders for money – in other words the sin of simony. When Turlough's son, Muircheartach, assembled a synod at Cashel in 1101, he did not address the divorce anomaly – perhaps in order to avoid too strong a reaction among the Irish, for this was not a purely ecclesiastical gathering but rather a synod of clergy and laity of the kind practised by the continental Franks before the Hildebrandine reform.

The most important happening of the synod was Muircheartach handing over the Rock of Cashel to the Church as a free gift. But the synod also tried to come to grips with bringing the Irish Church into conformity with Rome by legislating against simony, marriage within the forbidden degrees of kindred, the presence of two ecclesiastical heads in the same church and laymen ruling Irish churches. This last decree struck at the very heart of the Irish system where the layman had too much power and the bishop too little, and signalled the beginning of its end – and disaster for old Irish culture. The effects of these Cashel edicts may at first only have been felt in the southern half of the country, but the enthusiasm for reform was soon taken up in Armagh when Cellach was consecrated as the 'noble bishop of Armagh' in 1106.

Five years later another synod was convened at Rath Breasail, not far from Cashel. It was attended by 50 bishops, 300 priests and 3000 ecclesiastics, and presided over by a papal legate in the person of Gilbert, the new Bishop of the Norse town of Limerick, whose consecration had showed Canterbury for the first time that Ireland and the Norse towns were now able to consecrate their own bishops. In the same way that England was divided into the two archbishoprics of Canterbury and York, Rath Breasail divided Ireland into two halves, represented respectively by the new province of Armagh for the north and Cashel for the south. Each of these was allotted eleven suffragan bishoprics, the boundaries of which were certainly influenced by local politics. For the first time, Ireland was now ecclesiastically organized along European lines and Gilbert, in a treatise which he wrote around the same time, affirmed that the bishop was now to have authority over both parish and monastery, that Cashel was to be subject to Armagh and that all should be subject to the pope in Rome.

With the death of Muircheartach O'Brien in 1119, the reform movement lost much of its impetus in Munster, and Cellach in Armagh became the main standard-bearer for Church reform throughout the country. He found support in the man we know today as St Malachy, canonized in 1190, who came south to the venerable monastic school at Lismore in County Waterford to seek spiritual encouragement. He was subsequently to found a (temporary?) monastery in the province where he was frequently visited by Cormac MacCarthy, who built Cormac's Chapel on the Rock of Cashel (1127–34).

Cellach was both Archbishop and '*comarb* of Patrick', the latter being the hereditary leadership which had been in his family for seven generations. But when he died, the two roles were split, and Malachy, who lacked the hereditary credentials, took over the office of archbishop in 1134. He felt uncomfortable on the archbishop's throne because of local anti-reform opposition, and resigned three years later to retire to the smaller Bishopric of Down. There he made the old monastery of Bangor his headquarters, and became the prime mover in the reform movement, though he again met opposition in trying to build a church in a new style, rather larger than those to which the Irish were accustomed.

Malachy's aim was to achieve the ultimate sanction by Rome for the reforms introduced at Rath Breasail in 1111 and, to this end, he set out for Rome in 1139 to request the pope to grant the pallium, the symbol of archiepiscopal dignity, to the two archbishops of Armagh and Cashel. His route brought him through France, where his visits to two monastic foundations were to be of immense importance for Ireland – Arrouaise, where he encountered the Augustinian way of life, and Clairvaux, where he struck up an immediate friendship with its great preacher-abbot, St Bernard. So impressed was he by the Cistercian rule of his new-found friend that, when he reached Rome, he requested permission from the pope to spend the rest of his life at Clairvaux, so that he could be a part of the all-conquering spirituality of St Bernard. Sensing that Malachy would be more valuable working in his homeland, the pope refused both his wish and the request for the pallium – but he made up for it by sending Malachy back to Ireland as papal legate. On the return journey Malachy left some of the younger members of his entourage at Clairvaux so that they could become acquainted with the Cistercian lifestyle. They returned to Ireland the following year, along with some French stonemasons and, with their help, Malachy set up the first Irish Cistercian abbey at Mellifont in County Louth, on lands granted by the friendly local king, Donnchad Ó Cerbaill. This was to be virtually the first of the many houses in Ireland that were founded for the continental religious orders and that were to play such a dominant role in the ecclesiastical life of Ireland up to the time of the Reformation. St Malachy's visit to Arrouaise was to bear fruit, too, in the introduction of the Arrouaisian canons who, as Augustinians, were to be incorporated into, and keep alive, some of the older Irish monastic foundations such as Clonmacnoise and Glendalough.

One of the probable reasons why the pope refused to grant Malachy the pallium was that he felt that the request should have come not from Malachy alone but from the Irish bishops as a whole. When these assembled on the island of Inis Phádraig off Skerries in 1148, they convinced a now-ailing Malachy that he should set off once more to Rome to make a formal request for the pallium.

Malachy only got as far as Clairvaux, where he died shortly afterwards in the arms of his friend Bernard, who thereupon did him the signal honour of writing his *Life* and, on his own death five years later, had himself buried beside St Malachy in front of the high altar at Clairvaux. Malachy's final voyage was not in vain. When a synod was convened in 1152, starting at Kells and subsequently moving to Mellifont for its closing session, it was rewarded by the papal legate, Cardinal Paparo, bringing with him not only the coveted pallia which Malachy had wanted for Armagh and Cashel but two more in addition – one for Dublin and the other for Tuam.

This synod at Kells made certain changes to the organization and territories of bishoprics laid down at Rath Breasail forty years earlier, and had a permanent effect in that its scheme has – with only minor changes – remained intact down to our own day, with Armagh being formally granted the primacy as proposed in Gilbert's treatise. The synod also dealt with a number of further reforms passed over at Rath Breasail: the putting away of concubines, the denial of payment for bestowing baptism and an order not to take payment for church property – but that tithes should be paid punctually. Kells set the seal on the reform movement, and its spirit was to be continued in the following generation by another canonized Irish saint, Laurence O'Toole, Abbot of Glendalough and later Archbishop of Dublin – who, as it happened, was also the brother-in-law of Diarmuid MacMurrough. He shared with Malachy the distinction of having his *Life* written by a continental author after his death.

The Irish Church prior to reform is often seen as having had more abuses than virtues, yet it was not all bad. The earlier monasteries had been keepers of the old Irish tradition of learning, and during the twelfth century they succeeded in producing three great manuscript compilations of religious and secular texts, *Lebor na hUidre*, or the *Book of the Dun Cow*, the manuscript Rawlinson B. 502 now in the Bodleian Library in Oxford – both apparently written in Clonmacnoise – and the *Book of Leinster*. These are vitally important for preserving lore, which went back many centuries, including the great epic known as *Táin Bó Cuailnge* – the Cattle Raid of Cooley. They represent a kind of Indian summer, but also the best of the old Irish monasteries, for the reform movement which centralized power in the diocesan bishops had the effect of draining the life-blood of the Irish culture embodied in the monastic tradition. But, before they declined, the Irish monasteries experienced a revival in architecture and in the art of metalwork in the late eleventh and the first half of the twelfth century. This revitalization saw the enshrinement of relics of earlier saints – St Patrick's Bell, the crozier of the abbots of Clonmacnoise, St Lachtin's arm from Freshford, Co. Kilkenny, and the first recorded relic of the True Cross in Ireland enshrined in the Cross of Cong – all now preserved in the Treasury of the National Museum in Dublin. Other splendid reliquary shrines of the early twelfth century include the *Bearnán Cuilean*, an encased bell from Glankeen, Co. Tipperary, now in the British Museum, and the roof-shaped St Manchan's Shrine from Lemanaghan in County Offaly, now preserved in the Catholic church at Boher nearby.

The creation of such great artworks must also be partially attributed to the desire of centralized kingship to show its munificence in commissioning them, and to demonstrate that these kings, most notably the O Conors, were the embodiment of the revival of the Golden Age of the Irish past. Politically, this was manifested by Turlough O Conor and his son Rory recalling to life the old traditional fair known as the *oénach Tailten*, probably in the belief that they were once again exercising the prerogative of the King of Ireland. The reappearance of High Crosses, albeit in a different form, notably in the O Conor stronghold in Tuam but also elsewhere in Connacht and Munster, should also be seen as a renewed manifestation

of the earlier Golden Age of High Crosses, when the Clann Cholmáin Kings of Meath erected crosses at Clonmacnoise and elsewhere more than two hundred years before.

The Tuam crosses are infused with the Viking style of animal ornament emanating from Dublin, and one wonders if it was seen as symbolic of the reform movement, which had partially come about through the christianization of the pagan Ostman city. Cormac's Chapel at Cashel was the result of the generosity of a MacCarthy King of Munster in the heart of reform territory, and regal commissions may also have been responsible for at least some of the series of beautiful Romanesque churches which followed in its wake. The Diarmuid whose name is inscribed on the portal at Killeshin is likely to be that of the same MacMurrough who invited the Normans to Ireland and who was also responsible for the founding of Mellifont's daughter-house at Baltinglass in County Wicklow.

One further factor which may have precipitated the spate, and the location of, Romanesque churches in twelfth-century Ireland was pilgrimage. During this period, pilgrimage was the most popular activity in the rest of Europe and, as Ireland is likely to have participated in the

LEFT AND RIGHT (detail) St Cuilean's Bell – in Irish, *Bearnán Cuileain* – is said to have been found in the hollow of a tree at Glankeen, Co. Tipperary, and is now in the British Museum. When the bell was enshrined some time around 1100, it was decorated with interlacing as well as human and animal heads damascened with inlaid silver strips and niello.

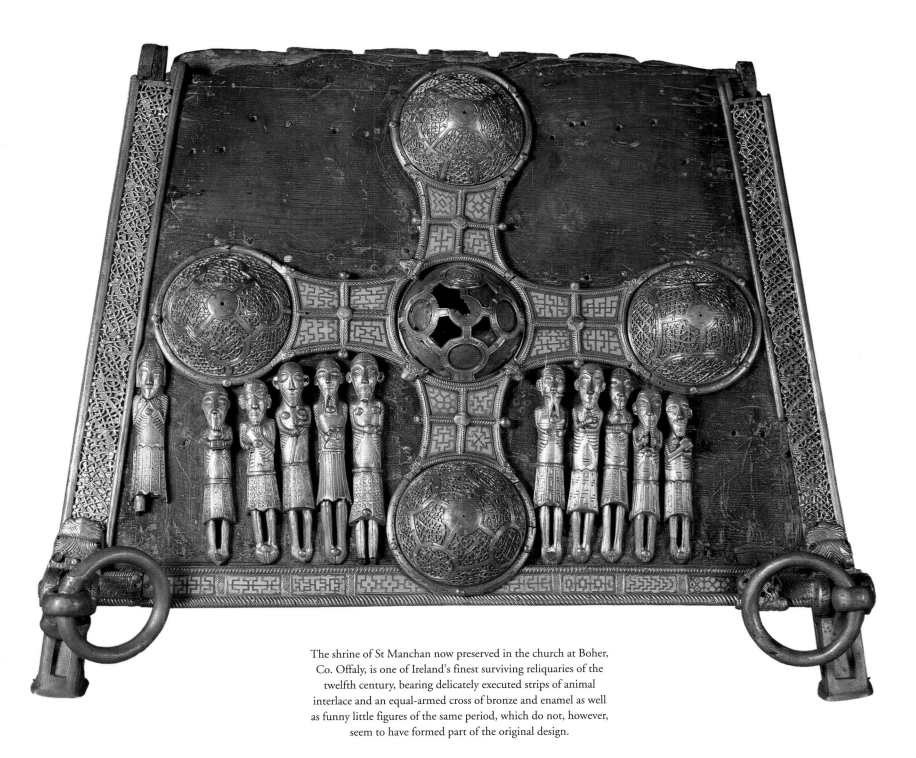

The shrine of St Manchan now preserved in the church at Boher,
Co. Offaly, is one of Ireland's finest surviving reliquaries of the
twelfth century, bearing delicately executed strips of animal
interlace and an equal-armed cross of bronze and enamel as well
as funny little figures of the same period, which do not, however,
seem to have formed part of the original design.

same trend, the presence of Romanesque churches on many of the old
monastic sites may well be a reflection of the desire to cater for the
doubtless numerous Irish pilgrims who came to venerate the relics of the
old Irish saints in their own foundations. The pilgrimage which was to
make Ireland famous throughout Europe in the later Middle Ages – that
to St Patrick's Purgatory in the Donegal Lough Derg – can also be
traced back to the twelfth century. The veneration of Irish saints' relics
on these old monastic sites may possibly represent a combination of the
conservative Irish tradition with the new religious fervour which swept
the country during the twelfth century.

But the pilgrimage activity of the native Irish is likely to have been
dampened by the spread of the Normans in the late twelfth century, and it
is significant how the old Irish tradition of decorative metalwork in the
enshrining of older relics finds its last great expression during the first half
of that same century. The new continental religious orders, and the Normans who came in their wake, caused a weakening in the old Irish manuscript and metalwork tradition. Instead, they brought the country into the
stream of pan-European styles, as seen particularly in the architecture
which accompanied them, though the old Romanesque style remained vig-
orous in Connacht until the Normans moved in there around 1235.

ROMANESQUE CHURCHES AND DECORATION

From the architectural point of view the twelfth was the most remarkable century of the Irish Middle Ages, as it combined extraordinary variety and rapid change in ecclesiastical building styles. Since the ninth century the simple rectangular churches had remained much the same whether they were built in wood or stone, and the surviving stone examples give little indication of any great interest in decoration, though this could of course have been applied in the form of internal wooden furnishings, wall-hangings and possibly even frescoes and pictures, long since disappeared. The twelfth century was to change all that.

The renewed spirit of the age – evident since Christianity realized that the world was not going to end with the year 1000, as many feared it might – began to manifest itself in a novel sense of decoration, infused with a feeling of new-found elation but also imbued with enchanting mystery. It was in France of the eleventh century that the new experiments began to be made, not only in sculptural decoration but also in daring efforts to vault over the ever-widening naves and chancels. The great Burgundian monastery of Cluny played its role in the expansion of this appealing style

Curious capitals and neatly joined masonry in the interior east window of Kilfenora Cathedral typify the School of the West's continuation of the round-headed Romanesque style in Clare and Connacht into the first quarter of the thirteenth century.

of Romanesque architecture by encouraging the building of many small churches sculpted liberally with mysterious humans and beasts, and much admired by pilgrims on their way to visit the relics of the Apostle James at Santiago de Compostela in north-western Spain. In time this new Romanesque style – deriving its name from the use of the rounded arch as practised by the ancient Romans – began to spread beyond the bounds of France and Spain, and duly found its way to Ireland, with England acting initially as an important staging post. Subsequently, French influence would also manifest itself in the use of human and animal heads decorating the voussoirs of round-headed doorways.

In its Round Towers Ireland had shown that it was capable of erecting tall buildings, but its innate conservatism was not yet ready to make the great leap forward to create the large and lofty vaulted churches built by the English and continentals. Nevertheless it succeeded in making a daring start with Cormac's Chapel on the Rock of Cashel, and it was the spirit of religious reform which gripped the country after the Synod of Rath Breasail in 1111 that laid the foundations for the subsequent popularity of the new style, initially in Munster but later in the midlands and further north. Even after the greatest Irish reformer of the age, St Malachy of Armagh, had introduced the continental monastic orders which were to build the first large stone churches in Ireland from the 1140s onwards, the old Irish establishments kept to church sizes which were only marginally larger than those of the three preceding centuries. The difference now, however, was that the Irish enthusiastically took to the idea of decorating the doorways, chancel arches and occasionally the windows of these smaller churches with ornament and sometimes figure sculpture, all in high-quality craftsmanship matching that of the High Crosses two centuries before. Despite the growing popularity of the larger Gothic churches among the Normanized towns in the eastern half of Ireland after the year 1200, the Irish west of the Shannon retained the Romanesque style of church decoration into the first quarter of the thirteenth century in what Leask called 'the School of the West', which produced high-quality masonry and carving of a kind already developed in the previous century.

It would, however, be a mistake to equate Romanesque entirely with the twelfth century. One whole quarter of that century had already passed before Romanesque made its mark with Cormac's Chapel, and it may well be that the twelfth century in Ireland still occasionally saw the continuation of the earlier style of simple, undecorated churches, as suggested by the use of the old *antae* in churches built possibly as late as the thirteenth century.

THE ROCK OF CASHEL
Co. Tipperary

The Rock of Cashel must be the most impressive cluster of medieval monuments in Ireland – a Round Tower, Cormac's Chapel, a High Cross, a cathedral and the late-medieval Hall of the Vicars' Choral – all perched on a dome of rock which rises up dramatically from the Golden Vale. Its defensive possibilities made it a natural choice as the seat of power for the early Eóganacht kings of Munster. In 1101 the Munster King Muircheartach O'Brien 'granted Cashel of the kings to the religious, without any claim of layman or cleric upon it, but to the religious of Ireland in general', an act calculated to create Munster strength as a southern counterbalance

The Rock of Cashel in the Golden Vale of County Tipperary was transformed from an ancient centre of Munster kingship into a hub of ecclesiastical reform when it was handed over to the Church in 1101. The architectural expression of its new-found role was Cormac's Chapel (1127–34), which exudes a warm sandstone glow at the centre of the picture above, in contrast to the colder limestone of the thirteenth-century Gothic cathedral overshadowing it behind.

to the power of Armagh in Ulster. There are, however, growing indications that there was some kind of ecclesiastical activity on the Rock before 1101 – ninth-century religious antiquities of bronze and stone, a Round Tower built possibly before 1100, and the presence of wooden and stone structures with accompanying burials beneath both Cormac's Chapel and the cathedral. It is the existence of these earlier buildings which may help to explain some of the peculiarities of the chapel which Cormac MacCarthy built probably for the Benedictine monks between 1127 and 1134. These include an off-centre chancel, a main entrance from the north, two further doors – neither of them in the west wall as one would have expected – and two tall square towers instead of transepts. The exterior south wall has a series of

LEFT Cormac's Chapel, built on the Rock of Cashel between 1127 and 1134, was probably Ireland's first Romanesque church, and at the time it must have embodied so many novelties – height, three doorways, superimposed blind arcading, stone roofing and transeptal towers – that it must have astonished the Irish with its ingenuity.

RIGHT A Norman-style helmet worn by the centaur attacking a lion on the tympanum of the north doorway in Cormac's Chapel at Cashel provides a hint of the English origin for many of the novel ideas contained in this unique structure.

ABOVE Twelfth-century frescoes with impressive colouring, but portraying figures not complete enough to be identified conclusively, have recently been revealed as Ireland's earliest surviving wall-paintings.

superimposed blind arcades, and the roof is made of stone, prevented from collapsing inwards by a pointed arch in a small chamber above the nave. The original main doorway, a deep porch to create an atmosphere of importance, was surmounted by a triangular 'tangent gable' decorated with horizontal and vertical bands of chevron (zig-zag) with rosettes between – probably imitated from a timbered model. Another unusual feature of this porch is the existence of a tympanum over the door, carved with a large lion being shot at by a centaur wearing a Norman helmet – our first hint of English influence in this building. Opposite the north entrance there is a south door, and there was a third entrance (now blocked) in the east wall of the north tower, probably to allow access to the clergy celebrating mass.

The nave has a barrel-vault borrowed possibly from West of England churches and supported by internal columns and capitals. The chancel arch is richly decorated with heads and painted 'floral' motifs. The rib-vaulting of the chancel shows the builder keeping abreast with the latest architectural developments elsewhere. Recent conservation work has brought out high-quality Romanesque frescoes with figure scenes (including Solomon and his Temple?) using a palette of colours reminiscent of Canterbury.

For the archaeologist Liam de Paor, Cormac's Chapel is an entity, 'a piece of Romanesque *architecture* as hardly any other Irish Romanesque church is', and most authorities have now accepted his view that it is the earliest surviving Irish church in the style. It certainly set Irish Romanesque architecture on its way with a breathtaking start, and it must have created a great stir when it was consecrated in 1134. It was so full of innovations, many inspired by the West of England as Roger Stalley has rightly argued, that it must have taken the Irish very much by surprise for they were accustomed at the time to much smaller churches with scarcely a trace of stone-carved decoration. The chapel's grandeur must have struck such awe into its beholders that they found it difficult to comprehend its combination of scale and decoration. Its multiple entrances, its towers and the richness of its interior decoration found few imitators. But where it did make its mark was with the introduction of decorated entrances and chancel arch, its stone roof construction and, above all, in the details of its carved ornament which finds consistent echoes throughout the twelfth century in Ireland.

Today, the warmth of the red sandstone of Cormac's Chapel contrasts with the colder limestone of the thirteenth-century cathedral which dwarfs it and prevents us seeing its original west end. The cathedral, probably standing on the site of a predecessor of *c*.1170, is built in the early Gothic style, with tall lancet windows in the chancel. Unusually the nave is shorter than the chancel, but that came about because the west end was made into a fortified residence in the later Middle Ages. The fear of attack which brought this about was not unjustified, for it is recorded that the Earl of Kildare set fire to the cathedral in 1495 thinking that the archbishop was inside at the time! However, the cathedral remained in use until 1749, when Archbishop Price found it too arduous to climb the Rock to hold divine service there, and replaced it with the present St John's Cathedral in the town.

LEFT The interior of Cormac's Chapel creates an illusory perspective of considerable depth in a comparatively short church where the off-centre chancel is a notable feature.

KILMALKEDAR CHURCH
Co. Kerry

Irish Romanesque established itself first in Munster, and Cormac's Chapel in Cashel found imitators in churches in the south-west of the province before its influence cast a wider net. This is seen to good effect in two churches associated with one of Ireland's best-known medieval saints, Brendan the Navigator, whose fantastic travels related in the *Navigatio Brendani* made his name famous throughout Europe. One is Ardfert Cathedral; the other church is dedicated to a local saint, Maolchethair (anglicized Malkedar), who died in 636, but its connection with the Navigator stems from the fact that it lies on the Saint's Road which led those making the pilgrimage in honour of St Brendan from their starting point at Ventry Harbour to their goal on the top of Mount Brandon. The church is romantically sited in a great arena, subdivided by stone walls and fuchsia bushes, and looks out over the incomparable scenery of Smerwick Harbour at the end of the Dingle Peninsula. It retains elements of earlier church architecture in having *antae* at all four corners of the nave, and Leask recognized its derivation from Cormac's Chapel by the presence of a tympanum (carved only on the inside – with a bovine head), a stone roof (now largely gone) and a blind arcade at about 3 feet (0.9m) above ground level on the interior nave walls, where it is decorated with scalloped capitals. The chancel arch, springing from bases at about the same height and decorated

ABOVE AND LEFT Close to the end of the then known world, Kilmalkedar Church near the tip of the Dingle Peninsula has features, such as the stone roof, which were probably borrowed from Cormac's Chapel in Cashel – but its own individuality is expressed in details like the external *antae* and the finials on the gables.

RIGHT Romantic lake-side scenery provides the backdrop for the church and doorway at Aghadoe near Killarney, where the building date of 1158 offers us one of the few chronological fixed points for twelfth-century Irish architecture.

ABOVE The elegant sundial at Kilmalkedar, Co. Kerry, is probably contemporary with the nearby church, and remains one of the few surviving early examples of its kind in Ireland.

underneath with interrupted lozenge motifs, leads to a chancel (also stone-roofed), which replaced an earlier one. On top of the two gables are finials. Associated with the church are a number of smaller but interesting antiquities. Placed beside the chancel arch is a cross-decorated stone bearing a carved alphabet said to date from the sixth century. In the churchyard are also an Ogham stone, a stone cross and a beautifully carved sundial.

AGHADOE CHURCH
Co. Kerry

The writer of the *Annals of Inisfallen* noted for the year 1282 that 'there was many a violent windstorm, and ricks and many houses were damaged; also the great church of Achad Déo (which had been standing undamaged for six score and four years), its holy cross, too, being broken – which I much deplore.' The church to which he referred was that at Agha-doe, situated on a sloping hill overlooking the scribe's charming island monastery in the midst of Killarney's sublime lake scenery – proving, if proof were necessary, that the old Irish monks had a special relationship with the beauties of nature. The man who chose the location for the origi-

nal church with this splendid scenic panorama was one of the many St Finians (perhaps 'the Leper'), who may have lived in the seventh century.

An heir-apparent of the ruling Eóganacht dynasty was dragged out of a stone church here in 1061, and the large stones now built into the north-western corner of the present structure may have belonged to that church, which stood close to a Round Tower whose butt still survives nearby. But the church damaged in 1282, after a life of only 124 years, was almost certainly the one we see still ruined today with the ornate Romanesque door-way in the west wall – its date of 1158 giving us one of our few anchoring points for the chronology of Romanesque churches in Ireland.

The doorway, which may once have had a tympanum and has suffered at the hands of earlier 'restorers', is of three orders, the outermost with zig-zag ornament on the column, and the middle one with a battlement-like vertical decoration on its jamb. The outer ring of the arch shares pellet decoration with Kilmalkedar, another of the County Kerry churches bearing testimony to the importance of the southern province of Munster in the development of Irish Romanesque architecture. The lancet windows in the east gable suggest an extension of the church in the thirteenth century, the interior being later subdivided at some period unknown by a cross-wall.

ST CRONAN'S CHURCH
Roscrea, Co. Tipperary

Some time in the sixth century St Cronan founded a monastery at Roscrea which continued to exist until at least the twelfth century. Roscrea was also included as a suffragan of Cashel in the list of bishoprics which the papal nuncio, Cardinal Paparo, took off with him to Rome after the Synod of Kells in 1152. One Isaac Ó Cuanain is recorded as having died as Bishop of Roscrea in 1161, and he may well have been the builder of St Cronan's Church in the town, a structure worthy enough to have acted as a cathedral for the short-lived diocese which is not heard of again after the 1160s. A date shortly after the middle of the twelfth century would thus not be out of place for a church which bears echoes of Cormac's Chapel at Cashel, completed in 1134.

Most of the church was demolished in 1812, but fortunately not the sandstone west gable, which was worn away instead by fumes of the heavy motorized traffic that passed in front of its very portal. The moulded *antae* stand sentinel on its corners like guards of the central doorway, which is flanked on either side by two blind arcades, all linked together by an impost moulding which runs right across the whole facade. The doorway, with two orders of chevrons, is twice the width of each arcade, and the tangential gable above it is also about twice the height of those over the arcades, thus displaying a mathematical finesse in the facade design. Rosettes like those of the north doorway at Cashel flank the tall figure of a saint above the entrance – doubtless St Cronan – who is carved in high relief on a number of stones forming the fabric of the church. Further rosettes are found higher up the gable, but their position is not original as the gable was partially rebuilt in the nineteenth century and must once have been higher than it is now. Though worn, the carving at Roscrea is of a quality matched by that of the fragmentary High Cross to the south of the church, which time has also dealt with harshly. On the far side of the roadway is a Round Tower, which may be roughly contemporary with the church, even though it bears no sign of Romanesque decoration.

DYSERT O'DEA
Co. Clare

The Michael O'Dea who 'repaired' the High Cross at Dysert in 1683 (p. 92) must have been something of a miraculous magpie. Not only did he conjure together two apparently separate fragments to form a single cross, but he also garnered what must be pieces from two different churches and compressed them into a single one. He must have taken parts of the church to act as supports for the High Cross in the adjoining field, and he is certainly the most likely candidate to have created the incredible jumble that is Dysert church today. As one can see from the multifarious window fragments built into the west gable, the decorated stonework as it stands is too plentiful and varied for it all to have come from a single church. G.U. Macnamara was probably right in suspecting that the carved stones from the original Dysert church must have been complemented by further material brought (doubtless by Michael the 'magpie') from a ruined Romanesque church at Rath 2 miles (3km) away to make up the hotchpotch *suprême* of the church – the Romanesque doorway in the south wall.

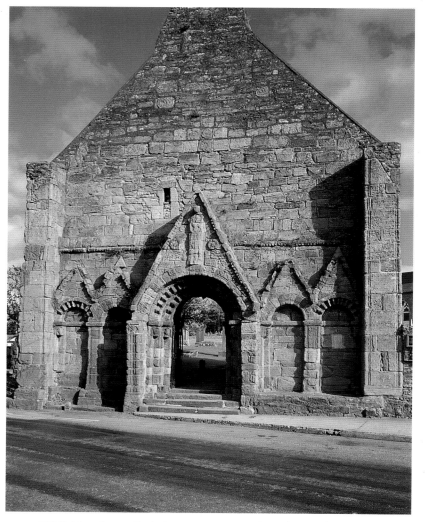

ABOVE Old-fashioned *antae* flank the gable enclosing the more up-to-date and elegant Romanesque surrounds of the mid-twelfth-century doorway at St Cronan's Church in Roscrea, Co. Tipperary.

RIGHT Carved stones from at least two different Romanesque doorways are apparently jumbled together in the south wall of the church at Dysert O'Dea in County Clare – including voussoirs bearing human heads, which may copy French ideas.

In four orders the doorway's columns have been cleverly patched together with fragments bearing foliate scrolls, animal interlace as well as beaded and chevron ornament, this latter also found in the arch above. Its best-known element is the outer order of the arch – a curious compendium of animal and human heads deriving probably from two separate doorways. The human heads, carved in the local hard limestone, have high cheek-bones, prominent eyes and high ears; they vary considerably in expression – one of the faces, with flowing moustache, having a distinctly oriental appearance. Heads were already built in above the chancel arch in Cormac's Chapel, but here they may have been more strongly influenced by similar features found in churches in the Bordeaux area of western France, where the patron of the Dysert (and Rath?) doorway may have seen them on a pilgrim journey to or from Santiago de Compostela.

THE NUNS' CHURCH
Clonmacnoise, Co. Offaly

No matter how much they were secularized, Irish monasteries probably had convents of nuns established outside the monastery's walls, and the most striking example of this is the Nuns' Church at Clonmacnoise, situated beside the Pilgrims' Way about one third of a mile to the east of the main enclosure. The compact nave-and-chancel church was completed in 1167, perhaps replacing an earlier church, remnants of which survive in a nearby field-fence. The benefactress of the church was Dearbhforgaill, better known as Dervorgilla, wife of Tighernán O'Rourke, King of Breifne, whose (apparently not entirely involuntary) abduction by Dermot MacMurrough in 1152 led fourteen years later to the latter's banishment from his Leinster kingdom and, ultimately, to the arrival of the Normans in 1169.

In its present form the church is the result of a reconstruction undertaken by James Graves and the Kilkenny and South-East of Ireland Archaeological Society in 1865, with the assistance of private subscriptions. Graves and his advisers replaced the missing parts with limestone, which contrasts neatly with the warm sandstone colouring of the original Romanesque work that is spread so profusely over the doorway and chancel arch. The doorway features animals in many situations – biting a bar which arches above the door, forming the end of a hood moulding or swallowing smaller fry at the top of one of the chevrons of the doorway. The chancel arch is even more heavily ornamented, and the capitals are carved overall with a variety of patterns displaying a severe case of *horror vacui* – fear of empty spaces. Some of the decoration is of a geometric nature with masks on the corner, one looking like that of Agamemnon. The proliferation of floral and animal decoration seems purely ornamental rather than being architectural sculpture. The arch is filled with pel-leted chevron ornament, often enclosing triangular foliate patterns and, in one instance, a female figure exhibiting her hind-quarters, who, however, is not to be confused with a sheela-na-gig.

ST DOULAGH'S CHURCH
Balgriffin, Co. Dublin

The fascinating church of St Doulagh, standing out so prominently beside the Dublin–Malahide road, presents more architectural puzzles than any other church of its size in the country, because of its many unusual features which are difficult to piece together. It may seem strangely out of place in the midst of all the decorated Romanesque churches in this section, but it is inserted here because its earliest portion still reflects the influence of Cormac's Chapel in the stone roof supported by a croft above the vaulted chancel. It is only the eastern end of the chancel, the section closest to the road, which may be ascribed to the twelfth century. About half way along its length, the vault displays a cleverly hidden joint with the later Gothic parts of the structure which were added when the other parts of the twelfth-century church were demolished to make way for it. Another connection with Cormac's Chapel is the occasional use of a very lightweight stone known as tufa, as Maurice Craig has pointed out.

There are no traces in or around the church of any stones carved in the Romanesque style, so we may conclude that the original church was simple in style, like St Kevin's Church at Glendalough, which is vaulted in a similar manner. Having a particularly Irish form of stone roof, the eastern part of St Doulagh's may have been built shortly before the Normans occupied the area in the 1170s. The Doulagh to whom the church is dedicated was once thought to have been a Dane, until it was demonstrated in 1859 that he was an obscure Irish saint who probably died *c*.600.

LEFT Dervorgilla, whose abduction ultimately led to the Norman invasion of Ireland, is said to have endowed this so-called Nuns' Church at Clonmacnoise, completed in 1167. Its profusely decorated doorway and chancel arch demonstrate just how much of these small twelfth-century structures bore Romanesque ornament.

RIGHT Parts of the narrow, stone-roofed chancel of St Doulagh's Church at Balgriffin, Co. Dublin, are Romanesque in date if not particularly in style, but the remainder consists of later additions both medieval and Victorian.

LEFT Shut away in a much later tower, the twelfth-century lintel at Maghera, Co. Derry, is one of the rare examples where the Crucifixion features in architectural sculpture of the Romanesque period anywhere in Europe.

RIGHT Venetian colouring is provided by the use of different hues in the stone of the gabled Romanesque doorway at Killeshin, Co. Laois, built perhaps at the behest of Dermot MacMurrough, King of Leinster, shortly after the middle of the twelfth century.

THE LINTEL AT MAGHERA
Co. Derry

The tympanum at Cormac's Chapel (p. 117) is an early Irish example of true architectural sculpture, but another and slightly later instance is provided by the lintel that formerly adorned a Romanesque church doorway but is now housed darkly in a seventeenth-century tower at Maghera, Co. Derry. This presents us with a coherent series of scenes illustrating the events of Christ's Passion during Easter Week. The central feature is the Crucifixion, showing Christ wearing a loin cloth and with very long arms, seen against the background of an even longer cross-arm. Blood flows from the wound in his right side onto the figure of Stephaton, the sponge-bearer, who is balanced on Christ's other side by Longinus, holding his lance. Standing on the heads of these two figures are the two thieves, whose bodies extend upwards between Christ's arms and those of the cross, so that their heads emerge beside the angels above the cross-arms. The figure of Mary can be seen standing behind Stephaton. The other figures on the lintel are more difficult to identify, but those on the extreme left may represent the Mocking of Christ, while those on the right may well show a Centurion, the Soldiers parting Christ's Garments, and the Holy Women coming to the Tomb. While not being a carving of very high quality, the crowded figures surrounding the Crucifixion seem to be following a European trend in frescoes of *c.*1100, though, along with a fragmentary lintel at Raphoe in County Donegal, they represent some of the very few examples of the Crucifixion forming part of architectural sculpture in European churches of the twelfth century.

KILLESHIN
Co. Laois

The monastery at Killeshin, only a few miles north-west of Carlow, had two patron saints, Diarmait, an early Leinster saint, and Comgán, a Munster saint whose name was attached to the monastery when the Dál Cais interfered in its affairs in the eleventh century. Further interference is likely to have occurred in the following century, this time from Dermot MacMurrough, King of Leinster (*c.*1133-71), whose name may have been inscribed on the doorway of the church.

The door stands in the west gable, which still retains one *anta* at the north-western corner. More than any other of its kind in the country, this doorway exudes colourfulness, using two different hues of granite and a brown sandstone. Under a tangent gable, its four orders present a considerable variety of motifs which avoid the overcrowding of the Nuns' Church at Clonmacnoise. The most striking features are the heads – beardless and clean-shaven – carved on the corners of the capitals, and with hair strands forming an interlace, which in one instance even develops into an Urnes-style animal interlace of Viking pedigree. Another striking bearded head stands alone at the centre of the innermost arch, presiding over zig-zag and chevron ornament in the orders of the arch, which are enlivened with foliate, quadruped and bird carvings in the spandrels.

The bulbous bases bear a considerable resemblance to those in the Cistercian church at Baltinglass, Co. Wicklow, which we now know to have been founded by Dermot MacMurrough in 1148, so that a date no more than a decade later may be assumed for Killeshin. As the fragmentary

inscription placed horizontally on the abacus above the capitals reads in part, 'D.AR . . . I LAGEN', possibly reconstructible as DIARMUIT RI LAGEN, Diarmuit (or Dermot), King of Leinster, there is a likelihood that he was also involved in commissioning this church too. There is a secondary inscription placed vertically on the north side of the doorway, but it has not proved possible to identify the 'Cellicami' mentioned in it with any known historical personage. The church once stood in the shadow of a Round Tower which was taken down in 1703 and which, if an old account is to be believed, is likely to have been one of the tallest in the country at 105 feet (32m).

ARDMORE CATHEDRAL
Co. Waterford

In addition to the Round Tower (pp. 106-7), Ardmore in County Waterford has another claim on our attention in the form of the high relief carvings built into the west end of the cathedral, which are the most extensive series of twelfth-century architectural sculpture remaining in Ireland.

The site is associated with St Declan, one of the so-called pre-Patrician saints of early Ireland, whose tomb-shrine survives in the form of a small, though much-mutilated, stone-roofed structure to the east of the cathedral. The cathedral is a multi-period structure, but where the carvings originally belonged cannot be ascertained satisfactorily because they have been built in secondarily into the exterior west wall of the cathedral at some period unknown. There they were fitted in a rather disjointed way into two large lunettes and a series of narrower arcades above them. The two most readily identifiable subjects are from the Old Testament – Adam and Eve in the middle of the left-hand lunette and the Judgment of Solomon in the upper part of the right-hand lunette. A harper on the right of the latter scene is quite probably Solomon's father, David, and it has been suggested recently that many of the other carvings may represent events in the lives of the same two biblical kings, including David's Battle with Goliath and the Building of Solomon's Temple. If correctly identified from a number of displaced fragments, Solomon's Temple would be a most suitable subject to adorn a cathedral.

A Bishop of Ardmore, named Eugene, is recorded as the signatory of a charter dating from 1172/9 and, as the first and probably the only Bishop of Ardmore, he is the most likely person to have commissioned the sculpted figures. He must have built them into a part of the cathedral which was subsequently demolished, but the fragments were obviously sufficiently important for them to have been taken down and reassembled in their present jumbled form in the west gable.

Arcades in the west wall of Ardmore Cathedral in County Waterford enclose a confused collection of twelfth-century architectural sculpture salvaged from an earlier building, including panels with recognizable subjects such as Adam and Eve and the Judgment of Solomon.

LEFT Monaincha Church was built in the later twelfth century on what was once an island in a now-drained bog, and was a famous centre of pilgrimage down to the seventeenth century.

BELOW One of the few examples of windows decorated externally in the Romanesque fashion is found on the church at Toureen Peakaun in the secretive Glen of Aherlow, Co. Tipperary, where there are a number of interesting monuments.

MONAINCHA
Co. Tipperary

One of the most appealing of all the smaller Irish Romanesque churches is that at Monaincha, not far from Roscrea, built on what was an island in a lake drained in the early nineteenth century. The island was a hermitage of the ascetic Culdees and, according to Giraldus the Welsh historian, who visited the island in 1185/6, no female – human or animal – could live on the island. The church was probably constructed by the Augustinian canons in the last third of the twelfth century, but the inscriptions on the doorway are sadly too fragmentary to allow us to identify the personage who was responsible for its erection.

The west doorway, which inclines slightly in the old Irish fashion, is composed of a beautifully warm red sandstone and is decorated with chevron and foliate ornament, including scrolls and variations of the classical palmette. The arch above also has chevron and flower ornament. The chancel arch is better preserved and its carving, particularly on the underside, is still extraordinarily crisp. Above the scalloped capitals, finely chiselled zig-zag ornament is flanked by a roll moulding terminating in dragon heads, and the varying rhythms of the chevron ornament are interspersed with flower motifs. The windows in the south wall were inserted in the thirteenth century and the small window above the west door shows that the church was still in use two centuries later.

From early times Monaincha was an important centre of pilgrimage and one pilgrim came all the way from Germany to visit it in 1591. In the seventeenth century thousands of others are recorded as having congregated here, saying their pious prayers and doubtless kneeling in front of the twelfth-century cross now reconstructed outside the west door.

TOUREEN PEAKAUN
Co. Tipperary

One of the most intriguing archaeological sites in the enchanting Glen of Aherlow is Toureen Peakaun, which contains a number of early medieval monuments. The name 'Peakaun' comes from the old monastery's founding saint, Beagán, latinized Beccanus, who appears to have been an early Irish anchorite whose special form of asceticism was to recite the whole Psalter daily while standing with his hands outstretched in the form of a cross. The church, illustrated here, was probably built in the twelfth century, about five hundred years after his death, and is unusual in having Romanesque foliate decoration on the exterior face of the south window.

Up to thirty cross-decorated memorial slabs inscribed with personal names have been recovered from the site, including a number found during an excavation in 1944, but none of them can be identified satisfactorily with historically recorded personages. One interesting stone cross, with an Irish inscription using capital letters of a kind inscribed on the Ardagh Chalice (p. 53) but not yet fully deciphered, seems to imitate carpentry techniques, suggesting that it was copied from a wooden original, perhaps some time around 800.

TUAM CATHEDRAL
Co. Galway

Reflecting the fact that it was the seat of the O Conor dynasty which provided Ireland with two High Kings in the twelfth century, Tuam preserves a number of important monuments of the period, of which three

High Crosses are now housed in the Protestant cathedral. In the cathedral itself there is the chancel of a Romanesque predecessor which served as the seat of the archbishopric created at the Synod of Kells in 1152. With a span of 16 feet (5m), the chancel arch is the widest of its kind in Ireland. The capitals are decorated with animal interlacing imitating the Urnes-derived style found on the Market Cross now in the south transept nearby, and there is a wonderful smiling mask on the inner face of the innermost order. The moulded abacus above the capital is a feature which occurs late in the development of Irish Romanesque, supporting Roger Stalley's suggestion that the whole chancel, including the interior east windows carved with a curious sword-bearing figure, was erected after a fire in 1183.

What was originally the chancel of the Romanesque cathedral was converted in the fourteenth century to become the porch of a building added on to the east, which Maurice Craig has described as a 'retro-choir'. This building acted as the choir of the medieval cathedral, and the central east window of the Romanesque chancel was broken through to act as an entrance doorway to it. It was blocked up after the present nave of the modern cathedral was erected in 1861 over the site of the original nave.

RIGHT AND BELOW (detail)
Tuam Cathedral, well endowed by the O Conor High Kings in the twelfth century, was provided with Ireland's broadest Romanesque chancel arch probably some time after a fire in 1183. Not having been exposed to the elements, the carvings – such as the mask-heads on the capitals – have retained an unusual crispness of detail.

CLONFERT CATHEDRAL
Co. Galway

The great west doorway of Clonfert Cathedral is generally regarded as the high point of the Romanesque style of ornament in Ireland. 'Baroque' in its exuberance, it scarcely leaves a square inch of its surface undecorated. The reason for such an elaborate portal is that it acted as the entrance to the relics of that remarkable Irish saint, Brendan the Navigator, renowned throughout Europe, who lies buried here so far from the sea which he loved. The saint had died in another monastery he had founded at Annaghdown beside Lough Corrib (where there are also late Romanesque fragments), but his body was brought here for burial in 577 or 583.

The doorway is an insert into an already existing gable with *antae*, to which some earlier-looking Romanesque fragments inside the cathedral may have belonged. The doorway inclines slightly as it rises, but this has been partly 'rectified' in the fifteenth century by the insertion of an inner-most order of limestone with a vertical doorcase bearing floral ornament and the figures of two bishops.

The portal bears a great variety of motifs: animal interlace ultimately of

Built in honour of St Brendan the Navigator, who was buried here in east Galway far from his beloved sea, Clonfert Cathedral was provided with a gabled doorway that represents the zenith of Irish Romanesque sculpture. Exuberantly decorated with interlacing and bosses of 'baroque' whimsy as well as human heads (in the gable), it includes an innermost order – possibly with a carving of the saint himself – which was added in the fifteenth century.

DOORWAY IN KILLALOE CATHEDRAL
Co. Clare

Killaloe had a Romanesque cathedral which was demolished, but the fine west doorway was preserved and reconstructed in the south-western corner of the Gothic cathedral. Its forceful carving, much of it in high relief, must have argued persuasively in favour of its retention.

Its jambs proliferate in curving pelleted mouldings, chevron ornament with foliate scrolls, mouldings terminating in fantastic animal heads and, in one instance, a whole animal facing downwards to bite a roll moulding. The capitals are a developed form of the scalloped capital, enlivened with asparagus-like additions and spirals above. The arch also has chevron orna-ment, but one order is unusual in having human faces and animals carved in high relief. Many of the details of this doorway recur on carvings of the 'School of the West', as at Ballintubber, Boyle and Corcomroe, so that it can be seen as a seminal element in the development of that school during the first quarter of the thirteenth century. Tessa Garton's date of *c.*1200 would therefore seem appropriate for this Killaloe doorway, which demon-strates a lively inventiveness in the late Romanesque carving that was con-tinuing in the west of Ireland when the Gothic style was already spreading in the east of the country.

Scandinavian origin, classical palmettes, floral patterns and scrolls, chevrons, bosses, as well as animal heads – some eating jamb-columns, others standing out in high relief as masks or grasping a torus moulding forming a semi-circle in the arch. The three outer orders of the arch bear high relief bosses, and in the inner three the effect of light and shade play a prominent role. Above the arch, the tangent gable of Cormac's Chapel makes its last and most grandiose appearance, with half a dozen heads at the top of an arcade and, at the apex, a pattern of flat triangles alternating with human heads in sunken relief – and there are a few more heads thrown in here and there for good measure. These heads, which some authors imagine to be a throw-back to the *tête-coupée*, or severed head, revered by the pagan Celts, range from the stylized and bearded to the clean-shaven and almost portrait-like, suggesting that we are here at the threshold of the transition from Romanesque to Gothic, probably some-where in the final two decades of the twelfth century. Much of the nave and chancel appear to belong to the early thirteenth century, though the friary-like tower over the doorway, the transepts (of which the north one has vanished) and the sacristy belong to the later medieval period, when the chancel arch (with helmeted head) was inserted.

Preserved in the south-western corner of the nave of the Gothic Killaloe Cathedral is the doorway of a Romanesque predecessor, which must have inspired 'School of the West' sculptors in the early thirteenth century.

CHAPTER FOUR

THE ANGLO-NORMANS, 1169–1400

THE POLITICAL SCENE

In 1175 the English King Henry II concluded the Treaty of Windsor with the Irish 'High King' Rory O Conor, in which the latter pledged to pay an annual tribute while Henry agreed to leave O Conor as High King of the territory which remained unconquered by the Normans. But neither party kept – or could keep – the bargain, O Conor because he was simply not accepted as High King throughout all of Gaelic Ireland, Henry because he could not restrain his rapacious barons from grabbing more of the better agricultural land, while leaving the bogs and forest uplands to the Irish. King Henry kept Dublin and its hinterland for himself, as well as the maritime cities of Cork and Limerick, and his barons did not long remain idle in their own interest. Hugh de Lacy organized the taking of Meath from the Shannon to the Irish Sea, while John de Courcy marched into Ulster, took Downpatrick and created new

centres of power in Carrickfergus and Dundrum, among other towns. Munster was divided up between a number of foreign knights, thereby becoming almost as French as France itself. It was not until 1235 that the Normans went beyond their Shannon castles to invade Connacht – scarcely a fair fate for its O Conor kings who had remained allies of the English monarch, and who now saw their lands being distributed among de Burgos, de Lacys and FitzGeralds. Norman towns sprang up at Galway and Athenry, the old Norse town of Limerick was fortified and many other towns such as Youghal were to have town walls built around their settled areas. By the middle of the thirteenth century three-quarters of Ireland was in Norman hands. The remaining quarter – the north – was to remain independent for more than three centuries.

The Normans conquered because of their rigid military discipline and their superior weapons and armour, though in time they reduced the weight of their armour to suit Irish fighting conditions. Unlike the native

John de Courcy was probably the first to have fortified the site of Dundrum Castle, Co. Down, in his efforts to retain those parts of Ulster that he had conquered in 1177. Nevertheless, much of the present structure may not have been built until early in the following century.

Among the early Norman intruders into north Cork were the Condons and the Roches, who, between them, seem to have built most of this castle at Glanworth in the second half of the thirteenth century.

Irish, for whom war was mostly about cattle-raiding, the Normans kept what they won by the sword. To provide advance offensive positions and subdue, yet impress, the conquered Irish, they built earthen motes, or mottes, with accompanying baileys to accommodate cattle and horses. But already before the end of the century they were erecting ringworks – enclosures defended by ditch and palisade, and guarded by a gate-house – while, at the same time, embarking on the construction of more ambitious stone castles to consolidate their territorial gains. Rather than ejecting the Irish from the territories they conquered, they retained them to work the land, yet regarded their kings as equals to whom they began marrying off their daughters, for the conquering barons ran out of male heirs surprisingly quickly.

One of their major contributions was the strengthening and organizing of the old Norse towns of Dublin, Wexford, Waterford, Cork and Limerick, providing them in due course with stout walls. In the case of Dublin they built a strong castle as well, which was started in 1204 and was to remain the centre of English-based power in Ireland for more than 700 years. They set up markets, minted their own coins, established manors, workshops and churches, and in the larger towns built new and imposing cathedrals and churches at the same time as encouraging the newly arrived

Dominican and Franciscan friars to establish themselves in urban centres where they could preach to the townspeople.

Ulster west of the Bann remained in Irish hands because the Norman urge for conquest began to run out of steam, and fighting men had been syphoned off to to do battle in Britain and France. While the Normans still registered some notable victories in the second half of the thirteenth century, the Irish – for the first time – began to stem the tide, particularly in the south-west and in Connacht.

By 1300 the Normans had set up a framework of administration, instituted a parliament together with the necessary legal officials and encouraged an improvement in agricultural production through efficient ploughing and extensive forest clearance, though for centuries to come the country remained much more extensively wooded than it is today. Much wheat was harvested, thanks to a climatic optimum which was, however, to decline considerably in the following century. A somewhat neglected aspect of the Normans in Ireland is the development of their own literature and the creation of schools largely associated with the monastic orders, though the leaders in society sent their sons off to Oxford and Cambridge for their higher education.

Things started to go sour for the Anglo-Irish as the fourteenth century

ABOVE St. Mary's Church in New Ross preserves this effigy of an unidentified layman, representative of the rich burghers of the newly founded Norman towns that began to flourish in the thirteenth century. The stone itself was imported, perhaps already fully carved, from the Normans' homeland in the West of England.

RIGHT Greencastle, otherwise known as Northburgh or Newcastle, was built in 1305 on the Inishowen Peninsula in Donegal by Richard de Burgo, the 'Red' Earl of Ulster, with the intention of making it into the Normans' main fortress in the north-west of Ireland. But the aspiration was short-lived, as the castle was captured by Edward the Bruce's Scots in 1316 and a century later fell into Irish hands.

progressed. Edward the Bruce came over from Scotland in 1315 (to be followed two years later by his brother Robert), and he was crowned King of Ireland by the natives, but his campaigns left the country ravaged before he was killed at the end of a three-year campaign. By the mid-1320s half of the colonized lands belonged to absentees who had retired to England, and their defences deteriorated rapidly for want of repair. Much worse was yet to come in the form of the bubonic plague, better known as the Black Death, which wrought havoc particularly in the towns between 1348 and 1350. Friar Clyn of Kilkenny wrote a harrowing account of the plague which tailed off as he succumbed to it himself. It has been estimated that about one-third of the urban population of Ireland perished as a result of the Black Death; rural manors and villages were hastily abandoned, fields were left untilled and many of those who managed to survive returned to England. After the Black Death the area of Anglo-Irish domination contracted, while Gaelic Ireland began to show signs of revival, having been left comparatively unscathed by the mid-century plague.

Gaelic Ireland had remained thinly populated, perhaps not exceeding half a million souls. It had a pastoral economy, though with some land under tillage, but the settlements remained scattered and often impermanent. In the late twelfth century Giraldus Cambrensis, a rather biased and unflattering observer, could say of the Irish that 'woods were their forts, and swamps their ditches'. They abandoned the castles built by the O Conors before the Normans arrived, and a description of one of their palaces paints a picture of something decorative but perhaps in reality little more than a large wooden house. A Cistercian abbot ridiculed the Irish kings for living in wattle huts. Politically, Gaelic society was unstable, torn by rivalries and possessing a system of leadership which kept replacing itself from the top downwards, whereby recent off-shoots took over from the former chiefly houses. Little of what documentation there was has survived, so that our knowledge of medieval Gaelic Ireland is much sketchier than that of the better-documented Anglo-Norman society. But what did survive were the nucleated settlements which had grown up long before the Norman invasion at sites such as Clonmacnoise and Armagh, though there were probably small settlements, with craftworkers, around some of the lesser religious foundations. Crannogs, of the kind used in pre-Norman times, do, however, appear to have continued in use – at least in Ulster – until around 1600.

Symptomatic of the cultural resurgence of Gaelic Ireland after the Black Death was the great meeting of poets, bards and harpers at the house of O'Kelly in Connacht in 1351. For more than half a century Gaelic nobility acted as patrons for a new generation of poets in the Irish language who tried to recreate a past as if the Normans had never existed. Paradoxically, one of the greatest of these poets was of Norman stock himself, the third Earl of Desmond, better known as Gearóid Iarla (pronounced 'Gyar-o-id Eer-la). Great codices, such as the *Book of Ballymote* and the *Yellow Book of Lecan*, came to be compiled around 1400, each in its own way 'a library of Gaelic learning' in the words of Donnchadh Ó Corráin. New commentaries were written on the by-now largely incomprehensible early Irish law

FAR LEFT AND LEFT Effigies in Gowran, Co. Kilkenny, taken to be those of James le Butler, first Earl of Ormond and his wife Eleanor de Bohun, betray a rigour reflecting the decline of Norman Ireland only a decade or so before the Black Death began to take its toll in 1348.

tracts, and Irish translations were prepared for astronomical treatises and continental tales of chivalry. Gearóid Iarla symbolizes for us the increasing tendency of the old Anglo-Irish families to adapt Irish customs and dress, which had become such a worry to the English government that – even before the days of the poet earl – the Statutes of Kilkenny, introduced in 1366, forbade this gaelicization among the colonists. But the statutes proved to be of little avail, for they were honoured more in the breach than in the observance. Shortly afterwards, William of Windsor tried to stem the flow by ordering absentees to return in order to rebuild the decaying defences, or at least to pay for their reconstruction – but this only led to many of them selling their Irish estates. Richard II came over twice from England in the 1390s, but had to return to England where he lost his life and his head, largely because of his unsuccessful attempt to stem the Gaelic resurgence. By 1400 most of Ireland had effectively passed out of English control, and the dwindling colony was left largely to its own resources to defend itself.

CANTWELL KNIGHT AT KILFANE
Co. Kilkenny

The medieval parish church at Kilfane in County Kilkenny preserves a superb effigy of a Norman knight, described by Roger Stalley as 'one of the best of its kind in either Britain or Ireland'. With a length of nearly 8 feet (2.4m), it is also the largest, 'a colossus among medieval effigies', again in the words of Roger Stalley. The knight is defended by a coat of mail of many parts, a coif around the head which probably covered a metal skull-cap, a hauberk protecting the torso down to the knees, coverings for the legs and mittens for the hands. Over the hauberk the knight wears a surcoat with deep folds, and draped over it is a belt which held the sword visible between the legs. The long, triangular shield which he holds in his left hand bears the arms of the Cantwell family, who

LEFT This tall effigy of a Cantwell knight (known as 'Cantwell Fada' or 'Long Cantwell') at Kilfane, Co. Kilkenny, epitomizes the superiority and dominance of the Normans in many parts of Ireland for a century and a half after their invasion of the country in 1169.

RIGHT Two knights, known as 'The Brethren', unusually incised together on a tombstone at Jerpoint Abbey, Co. Kilkenny, demonstrate varying fashions in head armour used by the Normans in Ireland during the later thirteenth century.

formed part of the entourage of Theobald Walter when the Normans came to Ireland in the later twelfth century.

But which member of the family does the knight represent? Because of the rowel spurs which are worn on the ankles, John Hunt suggested that it is perhaps Thomas Cantwell, who died around 1320. But Roger Stalley has argued cogently on stylistic grounds for a date some seventy years earlier, even if this does not solve the problem as to which Cantwell is represented. But whichever one he may be, this imperious knight, with his proud movement of crossed legs and assured glance, gives us a splendid impression of the appearance of those Norman knights in full panoply who – like his companions known as 'The Brethren' in Jerpoint – dominated the east of Ireland throughout the thirteenth century. Though carved from local limestone, he may have been sculpted by a craftsman from South Wales.

NORMAN MOTTES AND CASTLES

Within decades of their arrival in Ireland in 1169, the Normans began to defend their newly conquered territories with both earthen and stone fortifications. Even with a comparatively untrained work-force, it would have been possible to erect earthworks quickly and effectively, and these come in two forms – the motte and the ringwork. The motte, as at Knockgraffon, is a large mound of earth on the flattened top of which a wooden tower, or bretesche, was built to store arms and to keep an eye out for potential attackers. Earth for the motte was provided by the excavation of a deep ditch around its base, and just outside the ditch there was often a bailey – a flat area also defended by a ditch and presumably a wooden palisade – where soldiers were quartered and cattle found protection. The ringwork was a rounded enclosure surrounded by a bank, and sometimes with a height-ened interior. Stone castles were occasionally built upon them later. As has been pointed out, the structure of Irish society in the twelfth century was following the European trend in becoming feudal in character, and some of the ringworks – and possibly even the some of the mottes – may even have been built by the Irish, but so like the Norman examples as to be indistinguishable from them.

Quite clearly Norman in origin are the great stone castles which were initiated within a decade of the Norman arrival and which continued to be built in various forms for about 130 years. Among the first were also the strongest – Carrickfergus, Co. Antrim, and Trim, Co. Meath. Each was built by a Norman baron who conquered the territory in which they stand – Ulster's captor, John de Courcy, in the case of the former, and the first Hugh de Lacy, Lord of Meath, in the case of the latter. Both are characterized by a tall, square central tower, three storeys high, with an entry on the first floor which acted as a guard-chamber controlling access to the keep. The second floor would have been reserved for the lord's immediate retinue, while the uppermost level contained the lord's own private chambers. The fact that neither of these towers contained living quarters for the soldiers suggests not only that the large hall where lord and soldiers mingled must have been outside the central keep, but also that these towers were, among other things, status symbols to impress others how important the lord was. The towers' lack of certain defensive features, such as arrow slits in some instances, shows that the Anglo-Normans cannot have feared the vanquished Irish too much as foes to be constantly kept at bay.

One who did not want to be too much impressed was the King of England, who was becoming worried at this ostentatious show of pride by the barons – not only those who built Carrickfergus and Trim but others too, such as William the Marshal at Kilkenny and Geoffrey de Marisco at Adare. The king felt the necessity to act in order to establish his own central power, and around 1204 he ordered work to begin on Dublin Castle where a great hall was built to act as the centre of social activities. Perhaps

Mottes such as this example at Knockgraffon, Co. Tipperary, would originally have had a wooden look-out tower on top and may be included among the earliest Norman fortifications in Ireland, dating largely from the late twelfth century.

the king was reacting against the tower-power of the barons by having no central keep or donjon at Dublin, and the same was true of another royal castle, namely Limerick, where much work was undertaken immediately after King John's visit to Ireland in 1210. It, like Dublin, was an oblong area defended by a strong curtain wall with stout circular towers at the corners and along the walls, the entrance being defended in each case by two half-rounded drum-towers. Athlone, which was built at around the same time, did, however, have a strong central polygonal tower, in an effort to establish a Norman bridgehead immediately west of the River Shannon.

But experience in England had already shown that angular towers could be undermined, as King John was to demonstrate royally when his siege weapons demolished one of the square angle-towers at Rochester in 1215. Around 1200 Theobald Walter built the massive donjon of his castle at Nenagh in the form of a cylindrical tower almost 100 feet (30m) high – the stoutest of its kind in the country – and Dundrum, Co. Down, was to have a similar feature added within a decade. Not slow to realize the greater impregnability of the round as opposed to the square tower, the Normans developed a new form of castle in Ireland which was to remain popular in one shape or form until the sixteenth century. This consisted of a tall rec-

tangular block with a round bastion at each corner, of which Ferns and Carlow provide good – if half-demolished – examples. Kilkenny castle also conformed roughly to the type, but its wedge-shaped plan allowed for a large open area in the centre. While the rounded bastions continued to the end of purely Norman castle-building at places such as Ballyloughan, Co. Carlow, in the early fourteenth century, the tall gateway of Roscrea castle, of c.1280, reverted to the rectangular form.

The lie of the land was an important factor in dictating the shape of the early Norman castles, particularly when they were sited on rock outcrops, as at Dunamase, Co. Laois, and Carlingford, Co. Louth, both of which originated early in the thirteenth century. But as the century wore on, flatter ground was preferred for the type of rectangular castle with rounded corner bastions. Imitation being the greatest form of flattery, one can only presume that the strength of this castle type at Roscommon – built by the Justiciar Robert de Ufford in the later thirteenth century – so impressed the O Conor Kings of Connacht that they decided to construct a similar castle on flattish ground at Ballintober only 10 miles (16km) away early in the following century. Shortly afterwards, the Bruce invasion threw Ireland into chaos and brought about a virtual end to Norman castle-building in the country.

LEFT Theobald Walter Butler's 100ft(30m)-high donjon of c.1200 dominated his castle at Nenagh, Co. Tipperary, and the Ormond territory over which he held sway. Its walls were strong enough to resist a gunpowder explosion in 1760, caused by a farmer trying to get rid of sparrows which were ruining his crops, and the top floor was added about a century later.

RIGHT It was probably Hugh de Lacy who built the so-called 'King John's Castle' at Carlingford, Co. Louth, around 1200, attracted by the defensive advantages offered by its rocky promontory and the deep-water anchorage – and perhaps even by an oyster or two, still a local delicacy.

CARRICKFERGUS CASTLE
Co. Antrim

The most complete surviving castle of the Anglo-Norman conquest is undoubtedly Carrickfergus Castle, which stands on a rocky outcrop stretching out like a tongue into Belfast Lough. It may have been started by John de Courcy in 1178, the year he marched into north-east Ulster. Central to the construction of its earliest phase was a square tower some 90 feet (27m) high and with three storeys, only the top one of which is well provided with windows. Through them de Courcy would have been able to survey the goings-on in the yard below, which was enclosed by a curtain wall interspersed with an occasional tower. The tower, or donjon, stood at one corner of this polygonal yard, and on the eastern side of it – close to the original entrance – lay the hall where the soldiers would have congregated and been addressed by their lord and master as the occasion arose. De Courcy was able to enjoy the use of the castle until he was ousted by Hugh de Lacy – son of the original builder of Trim Castle – who, in turn, was expelled from the Earldom of Ulster when King John overcame the castle in 1210. The king took over the defence of the castle and garrisoned it the following year with ten knights, sixteen soldiers, five bowmen and a chaplain, a complement twice the size of that of any other Ulster castle.

Because of the weakness offered to any potential attacker by the exposed wall of the tower on the landward side, a further defensive wall was added to the north around 1220 in order to keep besiegers as far away as possible from the donjon. This still left a part of the tongue of land undefended, but by the middle of the century it too had been enclosed, making access to the whole castle possible only through a door flanked by two massive round bastions facing the land. Subsequent additions have not been very substantial, so that Carrickfergus remains essentially a splendid thirteenth-century castle.

It functioned as an administrative centre throughout the later Middle Ages, and saw no action until 1689, when Schomberg took it for King William of Orange, who chose Carrickfergus for his first landing on Irish soil the following year. The French commander, Thurot, took the castle by surprise from the sea in 1760, and some cannon now displayed in the castle were mounted to prepare for a Napoleonic invasion which never materialized.

TRIM CASTLE
Co. Meath

If Carrickfergus is the best-preserved Norman castle in Ireland, that at Trim, Co. Meath, comes a close second and is, in addition, the largest, as it covers an area of 3 acres (1.2ha). At its centre is a massive keep, or donjon, basically square in shape, but with the addition of a square tower to each of the four sides (one of which has disappeared) – thereby making an equal-armed Greek cross, a ground-plan unique among Norman castles. As this form gave a total of a dozen corners which could theoretically

RIGHT Water was diverted from the River Boyne to create a moat and extra line of defence for Trim Castle, which was further fortified by an outer wall, still partially surviving.

LEFT Carrickfergus is the most impressive and complete of all the Norman castles of Ireland.

be undermined by siege operations, it may well be that the tower was designed less as a pure fortification than as a statement of social status made by its original builder. Hugh Tyrell, whom Hugh de Lacy, Lord of the Liberty of Trim, had left in charge of the place in 1172, may have been responsible for the erection of an earlier fortification on the site, which he set on fire when it was threatened by the Connacht King Rory O Conor. This may have been the ring-work which was revealed in Alan Hayden's excavations beneath the castle in 1995. De Lacy however must have decided to start building the existing stone keep shortly afterwards, because the earliest tree-ring date obtained by the Office of Public Works from the wood of the scaffolding surviving within the castle walls comes from around the year 1174/5.

Further pieces of wood found higher up in the structure provided additional dates for the years around 1195 and 1204. If a break in the masonry half way up the walls is seen as being the result of an interruption in construction caused by the death of Hugh de Lacy in 1186, we may presume that the upper part of the tower was virtually complete by the time King John took the castle in 1210, though the final touches may have been added by William Peppard as late as 1220. It must have been around this time, too, that a plinth was added to the base of the tower.

But the real defences of Trim were the curtain walls, which form a D-shape along the banks of the River Boyne, some of whose waters were diverted to make a water-filled ditch around the curtain walls, thereby adding to the strength of the defences by making the whole complex into an island. Just inside the northern curtain wall, Alan Hayden recently uncovered a hitherto unsuspected large stone hall with a double line of pillars supporting a vault, probably dating from around 1300, and suggesting that a number of other stone or wooden buildings may yet remain to be discovered in the grassy area between the curtain wall and the central keep. The largely twelfth-century curtain wall was interspersed with towers, one being an entrance with a square tower on the western side, the others being rounded. One of these, facing south, was provided with a completely enclosed drawbridge, and is the place where tradition asserts that Prince Hal (later King Henry V) and the 'Good Duke' Humphrey of Gloucester were lodged for safety after King Richard II left the castle in 1399. The finds which David Sweetman made in these towers and the ditch suggested that the castle fell into disuse after the Black Death in 1348-50, when the fortunes of the Anglo-Norman colony fell into a decline in Ireland. Though repaired during the rebellion of Silken Thomas between 1536 and 1541, the castle did not play any further defensive role again until the 1640s, when it was twice taken, the second time by Cromwell's forces under Lord Inchiquin, after which it was finally abandoned. Lord Dunsany handed the castle over to state ownership as recently as 1993.

DUBLIN CASTLE

Today, we associate Dublin Castle with heavily guarded European Prime Ministers' meetings, presidential inaugurations in the State Apartments and official tribunals, not to mention the Revenue Commissioners. All of this might seem light years away from a medieval castle, and no longer quite fulfils the mandate which King John gave Meiler fitz Henry in 1204 to build him a castle in Dublin 'to hold his treasure, administer justice and defend the city with good ditches and strong walls'. The castle has roughly the shape of a rectangle with a round bastion at each corner, and the long walls had a semi-circular bastion on the south side and a two-towered entrance on the north. From the heavy urban clutter surrounding the castle today it is difficult to envisage that it was once washed on two sides by the River Poddle, which could bring boats from the Liffey up to a pool on the south side of the castle, and that water was diverted from the now-underground river to form a moat around the other two sides. In his excavations in the Powder Tower at the north-eastern corner, Conleth Manning found not only the moat and thirteenth-century tower, together with its junction to the main city wall, but also successive layers of Viking activity beneath, demonstrating that the Norman castle lay on top of centuries of Norse settlement and defences, for the tongue of land on which it stands was an eminently fortifiable site.

The castle acted as the centre of English power in Ireland from the time of its foundation until it was handed over to the Irish in 1922. During the intervening centuries it served many purposes: official residence of the Lords Deputy and Lieutenant and even of their kings – Richard II in the 1390s, probably James II and William III (both 1690), and George V in 1911; treasury and weapon store; seat of parliaments and courts of law; and prison for many Irish patriots (of whom Red Hugh O'Donnell was one of the few to escape, in 1592). Nothing now remains of the great hall burned in the seventeenth century. The towers on the south flank of the castle – including the Record Tower illustrated here – and parts of the intervening wall are all that remain visible above ground of the medieval castle, though the two corner towers on the northern side are viewable below ground after the 1980s excavations. One of these was the Corke tower in the north-western corner (near the present Conference Hall), excavated by Ann Lynch. Its collapse in 1624 was symptomatic of the general decay of the castle fabric at the time. However, a disastrous fire in 1684 accelerated the renewal which took place largely during the course of the eighteenth century – and that is essentially the castle which we can see and visit today.

KING JOHN'S CASTLE
Limerick

As the lowermost fordable position on the River Shannon, Limerick was first fortified by the Vikings possibly as early as the tenth century, and its strategic location facing the O'Brien Kingdom of Thomond was appreciated sufficiently by King John that he decided to fortify it in the years around 1200. As Lord of Ireland, he had granted a charter to the city in 1197, and this may have been the bugle call for the start of King John's Castle, one of the few royal castles to be built in Ireland before John visited the country as king in 1210. The castle forms part of the city walls bordering the River Shannon and overlooks Thomond Bridge, which is probably

the second successor to the one built by King John in the early years of the thirteenth century. The fortification forms a rough square, with massive circular bastions surviving on three of the four corners. The entrance faces north and is flanked by two rounded gate turrets.

Repairs were carried out in 1211-12, after which the castle was put under the charge of a number of successive custodians, the brothers de Braose, Geoffrey de Marisco and Richard de Burgh, but by 1226 all they had succeeded in doing was letting the castle fall into a state of chaos, so that it contained 'a lot of broken crockery'. The O'Briens and the Macnamaras threatened the castle on numerous occasions – and even succeeded in taking it once during the fourteenth century. Throughout the following hundred years, the condition of the fortifications continued to decline, despite being taken over by the merchants in the town. This comparative neglect of the castle during the fourteenth to the sixteenth century, documented by Sheelagh Harbison, was confirmed by David Sweetman in his excavations in the castle during the 1970s. By 1574 the Jesuit father David Wolfe could describe the castle as having 'been unoccupied for many years . . . the houses and roof of the castle are in decay'. The south-east corner had a new tower added by Josias Bodley in 1608-11, and nearby Kenneth Wiggins unearthed traces of pre-Norman occupation beneath the east curtain wall. This part of the defences is well preserved in the lower floor of a brash two-storey Interpretative Centre which was erected around 1991, after traces of the eighteenth-century barracks and ghastly 1930s local authority housing had been removed from the interior of the castle.

DUNAMASE CASTLE
Co. Laois

The Rock of Dunamase, geologically known as a 'hum', is splendidly located overlooking the plains of County Laois, and it is sad that the

LEFT The stout Record Tower is one of the least altered of Dublin Castle's defences since it was built in the thirteenth century.

RIGHT King John's Castle in Limerick probably seemed anything but placid and peaceful when erected around 1200 with the intention of cowing into submission the Irish who lived on the opposite bank of the River Shannon.

BELOW Perched on its dominant rock, Dunamase Castle in County Laois must have had a menacing – yet probably also fairy-tale – appearance when first erected in the thirteenth century, but it is now, sadly, a ruin.

condition of the castle perched upon it does not match the panoramic view which it provides. At the coming of the Normans in 1169, the Rock was in the possession of Dermot MacMurrough, King of Leinster, through whose daughter Aoife it passed by marriage to Strongbow, and through his daughter to William, Earl Marshal. He or Meiler fitz Henry may have initiated the fortification of the Rock, but it was probably William de Braose who completed it after he took over in 1231. The top of the Rock is enclosed by a curtain wall; within this is the central keep, which underwent many changes up to the sixteenth century. Defending the keep was an outer courtyard, triangular in shape, and entered through a round-faced gate-tower from a D-shaped bailey at the eastern end of the Rock.

During the remainder of the medieval period the castle was a constant bone of contention between the English and the Irish, the former keeping it well garrisoned to retain their interest in it. During the Cromwellian wars, the castle changed hands a number of times until Cromwell's generals, Hewson and Reynolds, blew it up, leaving it in its present sadly disjointed state. In the eighteenth century Sir John Parnell toyed with the idea of restoring it to its former glory – but nothing came of the plan, and his son allowed the castle to fall into permanent decay.

KILKENNY CASTLE

Kilkenny is one of the great medieval towns of Ireland, preserving within its ancient walls many buildings of the Middle Ages, of which the two finest are St Canice's Cathedral and Kilkenny Castle. For all its size and strength the castle features only rarely in early historical records. While William, the Earl Marshal, may have first started building on the site around 1192, the castle's trapeze-shaped plan scarcely evolved before the thirteenth century, when the massive rounded corner bastions were constructed, three of which survive. Like the castles at Dublin and Limerick, the central open courtyard does not appear to have had any free-standing tower within it. All four of the walls linking the towers were presumably extant when the Butlers, Earls of Ormond, bought the castle from its absentee owners in 1391/2. The only successful attack on the castle was launched by Oliver Cromwell in 1650, and the damage which he must have caused to the original entrance and adjoining wall on the south-eastern side was obviously so severe that this whole flank was later demolished, thereby opening up the vista to the extensive parkland which we enjoy today.

Shortly after 1698 a new entrance in classical style was provided by the second Duke of Ormond, who also remodelled the castle in the style of a French château. But, in the years after 1826, the first Marquess of Ormond undid much of the Duke's work in an attempt to restore the castle to its medieval appearance. His successor, the second Marquess, constructed the great two-storey picture gallery overlooking the River Nore to the designs of the Victorian architect Benjamin Woodward in the 1850s, thus completing the amalgam of styles we see today. After an uninterrupted occupation of the castle lasting almost 500 years, the Ormonds sold the contents in 1935 and transferred the castle and formal gardens to the state in 1967, for the nominal sum of £50.

RIGHT Ivy-clad Adare Castle, Co. Limerick, built overlooking the River Maigue in the thirteenth century, must surely get a prize for being one of Ireland's most romantic-looking fortifications.

LEFT Kilkenny Castle on the River Nore, focus of the enchanting 'marble city', has gone through many transformations – but also beautifications – since first erected in the thirteenth century.

ADARE CASTLE
Co. Limerick

The town of Adare, some 11 miles (18km) west of Limerick city, has one of the finest collections of medieval monuments in the country, including the fine castle which – like the royal castle at Limerick – fronts on to a river, in this case the Maigue. The somewhat dilapidated keep of the castle, with pilaster-like projections on two of its faces, forms part of the eastern curtain-wall of an inner ward enclosure which may have been a ringwork, or rectangular earthen-walled castle before the keep was built, probably sometime before 1226. This inner ward was entered through a gate, preceded by a bridge or drawbridge over a water-filled ditch which surrounded the inner ward. This ditch was probably deepened by the keep-builders and joined to the river so that it could have a constant supply of water. The bridge linked the inner ward to the outer ward where there are two halls standing parallel to the river. That further downstream, near the gate on the western side, is the earlier, having rounded windows which suggest a date around 1200, while the hall to the east was erected somewhat later in the thirteenth century.

The whole complex is usually called the Desmond Castle, probably because it was occupied by the Earls of Desmond in the half-century from 1536 to 1584. They were certainly not the builders – but who was? The manor of Adare was held by Geoffrey de Marisco in 1226, when the Crown granted him the right to hold a fair there and he may well have been the builder of both the keep and the earlier hall. An 'Inquisition' of 1329-31, taken on the death of Richard fitz Thomas, Earl of Kildare, described the castle as consisting of a chapel and a chamber, each roofed with thatch or shingles, a tower (the keep) covered with planks, and a kitchen covered with slates, but all was waste from 'recent' wars with the Irish, and in 1559 Simon Barnewall could speak of 'the old broken castle'. Although evidently dismantled forty years later, the castle was held by the royalists in 1641, and dismantled again in 1657, this time by the forces of Cromwell. In 1683 it was granted to Thady Quin, whose family, the Earls of Dunraven, still hold it.

THE TOWN WALLS OF YOUGHAL
Co. Cork

The town of Youghal offers one of the better-preserved stretches of medieval town walls in Ireland. The earliest-known murage charter, granted by De Clare in 1275, was for the repair of the walls, so that we may presume that the town had been fortified some time before that. The walls were repaired at various stages throughout the medieval period and again in the seventeenth and eighteenth centuries. During the 1970s Youghal Corporation ensured that stretches of the wall walks were made accessible from the grounds of St Mary's Church, itself an interesting medieval parish church (p. 158). The town acted as an important port for south Munster during the Middle Ages, and also in the late sixteenth and early seventeenth centuries, when Sir Walter Raleigh and the Boyle family lived there. Because the urban centre is located along a narrow coastal plain, the walls had to enclose part of a steep hill behind it, so that it would not be attacked from above.

FETHARD
Co. Tipperary

Founded in the thirteenth century, Fethard has a town wall described by Avril Thomas as 'the most complete of any Irish walled town'. The circuit, about two-thirds of a mile (1125m) long and with only a very few breaks, has five towers and as many gates, though only one gate now sur-

vives intact. The Protestant church of the Holy Trinity is largely fifteenth century in date, but it must have had a significant predecessor because those who built the walls in 1292 went out of their way to avoid going over church property. Further medieval monuments in the town include four tower-houses, and there are also other houses bearing the seventeenth-century armorials of their builders, particulary the Everards, once lords of the town, who had acquired considerable parts of it from the Archbishop of Cashel, its earliest recorded owner. Just outside the walls there was an Augustinian priory, still in use today (p. 207).

Its quiet location simply guarding a bridge over the small Clashawley river is one possible reason why Fethard might have escaped too much destruction in the turbulent centuries of Ireland's later Middle Ages. But another may well be that the town does not appear to have offered much resistance to Oliver Cromwell who, during his Irish campaign of 1649-50, described it as having 'a very good wall with round and square bulwarks, after the old manner of fortification'. But his entry was still remembered with bitterness by the burghers of Fethard in the mid-nineteenth century because, as the famous Victorian travellers Mr and Mrs S.C. Hall commented, 'there is a certain gate of the town through which a corpse is never carried, though in their direct course, because it was through that gate that Cromwell entered the town'.

THE NORMAN CHURCH AND NEW MONASTIC ORDERS

The arrival of the Normans in Ireland was to bring about considerable changes in the Irish Church. After the death of St Laurence O'Toole in 1180 the English king had virtual control of the appointment of bishops and archbishops to those sees which lay in the newly conquered territories. It is not surprising that this new trend started in Dublin with O'Toole's archbishopric, where John Comyn was appointed his successor, but it quickly spread outside the capital to dioceses such as Connor in north-east Ulster, where John de Courcy had conquered. Though expressly forbidden by the pope, the English policy was to exclude all the Irish from ecclesiastical dignities and, as each diocese fell vacant, they pushed for their own man to get in. Indeed, the distinction between the 'Church of the English' and the 'Church of the Irish' was the fundamental social and political reality in later medieval Ireland. In certain instances where a diocese had a reasonable balance of Irish and English inhabitants, special deans or deacons would be appointed where the two different languages were spoken. One Archbishop of Cashel, a learned savant, Michael Scot, resigned after only two days because he could not understand the language of most of his flock. By the end of the thirteenth century a greater number of sees were occupied by Englishmen, particularly after Connacht had come into Norman hands in 1235.

ABOVE RIGHT AND RIGHT (detail) Because medieval English Bishops of Armagh feared for their lives in their episcopal seat, which lay in Irish-held territory, they spent much of their time near this castle at the extreme southern end of their see at Termonfeckin, Co. Louth, where the turrets have corbelled roofs built on the same principle as that used some four thousand years earlier in the chamber tomb at Newgrange only 10 miles (16km) away.

Armagh did not have an English archbishop until the reign of Edward I (1272-1307), and even then he always lived in his castle at the southern end of his diocese, closest to Dublin, at Termonfeckin, rather than in Armagh, where he would have expected strong opposition. Church order and discipline down the line were provided through the holding of councils and synods, and the priests were virtually hired – but at wages little or no higher than would have been earned by an unskilled labourer in England. With the subdivision of dioceses into parishes in the thirteenth century, it is no wonder that the priests often resorted to pluralism, though many of them were probably affiliated to monasteries.

The administration of the Church of the English in Ireland in the fourteenth century was little altered from the previous century, but it covered a smaller geographical area and was pursued with less vigour. Chronic financial problems, and the fear of Irish sedition against the king, prompted the English king to seek papal permission to amalgamate certain dioceses. Although he obtained the approval, the scheme backfired and had little lasting effect because, as he later discovered, the 'mere English' were thereby absorbed into a diocese of the 'mere Irish', as was the case in Tuam. The king even went so far as to try to persuade the pope that no Irishman should be promoted to bishop or archbishop without royal assent. In practice, the pope rarely intervened, but he did approve a number of English appointments. One of these was William fitz John of Cashel, who is said to have fathered fourteen illegitimate daughters and married them off to increase his own power and oppress his clergy and flock. Another was Richard de Ledrede, his successor in the see of Ossory, best known for his relentless witch-hunt of Dame Alice Kyteler in Kilkenny on a charge of sorcery and heresy. The history of the Church of the English in Ireland during the fourteenth century was really a series of squabbles over the filling of bishoprics and archbishoprics.

The Archbishops of Dublin were frequently absentees or were often temporarily absent outside the country on business. One of them, Alexander de Bicknor, at least tried to get papal permission to establish a *studium generale*, or university, with a faculty of theology and law for St Patrick's Cathedral. Though the pope granted the petition, the plan failed, and Bicknor got himself excommunicated into the bargain for failing to pay his dues. Despite further efforts to revive the idea of the *studium generale*, Ireland had to wait until the foundation of Trinity College in 1592 before its first university was established. In Armagh David O'Hiraghty – appointed by Pope Benedict XII in 1333 – was to be the last Irishman to occupy the archbishopric for two hundred years. Another who filled the see of Cashel was David MacCarville (1254-89), who had studied Canon Law at Oxford and was thereby strongly influenced by the Anglo-Normans. Limerick succeeded in electing an Irishman, Cornelius O'Dea, in 1400. The most notable mid-fourteenth century Archbishop of Armagh was Richard fitz Ralph, an Anglo-Norman, best known for his tirades against the rising power of the mendicant friars.

The period of the Great Schism and the Avignon popes (1378-1417) was one of considerable confusion which left a legacy well into the fifteenth century. Most of the Irish gave allegiance to the Roman Popes Urban VI and Boniface IX, but there was considerable trouble in the Tuam archdiocese where some supported the alternative Pope Clement VII. By the end of the fourteenth century the area of influence of the Church of the English in Ireland had declined, whereas the Gaelic areas were coming to show the

increasing influence of Roman and Anglo-Norman ecclesiastical and social traditions. What was common to both the Church of the English and the Church of the Irish during the later Middle Ages were the monasteries and friaries, some of which actually supplied bishops and even archbishops to the various dioceses. On the whole, those in the Gaelic parts of Ireland were poorer than those in the English part, and some even had to close their doors because they were so poverty-stricken.

In the immediate aftermath of the religious reforms of the twelfth century the most important monasteries were those of the Cistercians. From the time of their first Irish foundation at Mellifont in 1141/2 until their last at Hore in 1272, a total of thirty-nine Cistercian houses was founded in Ireland, and here too the ethnic divide reared its ugly head. The earlier foundations, daughter-houses of Mellifont, were generally Irish, but of those founded after the coming of the Normans, some – such as Tintern and Dunbrody – were purely Anglo-Norman, while others at least had abbots who were Irish. Between 1217 and 1231 there was trouble in those areas conquered by the Anglo-Normans where the Irish had tried to retain control and preserve certain elements of the earlier native monastic system, leading to the 'Conspiracy of Mellifont' in 1227, after which all of the Irish abbots involved were deposed.

Malachy of Armagh was responsible for having introduced into Ireland not only the Cistercians but also the Augustinians of the rule of Arrouaise. This order, both canons and friars, made new foundations of its own, as

LEFT Richard de Ledrede, a Bishop of Ossory (1317-60) renowned for his witch-hunting activities, deserves credit for having started to repair the damage caused by the collapse of major parts of St Canice's Cathedral in Kilkenny, where his effigy lies.

RIGHT Hore Abbey near Cashel, Co. Tipperary, dating from 1272, turned out to be the last Cistercian house to be created in Ireland before the Reformation.

well as taking over – and breathing new life into – some of the older Irish monasteries, such as Clonmacnoise. Associated with the Augustinians were the hospitalling order known as the *Fratres Cruciferi*, or Crutched Friars, from the cross they bore on their habits, and these too had already established Irish houses before the end of the twelfth century. The oldest of all the orders, the Benedictines, had houses in Germany with some Irish monks (the so-called *Schottenklöster*) during the twelfth century, but very few in Ireland itself, where, apart from one associated with Cormac's Chapel on the Rock of Cashel, only that at Fore, Co. Westmeath, was of any significance. It may be noted, however, that two abbeys under the rule of St Benedict in the congregation of Savigny – Erenagh in County Down (1127) and St Mary's in Dublin (1139) – were founded with the encouragement of St Malachy before he introduced the Cistercians to Mellifont in 1142; five years later they joined the Cistercians themselves.

The great new continental mendicant orders springing up around 1200 quickly began to introduce their friars to Ireland during the first half of the thirteenth century – the Dominicans in 1224, the Franciscans at almost exactly the same time, the Carmelites within the next half-century, and the Augustinian or Austin friars (hermits) by 1282 at the latest. Convents of nuns were more frequent in later medieval Ireland than they had been in the earlier period; they were generally Augustinian, though some few belonged to other orders such as the Cistercians, Benedictines or Franciscans. In as far as their means allowed, the monasteries provided for the sick and the poor, and separately the Knights Templars and the Knights Hospitallers also offered hospital accomodation for the care of lepers. Their hospitality, however, also extended to the stranger and the pilgrim. Monasteries such as Holy Cross, Ballintober, Glendalough and Clonfert were regular places of pilgrimage for the Irish lay-folk, though St Patrick's Island in the Donegal Lough Derg was the only Irish place of pilgrimage well known outside the country. Many of the houses, and in particular the friaries, took on the schooling of younger people, producing some fine teachers and scholars, in fields such as theology, common law, the arts, computistics and old Irish lore. But, because of the lack of a university in Ireland, many went abroad to Oxford, Bologna, Padua and elsewhere for their further education.

GOTHIC CATHEDRALS AND PARISH CHURCHES

One of the great contributions made by the early English Church in Ireland was the number of important cathedrals they built in the towns which they controlled. These included not only the two Dublin cathedrals of Christ Church and St Patrick's but also St Canice's in Kilkenny, second only to Dublin in wealth and size. Even smaller dioceses with an English content, such as Ardfert, managed to

erect a cathedral of considerable size. It is difficult to visualize the village of Ardfert today as a lively medieval walled town, but that it was, and if we envisage it as such, we come to realize just how imposing these cathedrals must have been, towering over the single – or occasionally – two-storey wooden buildings crowded along the streets. Indeed, the cathedrals must have stood as notable landmarks for many miles around, like the Round Towers beside which they were sometimes built, as at Kilkenny and Kildare, but also at Ardfert, where the Round Tower fell in 1771. The Irish Church, too, built cathedrals in the new Gothic style as can be seen at Cashel and Killaloe.

The organization into parishes must have engendered the building of parish churches, such as the thirteenth-century examples at New Ross and Youghal and the largely fourteenth-century church of St Nicholas in Galway. While these churches would not be exceptional when compared to their English contemporaries, they do stand out in Ireland as among the largest parish churches of the Middle Ages. Most of the surviving medieval parish churches of Ireland were very much smaller in scale when built around the fifteenth century, and are usually bereft of any architectural decoration, except for a window or two moulded on the outside.

CHRIST CHURCH CATHEDRAL
Dublin

Christ Church Cathedral, in the centre of the old Norse and Norman city of Dublin, is not only the capital's oldest surviving stone edifice but also perhaps the most outstanding Norman contribution to Irish architecture. It was probably preceded by a smaller church, allegedly founded by the Norse King Sitric in 1038, but the existing structure was probably started around 1185-90 by John Comyn, the city's first Anglo-Norman archbishop. He can truly be said to have built a monument triumphally symbolizing the arrival of the Normans and paying a tribute to the land of their origin. There is indeed a great indebtedness to the West of England in the design and decoration of the cathedral, and even in some of its original decorated stone; this was quarried at Dundry near Bristol, from which city came the men to whom Henry II had granted Dublin.

Christ Church is the only cathedral of its kind in Britain or Ireland to have a crypt running the entire length of the building, doubtless necessary in order to provide a solid foundation for the superstructure to be built upon it. The first parts above ground level to have been completed were the choir and the two transepts. They were designed in a late Romanesque style, with archways bearing heavily undercut chevron decoration and capitals sculpted with warriors, dragons and entertainers, all probably carved by craftsmen who came from the Severn area. The choir was largely demolished in the fourteenth century, and its present form owes much to the restoration work undertaken by the famous Victorian architect George Edmund Street between 1871 and 1878, when some of the old medieval tiles were relaid.

After the completion of the original choir and transepts, there was probably an interruption of one or two decades before construction of the nave started. It was built to a very different, Gothic design in the Early English style, with a series of low arches in the arcade and a well-integrated vertical linkage of triforium and clerestory. Roger Stalley has suggested a date of c.1216-30 for all the bays except the most westerly, which can be ascribed to

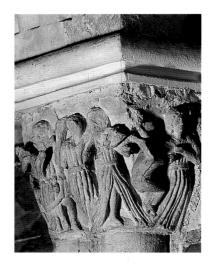

LEFT A late twelfth-century capital in the north transept of Christ Church Cathedral in Dublin reflects the sculptural style of the West of England.

RIGHT Nave and choir of Christ Church Cathedral, Dublin – the city's oldest church and one of the greatest Norman contributions to Irish architecture.

BELOW Coloured and line-impressed medieval floor tiles in Christ Church Cathedral, Dublin.

the years 1234-6. Once more, the style and the carving of the capitals can be traced back to the West of England. Sadly, however, the vault of the nave – doubtless the cathedral's crowning glory – collapsed in 1562, leaving the nave with only its north wall intact, but with an outward lean of 2-3 feet (0.6-0.9m), which might have proved fatal in the meantime had not Street added the external buttresses just over a century ago. The present south side is a complete reworking by Street, who may have very materially altered the appearance of the cathedral, but who has helped to give us some idea of its noble Gothic interior – thanks to the generosity of the Dublin whiskey distiller Henry Roe, who paid for the entire restoration undertaken by Street. It should be noted that Christ Church had monastic (Augustinian) canons, the foundations of whose chapter house can still be seen a short distance outside the south transept, where it would have formed one side of a cloister garth.

ST PATRICK'S CATHEDRAL
Dublin

If Dublin's Christ Church Cathedral was one of the finest expressions of Gothic architecture in Ireland, another was its near neighbour, St Patrick's, which, with an internal length of 286 feet (87m), was the largest church in medieval Ireland and, in the words of the American architectural historian Edwin C. Rae, 'one of the finest conceptions in late medieval insular architecture'. It must always seem strange to the outsider that Dublin should have two medieval Protestant Cathedrals within a few hundred yards of each other, both with naves constructed at about the same time in the thirteenth century and both restored one after the other in the nineteenth. The existence of two Protestant cathedrals in what is now a predominantly Catholic part of the country resulted from the Church of Ireland, which had been established at the time of the Reformation, taking over many of the larger parish churches and medieval cathedrals, and thereby assisting in their preservation down to our own day. In the thirteenth century, however, it was pressing administrative requirements more than jealous rivalry that were the real reasons why these two close neighbours came to exist in such close proximity to one another. Christ Church was a monastic cathedral with a chapter consisting of Augustinian canons, whereas the early Anglo-Norman archbishops felt the need for a secular chapter to run diocesan affairs. The church of St Patrick, on a small island in the River Poddle not far outside the city walls, was given collegiate status by Archbishop Comyn in 1192 – that is, it was established as a college of secular priests but with no episcopal see. Around 1220 his successor, Henry de Loundres, filled the gap by raising St Patrick's to cathedral status, with prebends rich enough to maintain able officials to carry on both secular and episcopal administrations. In 1225 preachers were sent out to collect alms for the construction of the cathedral, which was consecrated – and probably virtually complete – in 1254.

The religious rite used in the cathedral was that of Sarum, as used in Salisbury Cathedral, and Salisbury probably also played a role in the design of St Patrick's. Because it was built without a pause, St Patrick's is a more harmonious unit than Christ Church. However, perhaps because the preachers hadn't been able to raise quite enough money, the architecture became more severe as the building proceeded from east to west. Yet it is a gracious and spacious structure with square ambulatory at the east end and a nave of eight bays, where three horizontally separated storeys support a vault which fell in 1544 and is now simulated. A serious fire in 1362 damaged the western part of the nave, together with the tower which archbishop Minot replaced with the present tower in 1372. By the seventeenth century the whole edifice was in a semi-ruinous condition. Substantial restoration work was carried out at various times between 1832 and 1904, much of it paid for by the Guinness family, giving rise to the Dubliner's quip that whereas Christ Church was revived by whiskey, St Patrick's was restored on stout. Despite heavy restoration work, very considerable parts of the medieval structure, including the attractively decorated capitals, have remained intact, as a detailed study by Professor Rae has demonstrated. St Patrick's most famous dean was, of course, Jonathan Swift (1667-1745), who was buried in the nave – only a few feet away from his beloved Stella who, in Swift's own words, was 'the truest, most virtuous and valuable friend that I, or perhaps any other person, was ever blessed with'.

LEFT St Patrick's Cathedral, Dublin, seen in all its glory from the air.

RIGHT The choir of St Patrick's Cathedral, the oldest part of the structure, was built in the thirteenth century and rescued from ruination in the nineteenth.

ST CANICE'S CATHEDRAL
Kilkenny

The small Romanesque cathedrals in some of the Irish dioceses obviously proved too small for the expanding populations and ambitions of the new Norman towns. In Ardfert all of the Romanesque cathedral was demolished except for the portal and its accompanying arcade, which was left intact to provide an entrance for a much larger Gothic structure. In Kilkenny the entire cathedral was swiftly replaced by its beautiful Gothic successor, started by Hugh de Rous, Bishop of Ossory from 1202 to 1218, and probably completed by around 1260. With Christ Church and St Patrick's, Dublin had started the trend towards Gothic cathedral building, their lofty stone vaulting staying up almost miraculously like the gossamer of a spider's web. In Kilkenny, St Canice's did not follow suit, preferring wood for the roof of both nave and choir, thereby allowing more windows and less wall to create a luminous interior, particularly in the choir, which is lit by three tall and broad lancet windows. The nave arcade is low-slung with light piers, quatrefoil in plan, supporting broad arches and an uncomplicated series of clerestory windows above. The infusion of light, the simple clarity of design without too much fussy detail and the comparative lack of later defacements all go to making St Canice's the most successful of Irish cathedrals outside Dublin. To add further to its attractions, a high-quality sculptor carved sensitively smiling human heads and foliate motifs on corbels and capitals in various parts of the cathedral, both inside and out. Roger Stalley, who dubbed him the 'Gowran master' for his work on a church in the town of that name some

ABOVE The long, low nave and choir of St Canice's Cathedral in Kilkenny are graceful and numinous.

LEFT The best of Ireland's Norman cathedrals outside Dublin, St Canice's in Kilkenny was built in the thirteenth century on the site of an earlier monastery, represented by the free-standing Round Tower, which can be climbed to the top.

The dignified interior of St Brigid's Cathedral, Kildare, was restored by G.E. Street between 1875 and 1896. The unplastered walls of the nave in the foreground contrast with the smooth white Caen stone used in the east wall of the choir, as seen through the arches of the crossing tower.

8 miles (13km) away, describes him as 'perhaps the most gifted craftsman to work in Ireland during the thirteenth century' – and he may well have been both architect and craftsman combined. His artistic influence is felt particularly in a tomb-niche in the north transept and on two doorways of the cathedral, of which that in the west gable is the best preserved and also the finest early Gothic doorway in Ireland.

St Canice's, however, is also worth visiting for the wonderful collection of medieval tomb-sculpture which it contains, dating mainly from the fifteenth and sixteenth centuries. Sadly, the Cromwellians created such mayhem when they got inside the cathedral that very few of the effigies are likely to belong to the tomb-surrounds which support them. The Round Tower outside the cathedral is a reminder that the foundation of Kilkenny goes back beyond the time of the Anglo-Normans, the first monastery on the site having been founded by St Cainnech (hence Canice) of Aghaboe, who died around 600.

ST BRIGID'S CATHEDRAL
Kildare

The cathedral which Ralph of Bristol, the first Norman Bishop of Kildare, is recorded as having 'repaired and adorned' in 1223, was a successor to the church of St Brigid's double monastery in Kildare where, as described by her seventh-century biographer Cogitosus (p. 105), monks and nuns were kept out of mutual sight by a wooden partition. Ralph of Bristol, in contrast, brought the Kildare burghers of both sexes together in what must once have been one of the finest Norman provincial cathedrals in Ireland by the time it was completed, probably some time shortly after 1250. The build-

ing was cruciform in plan, with a stout tower above the crossing, and the chancel or choir curiously out of line with the nave. Its most characteristic features are the external nave buttresses enclosing pointed arches and supporting the 'embattled' or crenellated parapets. The general style of the tall, thin lancet windows throughout the building is typical of the early thirteenth century.

Despite further repair and beautification carried out by a later bishop, Edmund Lane, around 1482, the church fell a victim to time and the seventeenth-century wars. Around 1683, however, William Moreton of Chester, shortly after his consecration as bishop, appears to have re-roofed the choir so that cathedral services could be held there. By 1871 the general fabric had deteriorated to such an extent that the bishop, dean and chapter got George Edmund Street, who was just embarking on the restoration of Christ Church Cathedral in Dublin at the time, to prepare a report on the condition of Kildare cathedral. His candid comments pointed out that the choir's 'architectural character is of the poorest description' and that 'the rest of the church is in ruins'. It is a tribute to the local fundraisers that the money they collected allowed Street to rebuild completely the chancel and north transept on the old Norman foundations, to restore the nave and south transept on the basis of the substantial amounts of masonry still surviving, and to make the tower once more the cathedral's massive crowning glory. Street's ideas were executed by the diocesan architect, J.F. Fuller, so that when no less a luminary than Dr Benson, the Archbishop of Canterbury, came to dedicate the fully restored cathedral in 1896, he saw what was, in the words of T.M. Fallow, author of *Cathedral Churches of Ireland* published two years earlier in London, 'one of the most picturesque of modern ecclesiastical buildings in Ireland'.

ST NICHOLAS OF MYRA COLLEGIATE CHURCH
Galway

When it came to the distribution of dioceses in the twelfth-century synods, Galway City lost out not because it was too close to the regal and archiepiscopal city of Tuam but because it had not yet developed into the important maritime town it was to become in the thirteenth century, a status which it was to keep throughout the later Middle Ages because of its loyalty to the English Crown. By 1484 what had started out as the town's parish church had gradually developed into the collegiate church of St Nicholas, and from then on, until the Reformation finally reached Galway in 1568, services were provided by a college, or community, of priests elected by the municipal authorities.

The raising of the church to collegiate status had, however, been preceded by a century of unseemly squabbles, so that it is not surprising that the core of the church we see today, dating from around 1330, was not much altered or added to until late in the fifteenth century. Extensions to the aisles and north transept continued well into the sixteenth century, when a Blessed Sacrament chapel was also added. After the Reformation further improvements continued to be made, such as the spire, added in 1683 to the tower erected around 1500, and the parapets, which were not constructed until 1833. Inside, the church contains inter-esting architectural and tomb sculpture, including the sixteenth-century wall-tomb of the Joyce family in the south transept and the font of roughly the same period, while outside the eye-catching gargoyles are the most striking features.

ST MARY'S CHURCH
Youghal, Co. Cork

Dublin, Waterford and Limerick were Ireland's only maritime towns lucky enough to become diocesan centres at the Synod of Rath Breasail in 1111. The others contented themselves with large parish churches when the Normans swelled their population numbers in the thirteenth century, and St Mary's in Youghal is one of the finest examples to survive. It is a sizeable cruciform church with five-aisled nave and adjacent tower, and its main core dates back to the mid-thirteenth century. In the 1460s the church became attached to the college set up nearby by the eighth Earl of Desmond, who rebuilt the chancel and added the fine, traceried east window. In the course of time, the chancel duly lost its roof, so that John Wesley, when he preached there in 1763, could say that half the church was in ruins. But re-roofing around 1850 restored the church to its full extent and provided protection for the interesting collection of thirteenth- to seventeenth-century tombstones preserved within the church.

LEFT Gothic arches abound in St Nicholas of Myra, Galway city – a Protestant parish church that just went on growing organically, particularly in the fifteenth and early sixteenth centuries

ABOVE One of the few surviving large parish churches of medieval Ireland, St Mary's in Youghal, Co. Cork, has an unusually long choir, which was left roofless for centuries before being restored in the 1850s by a local architect.

ST MARY'S CATHEDRAL
Limerick

Early in the twelfth century Limerick played an important role in the Church Reform movement, with its Norse bishop Gilbert presiding as papal legate over the Synod of Rath Breasail in IIII (p. III), and late in the century it was to develop its own unique brand of cathedral architecture. After Dónal Mór O'Brien had thrown the Normans out of Limerick in 1176, he razed the city to the ground and was thereby able to obtain the choicest of locations for the construction of his new cathedral, which probably occupied him until his death in 1194. Not satisfied by any older Irish models such as those at Clonmacnoise and Glendalough – Christ Church in Dublin has scarcely yet begun – Donal turned to the excitingly large, if occasionally bleak, Cistercian churches of the previous few decades for the inspiration of his new structure, and the cruciform plan with arched side aisles reflects the ultimately Burgundian origin of the cathedral's style. What little interior decoration there is, as on the nave piers, follows Cistercian lines, but because Limerick Cathedral had to adapt the idea of an enclosed monastic church to an open urban environment, its west end received a decorated Romanesque doorway looking out on the River Shannon, though it is now only a fragment of its former self after its 'restoration' by J.F. Fuller in 1895.

During the fifteenth and sixteenth centuries in particular, wealthy

ABOVE St Mary's Cathedral in Limerick, constructed by that great church builder, Dónal Mór O'Brien, in the last quarter of the twelfth century, has Romanesque elements not uninfluenced by Cistercian architecture. But Gothic is the prevailing style of this edifice, which has crenellations giving it something of a fortified appearance.

RIGHT Tomb-niches and furnishings in the thirteenth-century choir of St Mary's Cathedral in Limerick include Ireland's only surviving medieval choir stalls, famous for their misericords (p. 220).

merchants of the city contributed to the cathedral by building chapels lit by traceried Gothic windows of various sizes. These chapels and other additions extended the side aisles and created further structures east of the transepts so that, by the time of the Reformation, the building had an almost rectangular ground-plan with the addition of 'embattled' parapets and a tall friary-like tower over the west doorway, as at Clonfert. Inside, the cathedral has a fine collection of funerary monuments from the thirteenth and subsequent centuries, and – alone of all the Irish churches and cathedrals – it has managed to preserve some splendid examples of medieval wooden choir stalls, with beautifully carved misericords (p. 220).

THE CISTERCIANS

The Cistercians were not actually the first of the continental monastic orders to set up house in Ireland, having been preceded by the Benedictines, including their branch belonging to the Order of Savigny, which, however, subsequently submitted to the Cistercians in 1147/8. But, even if not the first, the Cistercians were certainly the most important of the early wave of continental orders to come to Ireland and found houses whose architecture brought about radical change in Irish ecclesiastical building practices. In comparison to the simple Irish Romanesque churches of the day, the church which St Malachy started building at Mellifont in 1142 must have seemed most impressive – though that was not how some Irishmen viewed it. When St Malachy was building a large, no-longer-extant oratory some years earlier at Bangor in County Down, its size was described by a local detractor as a novelty, a superfluous frivolity and even as madness. Fortunately these words of a die-hard conservative were not to deflect Malachy from introducing the Cistercian building tradition which, after Romanesque, was to be the second important change in Irish church architecture during the twelfth century.

When they first arrived, the Cistercians continued to build in the Romanesque fashion, but it was the scale and order which was different – for they brought a logical organization into architecture which contrasts so markedly with the seemingly unplanned nature of the Irish monasteries which preceded them. Their monasteries were laid out around an enclosed, grassy garth, rectangular in shape and surrounded by a cloister, with the church at one end of the rectangle, facing the kitchen and refectory at the other end. On one longer side were the abbot's quarters and a chapter house, where the monks foregathered daily to deal with any business which required attention, while on the other side were store-rooms, above which the monks slept in a communal dormitory. The life of the Cistercians was one of humility, simplicity, prayer and self-sufficiency, and their buildings reflected the purity of their life-style. St Bernard, who railed against the grotesque menagerie carved on Romanesque churches, banished those weird and wonderful creatures from his churches because they distracted from prayer, though Irish houses such as Boyle and Corcomroe which were

ABOVE RIGHT AND RIGHT Grey Abbey in County Down, which was founded from Cumbria by Affreca, daughter of the King of Man and wife of John de Courcy, was among the first to have introduced the Gothic style of architecture into Ireland. Apart from its attractive monks' refectory, one of the abbey's best-known features is the Early English doorway (right) of c.1225 now in the west facade, though that was not necessarily its original position.

furthest away from St Bernard's Burgundian centre chose to avoid his strictures. Even if the Irish did not always want to learn, the Cistercians taught them to vault over large spaces in stone on a scale which makes a pygmy out of Cormac's Chapel. Using pointed barrel-vaults at first, the Cistercians later introduced ribbed vaulting seen to good effect at St Mary's Abbey in Dublin around 1200. But they were also responsible for one highly significant development in Irish architecture which was to have a lasting effect for centuries – the introduction of the pointed Gothic arch. Grey and Inch abbeys in County Down were among the first to have used it just before the close of the twelfth century, and early in the following century it had already reached a high level of sophistication at Graiguenamanagh. A monastery like Boyle shows the initially strong Burgundian influence giving way to Norman-induced elements spreading from England to the east of Ireland at first, before becoming popular over many parts of the country within half a century of the arrival of the Normans.

St Malachy obviously inspired such enthusiasm with his foundation at Mellifont in 1142 that daughter-houses were rapidly established at places such as Bective (1147), Baltinglass (1148) and Boyle, and many more were founded from English mother-houses under the influence of the Anglo-

Normans. By the early thirteenth century tension rose between the houses with Irish abbots and those ruled by the English, which after the 'Conspiracy of Mellifont' in 1227 led Stephen of Lexington to purge all abbots of Irish origin and to make English and French the languages of Cistercian Ireland. Religion was becoming politicized – but by then most of the Cistercian abbeys had already been built. The Cistercians were certainly the dominant monastery builders in Ireland during the eighty years after the foundation of Mellifont in 1142, and Holy Cross was one of the very few to experience substantial alterations and rebuilding in the next great age of monastic building in the fifteenth century (p. 208).

MELLIFONT ABBEY
Co. Louth

Mellifont, on the River Mattock in County Louth, was founded by St Malachy on land granted by Donnchad O Cerbhaill, King of Airgialla, in 1142. Malachy was assisted by monks who had come with him from Clairvaux in Burgundy with the blessing of St Bernard, and their influence can be seen in the alternating round and square side-chapels in

RIGHT AND BELOW (detail) Mellifont Abbey in County Louth, Ireland's earliest Cistercian foundation, preserves in its cloister garth the only extant Irish example of a lavabo, where the monks went to wash their hands before and after meals. The sandstone capitals of this two-storey structure, built around 1200, are delicately carved with foliage and bird motifs. Part of the cloister arcade was rebuilt in the 1950s.

Baltinglass Abbey, Co. Wicklow, founded by Dermot MacMurrough in 1148, must have taken about thirty years to build, and its nave arcade – with alternating square and rounded piers – still has capitals decorated with abstract ornament in a pure Romanesque style.

the east wall of the transepts. But finding the Irish lacking in discipline, the French soon returned to their homeland, leaving the Irish to get on with the construction of the first church, which must have been substantially completed when Cardinal Paparo, the papal legate, held the final session of the Synod of Kells there in 1152. By the following year the community was large enough to have created seven daughter-houses, and by the time of the Norman invasion, twenty years later, there were 300 lay-brothers in Mellifont to do the 'donkey work'. After the disturbing 'Conspiracy of Mellifont' in 1227, when Irish abbots were deposed and many monks banished, the number of lay-brothers was fixed at 60 and the monks at 50.

Most of the buildings we can admire at Mellifont today had already been long built by the time of the conspiracy. Little more than the foundations remain of many parts of the church, except the presbytery or choir, where the walls are preserved up to window level, though Liam de Paor's excavations in 1954-5 uncovered a unique crypt beneath the western end of the church. Adjoining the cloister garth are two better-preserved buildings – the chapter house with fine rib-vaulting of the early thirteenth century, repaired two centuries later, and the structure for which Mellifont is best known, the beautiful sandstone octagonal lavabo. Built around 1200, this originally housed a fountain, which was supplied with water by underground pipes fed from the River Mattock. The capitals of its rounded arches, while sadly much damaged, demonstrate the high quality of the monks' carving, which can also be seen in some of the capitals of the Romanesque cloister arcade reconstructed close-by. The church was remodelled on a number of occasions – diamond-shaped piers were inserted in the south transept crossing around 1320, and a tower was later added above. The number of monks had shrunk considerably by the time the monastery was dissolved at the Reformation, after which the buildings were altered to form a domestic fortified house around 1560. When finally abandoned in 1727, the abbey provided a rich quarry for stones, leaving it in the denuded condition we see today.

BALTINGLASS ABBEY
Co. Wicklow

The abbey of Baltinglass in the valley of the River Slaney was an early daughter-house of Mellifont, founded in 1148 with patronage from Dermot MacMurrough, King of Leinster. The church, good portions of which survive, shows its Burgundian ancestry in the square-ended presbytery and the low arcades leading to the transept. But the decoration of the nave arches, with alternating square and cylindrical piers, shows some Irish influence, too, in the interlace patterns on the scalloped capitals, and the Romanesque bulbous bases of the north-east crossing pier resemble those in the doorway at Killeshin, in the construction of which Dermot MacMurrough is also likely to have played a role. The church must have been finished by 1180, and in 1185 its abbot preached at a synod in Dublin complaining against the evil ways and bad example of the monks coming from England and Wales. No wonder, then, that the Irish community suffered at the time of the 'Conspiracy of Mellifont' in 1227, when its abbot was deposed and the monastery placed under the jurisdiction of an English house. Baltinglass was one of the first of the Irish Cistercian abbeys to be suppressed at the Reformation by Henry VIII. The chancel was later to be converted into a Protestant church, which continued in use until 1883.

JERPOINT ABBEY
Co. Kilkenny

Jerpoint Abbey in County Kilkenny did not become a Cistercian house until 1180, when it was made a daughter-house of Baltinglass, but there are strong indications that it had been founded by Donal MacGilla-patrick I, King of Ossory, some twenty years earlier. While the east end still shows traces of Burgundian severity, its nave arcade has the same alternating square and round piers seen at Baltinglass, and these are given an element of lively decoration in the scalloped capitals probably carved by masons who brought some of their designs with them from Baltinglass. The massive and ponderous tower above the crossing is a worthy fifteenth-century addition, but the vaulted sacristy and chapter house are part of the original building.

Much of the attraction of Jerpoint lies in its cloister arcade, which is later than the church and is the most richly decorated of its kind in the country. Its erection may well have benefited from money for indulgences granted in 1442 for the repair of the cloister and bell-tower. Its ornament consists of a variety of figures, clad in contemporary style and representing the Trinity, Apostles (Peter, James the Greater, Bartholomew and John the Evangelist), Saints Catherine of Alexandria and Margaret of Antioch, abbots and ecclesiastics, knights and their aristocratic ladies – as well as

RIGHT The cloister arcade at Jerpoint opens up a view of what is the tallest Cistercian church tower in Ireland, placed above the crossing of the abbey church.

BELOW The construction of Jerpoint Abbey in County Kilkenny was started before it formally joined the Cistercians in 1180. Its original Romanesque triple east windows were replaced in the fourteenth century by the single traceried window seen on the right.

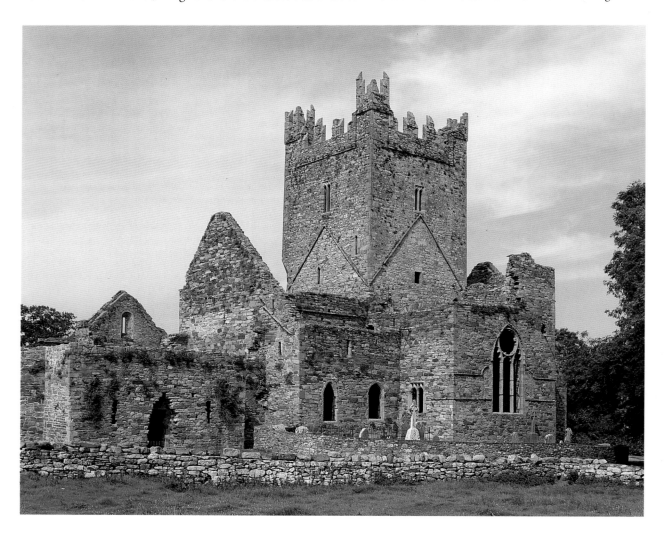

LEFT, BELOW FAR LEFT, BELOW LEFT AND BOTTOM Jerpoint's most unusual feature is its fifteenth-century cloister arcade, richly carved with a great variety of figures – saints, knights and their ladies, clerics, and others less easy to define – sometimes not without a certain sense of humour.

BELOW 'Weepers' carved by Rory O'Tunney and his workshop for a sixteenth-century tomb at Jerpoint Abbey include St Peter with his keys, St Andrew behind his saltire cross, and St James Major with his pilgrim's staff and shell-bedecked hat.

smaller figures and animals. Local products perhaps not of the highest quality, the cloister figures are nevertheless appealing, and the lesser figures and animals add a touch of gaiety unexpected in a Cistercian house – probably the result of patronage from the local Butler and Walsh families, whose arms the knights bear on their shields.

But Jerpoint also houses noteworthy tomb-sculpture, the earliest being the effigy of abbot O'Dulany, who died in 1202. Others worthy of attention are the two thirteenth-century knights known as 'The Brethren', (p. 136) incised on a slab now in one of the chapels of the south transept, and the Irish harper effigy of *c.*1500. Though St Bernard may not have approved of either sculpture or painting in his church, Jerpoint also has an example of late medieval fresco painting in the chancel, representing armorial bearings which have, however, hitherto eluded identification.

DUNBRODY ABBEY
Co. Wexford

Dunbrody in County Wexford was a daughter-house of St Mary's Abbey in Dublin, though it was originally affiliated to Buildwas in Shropshire when Hervé de Monte Marisco, Strongbow's uncle, donated the site on the shores of Waterford Harbour in 1171-2. Following in the footsteps of St Mary's, it took the side of Stephen of Lexington's English faction in the controversy surrounding the 'Conspiracy of Mellifont' in 1227. The church may not have even been entirely finished at the time, but it would at least have been well on the way to becoming the impressive pile it still is. With the exception of the massive square tower added in the fifteenth century, most of the buildings belong to the first half of the thirteenth century. Vast, and standing massively impressive in a very large field, it was more ornate than might at first appear, having had a fine triple-lancet window with 'plate' tracery above in the west gable, which, however, fell along with the south arcade of the nave in 1852.

Today's view from the nave shows a further set of three lancet windows in the east wall, and unusual double clerestory windows placed above the piers rather than the pointed arcades, as was so often the case in Ireland.

LEFT AND TOP A good example of an Irish Cistercian house dominated by English abbots was the thirteenth-century abbey at Dunbrody, which stands out like a colossus in a very large County Wexford field, and must have impressed the native Irish who had not previously been accustomed to churches on such a large scale. As in most Irish Cistercian churches, its twin-light clerestory windows (top) were placed over the piers of the nave.

ABOVE The view from the west end of Dunbrody Abbey church along the nave towards the crossing tower and the three tall lancet windows in the east wall. The south wall of the nave fell around 1852.

ST MARY'S ABBEY
Dublin

It is hard to believe – but true – that the chapter house tucked away almost invisibly off Meeting House Lane in Dublin is the only surviving part of the richest, and probably also the finest, of all the Cistercian houses in Ireland. It is roofed with four bays of low ribbed vaults of around 1200, and adjoining it is a slype, or passage way. Much of the remainder of what survives of this very sizeable monastery is probably still preserved underground in the surrounding area, awaiting redemption – but the walls were heavily quarried for stone when Dublin north of the Liffey was being developed in the late seventeenth century. Sections of what are likely to have been its cloister arcade were discovered about twenty years ago on the far side of the River Liffey in Cook Street, and these are now displayed in the chapter house, along with some tiles found in the excavations in the 1880s.

St Mary's was originally founded as a house of the Benedictine Order of Savigny in 1139 – thus preceding Mellifont, but it became Cistercian in 1147. Having been subject to two separate English Cistercian monasteries – Combermere and Buildwas – and being located, unusually for the Cistercians, in the northern suburbs of a capital city, it was very English in its outlook. Had the buildings been better preserved for us, their architectural details would probably also show much English inspiration. A Gothic wooden statue of the Virgin, now preserved in Whitefriar Street south of the Liffey, is said to have come from St Mary's and is also likely to be English. For such a bastion of the English establishment, there was great symbolism when the king's deputy in Ireland, Silken Thomas FitzGerald, threw down the Sword of State in this very chapter house in 1534, declaring himself an enemy of the king, and initiating a rebellion which took the Tudor monarchs many bloody decades to defeat.

DUISKE ABBEY
Graiguenamanagh, Co. Kilkenny

Like St Mary's and Dunbrody, Graiguenamanagh – otherwise known as Duiske – Abbey belonged to the anglophile side of the Cistercians in Ireland, having been founded by William Marshal, Earl of Pembroke, in 1204, though the monks had tried out various sites before finally settling down at Graiguenamanagh on the banks of the Barrow. The church they built there was the largest of all the Irish Cistercian churches – 212 feet (65m) long – and also the one showing the purest English Gothic style, though sadly the vaulting of the presbytery fell hundreds of years ago. The splendid restoration undertaken by the parish in the years 1974-80, under the architectural supervision of Percy LeClerc, leaves the dressed stonework standing out from the whitewashed walls, and brings us closer than any other Irish Cistercian church to the noble simplicity which is such a hallmark of Cistercian architecture. It did not prove feasible to restore the original floor level, but small trapdoors in the present flooring allow us to peer down and see some of the original floor tiles still in position. The claustral buildings are hidden among – and under – Victorian structures, but when the day comes for them to be liberated, Graiguenamanagh will prove to be one of the finest and best-preserved Cistercian complexes in the country.

Little more than this rib-vaulted Chapter House of *c.*1200 remains of St Mary's Abbey in Dublin, once perhaps the finest and richest of Ireland's Cistercian houses.

Whitewashed walls and a fine oaken roof have transformed the parish church at Graiguenamanagh in County Kilkenny, recapturing the pristine glory of what was once the abbey of Duiske, the largest Cistercian church ever built in Ireland.

LEFT, BELOW AND ABOVE Rising out of a green oasis amidst the Burren limestone of north Clare, the early thirteenth-century monastery at Corcomroe is one of the lesser – but most appealingly sited of all – Irish Cistercian abbeys. So much effort and money must have gone into the making of the delicate stone vaulting of the choir (below) that not enough was left apparently to complete the building as originally designed. But the monks obviously felt sufficiently adventurous to ignore St Bernard's strictures about the distraction of figure sculpture and went ahead with carving heads among the foliage on the capitals (above).

CORCOMROE ABBEY
Co. Clare

Felicitously named the Abbey of the Fertile Rock, Corcomroe stands out like a spectral oasis in the incomparable setting of the crags of Burren limestone in north Clare. Founded by one of the O'Brien kings in the late twelfth century, the building belongs to the first three decades of the following century. The fact that it was never a particularly affluent foundation is mirrored in its somewhat reduced scale and the presence of only one chapel opening off each transept (of which one is sadly blocked). But the quality of the masonry and the fine carving in the eastern end more than makes up for it. The presbytery is decorated with herring-bone rib vaulting, and the taut stonework of the lancet windows still displays some traces of original colouring. The capitals bear unusually early naturalistic carvings of flowers, including the seedpods of the (opium) poppy and lily of the valley, which were probably cultivated in the monastery's herb garden. The capitals of the south transept chapel have fine human heads which seem far distant from St Bernard's requirements of simplicity in the churches of his order. The dragons which bite the string-courses on the exterior walls of the presbytery seem to be directly derived from those on the late Romanesque doorway in Killaloe Cathedral (p. 131). The idiosyncratic carving and the fine masonry of the east end at Corcomroe shows how lively and inventive sculpture and craftsmanship could be in the Romanesque swansong of the west of Ireland when Gothic was rapidly taking over in the eastern half of the country. By comparison the nave of Corcomroe is rather featureless and may never have been completed.

contains some of the best examples of the 'School of the West' style. Internally and externally the three lancet windows in the east gable are richly sculpted with chevron, animal and foliate decoration, and the capitals of the rib-vaulted chancel include some assured, deeply carved animals and leaves associated with the 'Ballintober master', some close in style to those at the western end of Boyle Abbey. The remainder of the church is more austere in character, but further work of the school is found in the doorways of the east range of the claustral buildings. Excavations carried out in 1963 showed that many of the remaining structures around the cloister were datable to the fifteenth century when a new doorway was inserted in the west gable of the church.

The abbey was founded close to a well (the 'tober' of the name) dedicated to St Patrick, and it traditionally acted as an assembly point for pilgrims setting out to climb Croagh Patrick (p. 58). There is a strong local tradition that Mass continued to be celebrated at the abbey even during the darkest of the penal days of religious oppression during the eighteenth century. An early attempt to put a roof on the nave came to naught with the Famine of 1847, but it was finally and nobly achieved for the 750th anniversary of the foundation in 1966, thanks to the exertions of the local curate, Fr. Thomas Egan, and the architectural guidance of Percy Le Clerc. Their work now helps us to imagine what a fine medieval Augustinian abbey in Ireland was like in its heyday – though the meditational 'stations' recently erected in the grounds would, naturally, not have formed a part of it.

CONG ABBEY
Co. Mayo

The final flowering of the 'School of the West' is found in the abbey of Cong, located between the lakes of Conn and Corrib. It had been the site of an early monastery founded in the seventh century, but it became an affluent house in the 1130s through patronage from the royal house of the O Conors, whose last High King, Rory, spent his final years in retirement at the abbey until his death in 1198. Five years later, the town and monastery were destroyed, and the best of what survives today is the result of reconstruction undertaken during the following twenty-five years. The fine north doorway is not in its original position, but the doorways of the eastern range

LEFT Pointed doorways in the Gothic style, though with ornament strongly influenced by late Romanesque, suggest that Cong Abbey in Mayo was among the last sites where masons of the 'School of the West' operated before the Normans finally overran Connacht in 1235.

RIGHT The Augustinian priory in Adare, Co. Limerick, founded by John, Earl of Kildare, in 1315, is impeccably kept by the Church of Ireland, which continues to use it for divine service. The view towards its altar and east window gives us a very good idea of the original appearance of an Irish medieval Augustinian interior.

of the claustral buildings – with their rich foliate ornament and undercut chevrons – are preserved *in situ* and may be classed among the last works of the 'School of the West'. Comparable work in Regensburg in Bavaria of around 1230 has led to the suggestion that some of the masons may have had to go as far as Germany in search of work, as their transitional style of ornament would have seemed curiously archaic among the Gothic buildings being erected in the more easterly parts of Ireland at the time.

ADARE PRIORY
Co. Limerick

No structure gives a better idea of what the interior of an Irish medieval priory church looked like than the Augustinian priory beside the River Maigue on the outskirts of the Limerick village of Adare. Founded by John fitz Thomas FitzGerald around 1315, the church was built about ten years later, consisting of a nave and chancel, with a tower inserted later between them, and an aisle to the south of the nave. The east window of the latter shows the thick bars used in the mullions of

fourteenth-century Irish ecclesiastical windows, and the attractive cloisters are fifteenth-century additions. The priory was officially dissolved in 1539-40, though the friars appeared to have lingered on there for another twenty years, and the church was restored to its former beauty when it was handed over to the Protestant community in Adare in 1807. The old monastic refectory was roofed to serve as a school house in 1814 and, twelve years later, the central part of the west wing of the domestic quarters was converted into the mausoleum of the Wyndham Quin family who, as Earls of Dunraven, have done so much to make Adare one of the great showpieces of medieval Ireland.

ATHASSEL PRIORY
Co. Tipperary

The most extensive and impressive of the Augustinian foundations and one of the largest monasteries ever to have been built in Ireland was Athassel, near Golden, in County Tipperary. Access from the road today brings the visitor over a bridge – a reminder that the River Suir was

LEFT The Augustinian foundation at Athassel, near Golden in County Tipperary, is the most extensive cluster of medieval monastic ruins anywhere in Ireland.

BELOW At first sight the towered curtain wall at Kells in County Kilkenny looks like part of a heavily defended castle, but in reality it protected the tenants and livestock of the Augustinian monastery founded there in 1192/3.

diverted to make Athassel into an island. This comprised not only the monastery but a whole town that grew up around it – though leaving few visible traces today because it was twice burned, once by adherents of the Earl of Desmond in 1319 and again by Brian O'Brien in 1330. The reason for this animosity towards it on the part of the Irish was because Athassel was a rich foundation supported by the Norman de Burgos, who had founded it around 1200, and who continued to give it patronage for a long time thereafter.

The Augustinians did not develop an architectural style of their own and – like Ballintober – the plan of Athassel priory owes much to Cistercian architecture. The church has a broad, aisled nave with an unexpected tower at the north-western corner. After the church was burned in 1447, the nave was left roofless. Each of the two transepts has two chapels which underwent subsequent alterations, though these – like much of the rest of the architecture of the monastery – are difficult to date. Leading to the

choir is a finely decorated doorway of c.1260, having above it in the wall an arched recess (later built up) which may well have held a great crucifix or rood. In the choir is an early fourteenth-century slab (subsequently reduced in size) bearing an attractively incised representation of a man and woman. Another important carving from Athassel is a late thirteenth-century tomb-front bearing figures of knights in relief, which, being of stone from a quarry at Dundry near Bristol, may have been imported in its finished state. It has now been removed to the Hall of the Vicars-Choral on the Rock of Cashel.

The extensive claustral buildings to the south of the church are partially later than the church itself, and outside the immediate monastic complex there are further walls and buildings (including a gate-house) enclosing an area of almost 4 acres (1.6ha). The monastery was dissolved in 1541, and sixteen years later it came into the possession of Thomas, Earl of Ormond, whom we shall meet again at Carrick-on-Suir (pp. 227-9).

KELLS PRIORY
Co. Kilkenny

Kells in County Kilkenny suffers undeservedly from being overshadowed by its more famous namesake in County Meath, after which the famous book in Trinity College, Dublin, is called. But the Kilkenny Kells very much deserves attention in its own right because it has one of the most surprising historic monuments in the country, which is not what it appears to be at first sight. The casual visitor, coming across it by chance, would be easily led to presume that it was a fortified castle because of the long stretches of curtain wall interspersed with what are virtually a series of

century. Excavations by the late Tom Fanning between 1972 and 1980 uncovered fragments of the original cloister arcade – one of the rare mid-thirteenth century examples of the type. Subsequently, considerable alterations were made to the church, which was extended at both ends, suggesting the presence of an increasingly sizeable population in and outside the community. Furthermore, towers were added outside the north-western and south-eastern corners of the church, the latter being probably the residence of the prior, who was also a Lord of Parliament. Sometime probably in the fifteenth century, the north transept was further extended and the monastic complex was surrounded by a wall stretching from the river to the ill-defended millstream which ran parallel with it to the south of the cloister. Finally, a tower was

tower-houses. These walls would have enclosed the tenants and livestock of what was, in fact, an important Augustinian priory, while at the same time acting as an outer defence of the core of the monastery which lies to the north, on the banks of the King's River.

The priory was founded in 1192/3 by Strongbow's brother-in-law, Geoffrey fitz Robert, who brought over four canons from Bodmin in Cornwall to set up this Augustinian house close to his 'castle', represented until its recent destruction by a motte about a third of a mile (0.5km) upstream. The monastic buildings, not quite so well preserved as the towered enclosure to the south, comprised a church, a cloister garth surrounded by the canons' domestic quarters, and various outbuildings including a kitchen, an infirmary and a water mill. The church has a long, narrow hall-like shape, akin to its Augustinian *confrère* at Athassel, but only the south wall of the nave, the side walls of the choir and almost the entire eastern range of the claustral buildings date from the earliest phase of construction in the earlier thirteenth

added above the crossing of the church, probably in the fifteenth century, which was also likely to have been the period when the 'Burgess Court' with those remarkable curtain walls and towers was constructed to the south of the millstream. The priory was dissolved in 1539, and plans are now afoot to reconstruct some of its buildings on the basis of Tom Fanning's excavations.

THE BENEDICTINES AND FORE ABBEY, CO. WESTMEATH

In terms of the family branches of Western monasticism, the Benedictine order was one of the oldest. Founded by St Benedict in the sixth century, its rule came with time to be interpreted in a rather lax fashion, and many of the important medieval monastic orders – including the Cluny monks in the tenth century and, more importantly for Ireland, the Cistercians – arose out

of a desire to return to the original spirit of St Benedict's rule. Because St Malachy placed such reliance on the Cistercians and Augustinians to carry through his reforms in twelfth-century Ireland, the Benedictines came to be overshadowed. They were, however, the basis for Irish monasteries – the so-called *Schottenklöster* – founded on the continent in the eleventh and twelfth centuries. Through them, the Benedictines went to Rosscarbery, Co. Cork, but, more significantly, became involved in the administration of Cormac's Chapel in Cashel. In Ulster John de Courcy replaced Augustinian canons with Benedictines in the cathedral at Downpatrick, but architecturally their only foundation of significance was Fore in County Westmeath. There, Hugh de Lacy, the Norman baron, had granted all the churches from the earlier monastery of St Fechin to the Benedictine abbey of St Taurin at Evreux in Normandy, and the monks combined the two saints as joint patrons of the

new abbey, which was built in the thirteenth century down on the plain away from the other churches. But the French connection with St Taurin worked against the interests of the monastery in the Anglo-French wars of the fourteenth and fifteenth centuries, when the king regarded Fore as an alien monastery. As a result Fore was never able to prosper, but, despite a reduction in the number of monks, the monastery was still in existence when surrendered at the Reformation in 1539. By a curious coincidence Ireland's only modern – and much more successful – Benedictine foundation, Glenstal Abbey, had a French-speaking mother-house in Maredsous in Belgium.

The church at Fore is a rather austere rectangular structure of around 1200, with little ornamentation either in its three large round-headed east windows or elsewhere within the surviving complex, which also includes parts of the claustral buildings to the north of the church.

LEFT Fore Abbey, Co. Westmeath, was surprisingly the only significant Benedictine foundation in later medieval Ireland.

by Maurice FitzGerald, and most of the early friars were probably Englishmen or would have originated in the Anglo-Norman colonies. After Dublin, their houses spread rapidly in the Anglo-Norman towns, where they were frequently located outside the town walls. While many of their early patrons were Anglo-Normans, the Irish also encouraged them to settle in their territories – the O'Donnells in Derry, the O Conors in Roscommon and Donnchad Cairbreach O'Brien in Limerick. Within a quarter of a century of their arrival in Ireland, the Dominicans already had a dozen houses and by 1300 that number had doubled. A move towards a stricter life-style, known as the Observantine Reform, was initiated in the Irish Dominican houses west of the Shannon, starting with Portumna in 1426, but more were formally approved when the Irish

RIGHT Originally Cistercian, the priory at Portumna, Co. Galway, became Dominican in the early fifteenth century, and was the first Irish house of its order to introduce the stricter Observantine Reform.

THE DOMINICANS

In the twelfth century the Benedictines and the Cistercians brought the advantages of their particular monastic way of life to an Ireland which had not previously experienced such religious orders. In the following century it was the turn of some of the mendicant orders, the Dominicans and the Franciscans, both founded by outstanding Italian saints whose names they bear. The Dominicans came to Ireland from England in 1224, but Ireland only became an independent province of the order in 1484. One early Dominican, Reginald, an Italian companion of St Dominic himself, was to become Archbishop of Armagh from 1247 to 1256, and others were to occupy episcopal sees in the following century. The first Irish Dominican foundation was in Dublin, where the order was encouraged to settle

Province became independent in 1484. By the time of the suppression of the monasteries in 1540, there were thirty-three Dominican foundations in Ireland and in the seventeenth century they were to take on a new lease of life in the country.

Preaching was the essential work of the Dominicans, and the shape of their churches reflected this activity. The church was really a long hall, subdivided by a stone screen (often with a tower above) from the mid-fourteenth century onwards, and there the pulpit was placed. The friars conducted their liturgy in the choir, while the people listened to the sermons in the nave, from where they could not normally see the friars at prayer. To facilitate larger congregations, a south aisle or transept was frequently added, and the conventual buildings usually lay to the north of the church.

KILMALLOCK PRIORY
Co. Limerick

Kilmallock is the best preserved of the medieval Dominican priories, though it was not without its initial difficulties. The friars had settled on the other side of the river from where the town lay, on a plot of land obtained from one of its burgesses, John Bluet, in 1291. But the Bishop of Limerick disapproved, and within seven weeks of the friars' arrival he sent a party to demolish the buildings they had begun. However, the friars immediately appealed to the king, Edward I, with whose consent they had initially acquired the land, and he duly confirmed their possession. Within a decade or so they had built the fine priory we see today, which lost its roof after the Reformation. Because comparatively little is known of the priory's history, it can only be concluded that its life was a comparatively happy one until its suppression in 1541.

The church at Kilmallock is of the long, hall variety, with half a dozen tall windows in the south wall of the choir, originally of two lights and with 'switch-lined' tracery, where parallel mullions branch off in curving pairs as at a railway junction. But the choir was further illuminated by a magnificent five-light window in the east wall, each light graded in height and all grouped together under an arch with a span of 18 feet (5.5m). The south aisle of the nave as well as the transept were both added in the fourteenth century. The fine traceried window built into the south transept during the fifteenth century is so large that inserting it must have necessitated the almost complete reconstruction of the wall. Though the Dominicans had a vow of poverty, they nevertheless had enough funds to decorate the church with a number of sculpted heads. The slender tower of the church was probably heightened in the fifteenth century, but the claustral buildings – different in plan from those of the Cistercians – probably date from a century earlier.

LEFT AND BELOW (detail) Kilmallock, Co. Limerick, is the best preserved of Ireland's medieval Dominican monasteries, with its tall slender fifteenth-century tower, traceried windows and finely carved heads dating from the time of the original foundation around 1300.

Too few medieval Carmelite churches survive in Ireland to show whether they developed an architectural style of their own, and the church at Loughrea, Co. Galway, differs little from the designs used by the other mendicant orders. One of the latest uses of twin lancet windows in the chancel suggests a building date shortly after the foundation in the early fourteenth century, but the traceried windows and the tower were inserted presumably in the fifteenth century.

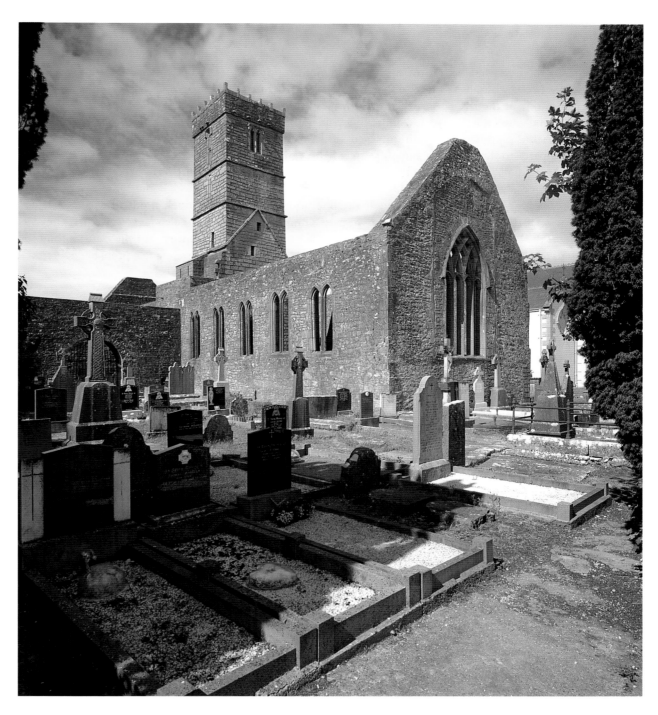

THE CARMELITES AND LOUGHREA FRIARY, CO. GALWAY

The last of the four major medieval mendicant orders to reach Ireland were the Carmelites, who took their name from Mount Carmel near Haifa, Israel. Originally eremitical, the order founded community houses when it started moving to Europe in the 1230s, and Crusaders introduced it to England within the following decade. The friars had certainly reached Ireland by 1271, if not before, settling initially at Leighlinbridge, Co. Carlow, and subsequently setting up their provincial house in Dublin. By the time of the Black Death in 1350 twenty Irish Carmelite houses had been established, and new foundations continued to be made as late as the fifteenth century. In 1458 the prior of one of these, at Kilcormac in County Offaly, commissioned a missal which is still preserved in the Library of Trinity College, Dublin.

Rathmullan, Co. Donegal, and Castlelyons, Co. Cork, preserve remnants of medieval Carmelite houses, but the best preserved of the order's Irish churches is that at Loughrea, Co. Galway. Here Richard de Burgo, second Earl of Ulster, founded the house where the Kilcormac missal was actually written and where the shrine of St Brigid's shoe, now in the National Museum in Dublin, was preserved. The modern Carmelite friary adjoining it was established in the nineteenth century.

CASTLES AND TOWER-HOUSES

Castles, and in particular tower-houses, are the most ubiquitous class of stone monuments to survive in the Irish countryside from the fifteenth and sixteenth centuries, though a few were built after 1600. They belong to a period when throughout Europe the scale and size of castles was being reduced. Gone were the days when the Anglo-Norman invaders had to build castles large enough to house not only the lords and their household retinues but also the soldiers they needed to defend them. The time had come more for fortified residences intended for family use, without the necessity of providing for a small standing army.

Even in the thirteenth century there were some smaller castles which were large stout towers built mainly for a lord and his domestic staff. The tradition was continued possibly in the fourteenth century and certainly in the fifteenth when large towers were built for family use, but it was increasingly the native Irish or the old Norman families who were building these

LEFT Deprived of his episcopal see of Down in 1441 for having lived an adulterous life in this castle at Kilclief, Co. Down, Bishop John Cely provided us not only with a tantalizing titbit of medieval scandal but also the earliest reliable date known for the existence of a tower-house in Ireland.

RIGHT While the two rounded towers in the foreground suggest that Dunluce Castle on the Antrim coast was initially built in the fourteenth century, it does not emerge into the light of history until the sixteenth, when most of the other existing structures were added by the MacQuillan family or by the Macdonnells who gradually displaced them. Additions continued to be made to the castle until it was apparently abandoned after the seaward end collapsed and fell away in 1639, bringing several members of the household with it to a watery grave.

larger structures. Among the latter were the Butlers, who constructed – or, to be more precise, almost completely reconstructed – the large castle at Cahir, Co. Tipperary, in the fifteenth century. This comprised a central keep, or large tower, which was defended by more than one set of walls in the form of inner and outer wards. Within the Pale, the area surrounding and defending Dublin from the native Irish, the Plunketts built a tall castle with rectangular corner towers at Dunsoghly, only 8 miles (13km) from the capital. In the Gaelic parts of Ireland, the recent Gaelic revival was beginning to express itself in the construction of large towers, such as that built by the MacCarthys at Blarney in County Cork. In north Munster the Macnamaras built Bunratty in County Clare around the mid-fifteenth century – a majestic castle also with corner towers and with a large arch at third-floor level on the outside, which supported a Lord's chamber above it. At Dunluce, Co. Antrim, at the other end of the country, the MacQuillans built a splendid defence on a small headland jutting into the sea. These castles were built for defence, but there was also an element of display in their make-up – the family status symbols of their day.

The larger castles were, however, more the exception than the rule, while the most common 'castles' of the fifteenth and sixteenth centuries were considerably smaller in scale. These are the tower-houses, which indicate the same combination of defence and status, but often somewhat further down the social scale. Their existence implies that everyone who could was left to protect his own interests in the absence of any central authority to defend him and his family. One Spanish agent reported to Philip II in 1579 that in Ireland 'every petty gentleman lives in a stone tower, where he gathers into his service all the rascals of the neighbourhood, and of these towers there is an infinite number'.

The typical tower-house is a four-storey tower, rectangular in shape and frequently with a slight batter (slope) in the walls as they rise. The lower floors are arched over with a stone vault, providing a solid stone floor for the storey above. Entrance was through a doorway leading into the vaulted ground floor, but along a passage with a 'murder-hole' above through which stones and other weapons could be showered down on unwanted intruders. Machicolations placed above the entrance, but at roof level, also served the same purpose. Just inside the entrance a stone staircase, often spiral, gave access to the floors above, one for the retainers and the top floor reserved for the owner. To judge by accounts of seventeenth-century visitors, furniture was kept to a minimum – a table, chairs or benches, and a bed, with the floor covered with rushes. The later examples often had more generous window openings, at least in the top floor, and the same applies to fireplaces, which could be quite elaborate if the occupiers were more opulent. There were stone gables in the later examples, and a wooden roof (of which Dunsoghly provides the only surviving example) covered with slates, around the base of which was a wall-walk. Occasionally the bases of the towers were sloped so that objects dropped from above could bounce off them onto potential attackers. Lower down the tower the windows were narrow slits to allow the defenders to fire on enemies, whose arrows or bullets would have little chance of penetrating them; and, when guns came into more widespread use, particularly during the sixteenth century, small gun loops were provided within the walls to provide cover from a variety of angles. Because of the often damp terrain, it was rarely feasible to carry cannon across country to attack tower-houses, but the advent of guns did encourage the building of a wall around the 'bawn', the open

The proximity of Kildavnet Castle to the seashore of Achill Island in County Mayo gave rise to its being linked traditionally with the name of Gráinne Ní Mháille, otherwise Grace O'Malley, the legendary pirate queen, who is said to have visited the court of Queen Elizabeth in London. But the simple tower-house is more likely to have been built by an ancestor, perhaps in the earlier sixteenth century.

space immediately adjoining the castle. This prevented muskets getting too close to the tower and also provided shelter for livestock against both human and animal predators – for the occasional wolf still prowled Ireland at the time.

Almost 3000 such tower-houses are known to have existed in Ireland, most of them south of a line from Drogheda to Westport, Ulster having very few. They are most frequent in Munster; Limerick had 400, Cork 325, Tipperary 250 and Clare 120. Here, as elsewhere, they must have been the houses of the local gentry with enough money to build a family defence but also to show neighbours how rich they were. Occasionally, to raise their status, there was a small element of decoration, particularly around the door and the top-floor windows, and the majority of sheela-na-gigs (see p. 224) are found built into the walls of tower-houses. Sadly, the keeping of records was not one of the occupants' specialities or else they have not survived, so that it is often difficult to know even the name of a family who built any one particular tower.

There has been an amount of discussion recently about the origin of these tower-houses, without any clear conclusion having been reached. They may well be a native version of the smaller, earlier Norman castle, developing a form of crenellated battlement on the skyline – the origin of which is equally uncertain. But the similarity in battlement styles to those on the towers of monastic houses led Leask to observe that the same masons may have worked on both.

CAHIR CASTLE
Co. Tipperary

Cahir Castle, on a rocky island in the River Suir, is one of the largest and best-preserved castles in Ireland, consisting of three parts – an inner, middle and outer ward, all defended by stout curtain walls. The entrance was – and still is – through the middle ward, from which one passed through a gateway with portcullis into the inner ward. This was the most heavily defended of the three parts, with square towers at the northern corners, a round bastion covering the entrance at the south-eastern corner, and a massive three-storey keep acting as a citadel on the southern side.

The foundations of the inner ward, the portcullis gateway and probably also parts of the keep, are among the few survivors of the earliest Norman castle on the site, built possibly by William de Braose, to whom King John had granted the lands hereabouts that had been in O'Brien hands before the Normans arrived. But in the following century the O'Briens took their revenge by regaining the territory and burning the town in 1332. In 1375 the castle was granted to the Butler Earls of Ormond, who retained it for centuries and built most of the fifteenth- and sixteenth-century castle we see today. In 1596 Thomas Butler, Baron of Caher, went over to the Irish in defiance of Queen Elizabeth, whose favourite, the Earl of Essex, managed to take the castle after three days in 1599 – cannon balls in the outer walls being a visual reminder of the siege. It was besieged again by Cromwell in 1650, but he captured it without a fight, as the defenders, under George Mathews, a half-brother of the Butler Earl of Ormond, marched out with banners flying, leaving the castle to the Parliamentary aggressors – but also helping to preserve it in good condition for posterity.

The Butlers later regained possession of the castle, and their descendants retained it – not without interruptions – until 1964, when the castle was

Cahir Castle, on an island in the River Suir, rests on earlier Norman foundations and is the most extensive of the later medieval Irish castles. Cannon balls from the siege of 1599 are still lodged in the outer walls.

taken into state care. One of the nineteenth-century Butlers, the Earl of Glengall, together with his Tipperary-born architect William Tinsley, restored the castle, including the great hall in the inner ward, reconstructed during the years 1840 to 1846 when Cahir Cottage was built at the southern end of the outer ward. The Commissioners of Public Works have undertaken among other things the praiseworthy reinstatement of the portcullis machinery and the provision of new floors in the keep, where temporary exhibitions are housed.

BLARNEY CASTLE
Co. Cork

Blarney is undoubtedly one of Ireland's most famous castles, not because of its good state of preservation, but because of a stone high up on the parapet which, if kissed on the underside as you lie on your back about 85 feet (26m) above the ground, is said to bestow the gift of eloquence. In the words of Father Prout, the nineteenth-century Cork divine:

> There is a stone there that whoever kisses
> Oh! he never misses to grow eloquent.

One suggestion about the origin of this curious custom concerns a sixteenth-century Lord of Muskerry, Cormac mac Dermot MacCarthy, whose silvery words seemed to please both sides in any dispute he was involved in, but which failed to convince Queen Elizabeth I, who described his eloquence as 'All Blarney'.

The castle is a mighty tower standing five storeys high on a prominent rock with two 'caves' within, one of which is thought to have acted as a prison. One stone supporting the parapet wall is said to have carried the inscription that Cormac 'the strong' MacCarthy built the castle in 1446, an ancestor of the silver-tongued Cormac. The Cromwellian commander Broghill captured the castle in 1646 but in 1662, after the Restoration of Charles II, it was returned to the MacCarthy Lord Muskerry, who had been created Earl of Clancarty four years earlier. But, with the defeat of James II in 1691, the family lost the castle, which was sold to the Jeffreys. This family then built a curious turreted mansion at the foot of the rock in the early eighteenth century, though much of its upper floors had to be demolished some years ago for safety reasons. The castle is now owned by Mr Charles Colthurst, a descendant of the Jeffreys.

BUNRATTY CASTLE
Co. Clare

Bunratty Castle, between Limerick and the modern town of Shannon, once dominated a medieval town, of which nothing save a parish church remains. It stands on what was formerly the island of Tradraighe on the northern bank of the Shannon where it could control shipping going to and from Limerick – a military function which it probably shared in tandem with Carrigogunnell Castle on the south side of the estuary. Bunratty is not the first, nor even the second, but the third castle on the site. It was built around the mid-fifteenth century by Síoda Mac-Conmara and completed by his son, Seán Finn, who died in 1467. In the

LEFT The solidly impressive tower of Blarney Castle, with its famous Stone of Eloquence, was built in 1446 and has survived much better than the dwarfed and slender turret remaining from an early eighteenth-century mansion in front of it.

RIGHT The third castle to have been erected on its riverside site, Bunratty Castle in County Clare was built by the Macnamaras in the mid-fifteenth century; subsequently, it came into the possession of the O'Brien Kings, and later Earls, of Thomond.

words of its restorer, Le Clerc, 'the castle is the most important civil building that has come down to us from the period'. Some time within the ensuing eighty years it came by marriage into the possession of the O'Briens, Kings and later Earls of Thomond. The fourth earl made it his chief seat around 1580, and the modern restoration has tried to recreate the castle as it would have been in his time.

The castle has four main floors of varying heights, including the basement with dungeons and storerooms and the Main Guard of the first floor, both being vaulted and the latter having been where the servants and soldiers of the earl kept watch. Above this there is the Great Hall, with a modern wooden roof, adapted from that at Dunsoghly Castle, Co. Dublin. In it the earl would have held court and dined – as do today's visitors to the castle who banquet there nightly, presided over by an 'earl' chosen from among the guests. In one of the window embrasures, a sheela-na-gig has been inserted into the wall, and in another there are fragments of stucco of

RIGHT The South Solar was reserved for the earl's special guests and was also the favourite room of Lady Gort, whose portrait by Philip de Laszlo (1933) hangs on the end wall. Her husband, Lord Gort, bought Bunratty castle in 1956 and magnanimously bequeathed it and its furnishings to the Irish nation.

BELOW High up in a corner tower of Bunratty Castle, the Earl of Thomond could sleep soundly in his well-appointed bedroom.

c.1600, a material which also decorates the chapel of the Great Hall. Finally, the uppermost floor contains the earl's private apartments, including his own private chapel, which are late sixteenth century in date.

In 1646 the papal nuncio, Cardinal Rinuccini, could say 'I have no hesitation in asserting that Bunratty is the most beautiful spot I have ever seen. In Italy there is nothing like the palace and grounds of Lord Thomond. Nothing like its ponds and parks and its three thousand head of deer.' But paradise gardens don't last forever. Shortly afterwards, Cromwell's Parliamentary forces wrested the castle from its defender, Admiral Penn, whose son William – the founder of Pennsylvania – may have experienced the siege before his father had to abandon it and sail

RIGHT The North Solar, high up beneath the parapets of Bunratty, was the Earl of Thomond's private apartment and now holds the so-called 'Armada Table'.

LEFT The lower, or public, chapel in Bunratty Castle has a rare Irish stuccoed ceiling of c.1600 and a variety of interesting ecclesiastical furnishings.

LEFT In the Great Hall of Bunratty Castle, the Earls of Thomond once gave as warm a welcome to their guests as their modern counterparts receive when they participate in the medieval banquet staged there nightly with appropriate ceremony.

off to Kinsale in 1646. The O'Briens never reoccupied the castle which was sold to the Studdert family, one of whose descendants sold it to Lord Gort in 1956. It was he and Lady Gort, advised by the famous art-historian John Hunt, who filled the castle with medieval furniture, eclectic in origin because very little Irish furniture of the period has survived the turbulence of intervening centuries. The castle and its furniture are now held in trust for the nation, and managed by Shannon Heritage, a subsidiary of the Shannon Free Airport Development Company, which has built a folk park and reconstructed a nineteenth-century Irish village in the grounds.

CARRIGOGUNNELL CASTLE
Co. Limerick

Carrigogunnell Castle is the most dominant medieval monument to enhance the skyline on the Limerick side of the Shannon estuary. It stands pre-eminent on a rock outcrop from which it could monitor – if it did not control – maritime traffic on its way upstream to Limerick, as Bunratty did on the Clare side. The periphery of the rock is protected by a wall which encloses an outer and lower ward, with the original entrance and a hall, and the inner ward with the remains of a keep. Forming an L-shape on either side of the keep are two fifteenth- or sixteenth-century buildings, up to four storeys high, in front of which is a paved court. The early history of the castle is unclear, but in the fifteenth century it seems to have passed from Norman ownership to the O'Briens of Thomond, who had to surrender it to the king's deputy, Lord Grey, in 1536, but later regained it. They were, however, dislodged by the Cromwellians under General Ireton, and the final act of ignominy to befall the castle was to have King William's henchman S'Gravenmore blow up most of it in September 1691. But for this wanton act of destruction, the state of the buildings might now match the superb siting which it still enjoys.

LEFT Carrigogunnell Castle is a romantic-looking landmark, standing ruined and ivied on a rock overlooking the Limerick bank of the Shannon estuary.

ABOVE RIGHT The fifteenth-century banqueting hall at Askeaton is seen here to the left of the ruined castle on an island in the River Deel in west Limerick.

RIGHT Malahide Castle was occupied almost uninterruptedly by the Talbot family from around 1200 until 1976. It is a very effective blend of medieval masonry and Georgian interior elegance, which is much appreciated by the visitors who flock to see it and the surrounding gardens.

ASKEATON BANQUETING HALL
Co. Limerick

Bunratty in County Clare may be the place we most associate with medieval banquets today, but it is the neighbouring county of Limerick which in reality has the virtual monopoly of banqueting halls of the period. Both Adare and Newcastle West have two; Maurice Craig suggests another at Tomdeeley but the best preserved of them all is on the bank of the River Deel at Askeaton. The land there, which King John had granted to William de Burgo around 1200, later passed to the de Clares before coming into the possession of the FitzGerald Earls of Desmond in the middle of the fourteenth century. It was doubtless one of the earls (the seventh, perhaps?) who built the banqueting hall to the west of the Desmond Castle, but within the bawn which stretches down to the river. Its architectural details are close to those of the Franciscan friary just downstream from the castle, and may thus date from the same period – the first half of the fifteenth century. The hall is a tall gabled building, with five vaulted rooms on the ground floor. A special staircase linked them to the upper floor, which was originally more subdivided than it is today. Now the wind passing through the ruined hall conjures up the noisy feasts which must have taken place when the noble earl and his guests could look out over the pastoral Limerick countryside and peer down into the River Deel flowing gently beneath the windows.

MALAHIDE CASTLE
Co. Dublin

Malahide Castle, bordering an inlet of the sea some 9 miles (14.5km) north of Dublin, has what is Ireland's only medieval hall kept in the style which it deserves. It was built perhaps by Thomas Talbot in the later fifteenth century and now houses many paintings of his descendants and others, forming virtually a National Portrait Gallery. The Talbot family were granted the castle by King Henry II towards the end of the twelfth century, and it was – with an interruption during the Cromwellian Commonwealth – one of Ireland's oldest sites to have been continuously inhabited by the same family. That was until 1976, when the last chatelaine, the Hon. Rose Talbot, was forced to sell the castle and contents to satisfy the requirements of a government not prepared to compromise over death duties in the interests of keeping together what was doubtlessly Ireland's greatest collection of art works and furniture. Fortunately, total disaster was averted when interested parties – private, public and commercial – bought many of the contents at the auction in order to have them reinstated back in the castle where they belonged, and where they can now be viewed and enjoyed by the public.

Very little of the great medieval hall is noticeable from the outside, where most of the features – the projecting entrance hall and the round turrets at the corners, for instance – are the result of major alterations made to the castle by two generations of the family during the reign of King George III (1760-1820). At the same period old tapestry-hung rooms were replaced by gracious classical interiors with stucco, perhaps by Richard West, and the Oak Room was decorated with older panelling and a much-revered Flemish carving of the Ascension of the Virgin, dating from around the early sixteenth century. This same room also contains a cabinet which came to the family through marriage with the Boswells of Auchinleck, in Scotland, and provided the world with one of its most sensational literary 'finds' of the 1920s, when it was found to preserve the unexpurgated manuscript of James Boswell's *Life of Samuel Johnson*. The later exterior casing of the castle visible today encloses what was the core of the old family home, a tower-house of the fifteenth century, which must be imagined as having stood out in the landscape above the great hall though not, of course, surrounded by the beautiful gardens in which the castle stands today.

ENNISCORTHY CASTLE
Co. Wexford

The castle standing on the southern slope of the Wexford town of Enniscorthy has a rectangular plan with four corner towers of a kind which goes back to the thirteenth century, when the Norman Philip Prendergast built a castle here which was later taken by the Irish Mac-Murroughs. The present structure was probably not constructed until the fifteenth or sixteenth century, during which period the alternation of ownership between Irish and English characterized its history. The poet Edmund Spenser, author of *The Faerie Queene*, leased the castle in 1581, but, fearing for his life, never actually lived there. It surrendered to the ubiquitous Cromwell in 1649, after which it was used as a residence – though it temporarily served as a prison in 1798, the year when the slaughterous Battle of Vinegar Hill was fought on the opposite bank of the River Slaney. In the nineteenth century the Earl of Portsmouth used the ground floor as his estate office, and leased the upper floor to a printing press company. The Roche family occupied it in this century until 1960, when the local historian Fr. Joseph Ranson (1907-64) opened the Castle Museum to house his extensive folk collection illustrating the history of the county.

RATHMACKNEE CASTLE
Co. Wexford

South Wexford is fortunate in having preserved a number of late medieval castles, one of the most complete being Rathmacknee, about 7 miles (11km) from Wexford town. Like some other castles in the area, Rathmacknee owes its origins to the Rosseter family, who came to Ireland with the Normans, settling in the Barony of Forth and making Rathmacknee their headquarters. While being staunch supporters of the English monarchy, they retained their old religion after the Reformation. Little survives from their earliest occupation of the site, but one of the Rosseters later built a castle there in the second half of the fifteenth century. Taken together with a nearby church and an old mill, it gives us a good picture of what a medieval Irish manorial centre was like, despite alterations necessitated by centuries of continuous occupation.

The tower stands at the south-eastern corner – and beside the gate – of a well-preserved high-walled bawn, in which a modern house still stands. An interesting feature of this bawn is the round 'bartizan' at the top of the north-eastern corner, supported by corbels and housing seven musket loops in the parapet. The tower itself, with its characteristic stepped battlements, had five storeys, with the probable addition of a roof attic. The two lowest floors were covered with a stone vault, the others having had wooden floors.

RIGHT The picturesque setting of recently restored Ross Castle beside the Lakes of Killarney makes it one of the most photographed tower-houses in Ireland.

LEFT Consisting of the typical Irish ground-plan of a rectangular tower with rounded corner towers, Enniscorthy Castle in County Wexford was built three or four centuries ago and has now been sensibly converted into an interesting museum of local bygones.

LEFT Rathmacknee Castle in County Wexford was built by the Rosseter family in the late fifteenth century and survives in good condition as an example of a solid tower-house with a well-preserved bawn or enclosing wall.

ROSS CASTLE
Killarney, Co. Kerry

Ross Castle must surely be classed among the most picturesque ruins in County Kerry, located on a small tongue of land beside Lough Leane, and in the sublime setting of the mountain scenery around the Lakes of Killarney. It consists of a tall tower-house surrounded by a bawn with rounded corner towers, some of which survive. Attached to the castle is a later building, which acted as a barracks in the eighteenth century when the castle was occupied by the Brownes, Earls of Kenmare.

The castle is a tower-house built by one of the O'Donoghue Ross chieftains of the area sometime around the sixteenth century. During the Cromwellian wars it was held by Lord Muskerry and the royalists for King Charles I. An old prophecy said that the castle could never be taken except by an attack made from the water by a sailing vessel known as a Man of War. Ludlow, the Cromwellian commander who laid siege to the castle, had a boat transported overland from the sea and launched it in Lough Leane, so that when the royalist defenders saw the vessel, they felt that the prophecy was fulfilled and abandoned the castle forthwith. Thus fell the last Irish castle to yield to Cromwell's forces. Extensive conservation works undertaken in recent years by the Office of Public Works, under the direction of Grellan Rourke, culminated with éclat when the castle was once again reopened to the public in 1994, making it look as fresh as the day it was built.

NEWTOWN CASTLE
Co. Clare

Most tower-houses are rectangular but, scattered around the southern half of the country, there are about fifteen round examples inspired perhaps by the circular bastions of earlier Norman fortifications, though their shape may have been determined as much by their striking visual appearance as by the need for a stout defence. Tipperary is the county with the greatest number of examples, but Clare can claim three, of which that at Newtown, illustrated here, has a unique pyramidal base.

Newtown was probably built in the sixteenth century for a branch of the O'Briens. But it later passed to the O'Loghlen family, known for centuries in the locality as the Princes, or even Kings, of the Burren, that lunar limestone landscape of County Clare at the northern foot of which Newtown is located, near the shores of Galway Bay. Abandoned around the early nineteenth century, the castle was bought in the 1980s by local hoteliers Michael Greene and his wife Mary Hawkes-Greene, who reconstructed it along traditional lines and added a conical roof to make it look as if it almost came out of a fifteenth-century *Book of Hours*. In 1994 the Greenes realized their dream by making the castle the centrepiece of the international Burren College of Art, which was formally opened by Ireland's splendid President, Mrs Mary Robinson, on one happy July morning in 1994.

LEFT, BELOW AND BOTTOM Newtown Castle, near the Clare shore of Galway Bay, was built before 1600 and restored in 1994 as the centre of the newly established Burren College of Art. Two floors are arched over with a stone vault, still bearing the imprint of the medieval wattle (bottom) used in their construction, while the conical oak roof (below) was prefabricated and dropped by a very tall crane into its crowning position on the parapets.

O'Loghlen Princes of the Burren also built rectangular tower-houses, such as Gleninagh beside the sea where, in the words of the song, they could watch 'the sun going down on Galway Bay' from their top-floor living quarters.

GLENINAGH CASTLE
Co. Clare

The drive along the road around the northern foot of the Burren, on the southern shore of Galway Bay, is enlivened by the presence of a tower-house at Gleninagh. Inhabited until the later nineteenth century, the castle belonged to, and was presumably built by, the O'Loghlen family who were known as the Princes of the Burren. The castle probably dates to the sixteenth century and was described by T.J. Westropp as 'a plain rudely-built structure'. The two lower storeys were vaulted in stone, like many of the Clare tower-houses, though, unlike them, the staircase is not within the rectangular structure of the tower but in a turret projecting out from it. Close by is a simple medieval church which was presumably supported by the castle's inhabitants.

DUNGUAIRE CASTLE
Co. Galway

Dunguaire castle is so photogenic that, thirty years ago, it would have been an ideal candidate for decorating the top of a biscuit box, and today it is the stuff of calendars and picture postcards. It has even formed the dramatic backdrop for a 1980 thriller film, *North Sea Hijack*, starring Roger Moore. The tower sits atop a knoll almost entirely surrounded by the Atlantic waters of Galway Bay, except for a small causeway joining it to the mainland and leading up to the broad entrance in the tall-walled and angular bawn. The tower takes up a goodly portion of the west wall of the bawn, and consists of two storeys above a vaulted ground floor. The roof is a modern reconstruction.

The castle was built probably in the sixteenth century by one of the O'Heyne family, Lords of Uí Fiachrach Aidhne. The same family had in *c.*1200 built a beautiful little church at Kilmacduagh in the same county, for a monastery donated to St Colman in the seventh century by his brother Guaire, who was himself a King of Uí Fiachrach Aidhne, famous for his hospitality; and from his fort – Dún Guaire – the castle gets its name. The tradition of hospitality still persists, as the present owners, Shannon Heritage, host banquets with a literary flavour there during the summer months. But earlier in the century, the castle was owned by two characters very different in their own way – firstly Edward Martyn of Tullira, poet and patron of the arts, who featured in the lives and writings of Lady Gregory, W. B. Yeats and George Moore, and secondly the flamboyant Christabel, Lady Ampthill, who featured in a famous law case decided by the House of Lords.

THOOR BALLYLEE
Co. Galway

> An ancient bridge and a more ancient tower . . .
> A winding stair, a chamber arched with stone,
> A grey stone fireplace, with an open hearth.

With these words, W.B. Yeats, the great Irish poet, described the tower-house which he bought in 1917, so that he could keep in close contact with his friends Lady Gregory and Edward Martyn, who lived nearby at Coole and Tullira respectively, forming the nucleus of the 'literary landscape' of south Galway. He had already discovered this sixteenth-century de Burgo tower on his first visit to Coole in 1896, and was attracted to it because of its romantic association with Mary Hynes, 'the shining flower of Ballylee . . . a beautiful woman whose name is still a wonder by turf fires', beloved of the early nineteenth-century poet, Anthony Raftery. Furthermore, Yeats was fascinated by, and wanted to discover more about, the great old, east Clare lady, Biddy Early, and her claim that there is a cure for all evil 'between the two mill-wheels of Ballylee' – which were actually rediscovered in Dominic Delaney's excavation of the mill in 1991-2.

Yeats got his architect, William A. Scott, that 'drunken man of genius', to restore the castle and design furniture for it, the craft furnishings being

RIGHT Dunguaire sits cosily and well protected by a bawn on its little promontory washed by the Atlantic waters of Galway Bay.

FAR RIGHT Thoor Ballylee in south Galway is a tower-house which will always be closely associated with Ireland's famous poet and Nobel laureate, W.B. Yeats.

made locally. With his family he occupied the castle intermittently between 1919 and 1926 and he found peace and tranquillity here in what were troubled times throughout the country. The building gave its name to his 1928 collection of poems entitled *The Tower* (*Thoor* being the Gaelic for 'tower'). For Yeats Thoor Ballylee was a 'fitting monument' and 'a permanent symbol of my work plainly visible to the passer-by'. But he also foresaw a time after he left when it would return to the semi-derelict state he found it in, and wanted this to be recorded on a stone in the wall bearing the following lines:

> I, the poet William Yeats
> With old mill boards and sea-green slates
> and smithy work from the Gort forge
> Restored this tower with my wife George;
> and may these characters remain
> when all is ruin once again.

Soon, all *was* ruin once again, without Yeats having inserted the stone. But, with the aid of two further Scotts, Michael the architect and Pat the artist, the stone was finally prepared and put in place in 1948. With the support of the Yeats family (who set up a trust for it) and aid from Bord Fáilte and Ireland-West Tourism, Mary Hanley of the Kiltartan Society got the tower restored – and opened by another poet, Padraic Colum, in 1965, the centenary year of Yeats's birth.

O'BRIEN'S CASTLE
Inisheer, Co. Galway

The Aran Islands are geologically a continuation of the limestone karst of the Burren in north Clare, and it is no wonder that Clare's ruling dynasty, the O'Briens, should have successfully taken over the islands in the centuries after the death of their greatest scion, Brian Boru, in 1014. There they became so powerful that Galway merchants agreed to pay them twelve tons of wine annually for the upkeep of a small navy to keep Galway Bay free of pirates. Perhaps because of all that wine, the fortunes of the O'Briens declined on the islands, but not before they had built a castle for themselves close to the eastern end of Inis Oirr, or Inisheer, the smallest island of the three and the one nearest to the Clare coast. The castle is a two-storey tower placed off-centre in an oval walled enclosure, which may well incorporate parts of a much earlier fortification, as hinted at by the castle's alternative name Dún Formna, 'the fort on top of the hill'.

LEFT O'Brien's Tower seems to fit like a cap on top of a limestone pyramid on Inisheer, the smallest of the three Aran Islands in Galway Bay.

JORDAN'S CASTLE
Ardglass, Co. Down

Ardglass, Co. Down, and Dalkey, Co. Dublin, are two towns which spring to mind as medieval urban centres lucky enough to have preserved a goodly selection of the tower-houses which their richer citizens had built to protect themselves and to store their goods. Jordan's Castle in the middle of Ardglass has dominated the harbour since it was built in the fifteenth century. Between the stone-vaulted basement and restored roof it has three floors, which were fitted up as a museum when the Belfast antiquary, F.J. Bigger, bought the castle in 1911. On his death in 1926 the castle was handed over to the state. It, and other County Down castles like Kilclief, have one feature unusual in Irish tower-houses in that entry was gained through a doorway on the inner side of one of the projecting corner towers, in which a spiral staircase provided access to the upper floors.

RIGHT Jordan's Castle, with Ardglass harbour in the background, is a fine example of a tower-house built within a medieval town.

DOE CASTLE
Co. Donegal

The name Doe has nothing to do with the graceful deer but comes from a title applied to the lands of the MacSweeney family who, from having been mercenaries of Scottish descent, became lords of the area around Sheephaven Bay in north Donegal, where the castle is situated. Standing out on a tongue of land projecting into the bay, the castle is thus surrounded on three sides by water, the fourth being protected by a ditch to hinder attack from the landward side. The castle itself consists of a four-storey tower located off-centre in a high-walled bawn. The castle is first mentioned in historical records when there was internecine strife in the MacSweeney family in 1544, so the castle must date from before that time. Its next appearance in the history books is in connection with a rather more dramatic and international affair – the Spanish Armada of 1588 – when some of King Philip's ships struggled manfully against the elements to regain their home port. Some sank, others were able to make an Irish landing, including a few whose crew found refuge in Doe Castle. When the Irish lost their land in the early seventeenth-century Plantation of Ulster, Doe was granted to one Captain Sanford, who lived there with his wife and four English families, who helped him to farm the 500 acres (202ha) attached to the castle. During the following two centuries the MacSweeneys regained and lost the castle a number of times, and it was here that Owen Roe O'Neill landed from Spain with one hundred veterans in 1642, before setting off for Charlemont, Co. Antrim, to take charge of the Irish army.

Some time in the late eighteenth century, the castle came into the possession of George Vaughan Hart, whose initials and coat of arms can be found above the entrance, and his descendants occupied the castle for about a century, until they abandoned it about a hundred years ago. The extent and quality of the repairs carried out on the castle by the Hart family were such that it is sometimes difficult to differentiate between the medieval and the modern. Built into the exterior north face of the tower is a grave-slab decorated with animals and an eight-pointed cross. It presumably marked the grave of one of the sixteenth-century MacSweeneys in the nearby graveyard, and was brought to the castle for protection in 1968.

Survivors of the Spanish Armada
found solace here in Doe Castle,
picturesquely sited on the shores
of Sheephaven Bay in
County Donegal.

THE CHURCH

By 1400 many of the monks in the Gaelic and Gaelicized areas of Ireland had abandoned the normal rules of life in the monastery and openly married. Repeating what had happened in the seventh century, the Irish monasteries of the fifteenth century became increasingly secularized – not helped by the pope himself appointing superiors more for their money than their talent, many of whom rushed to Rome to get preferment ahead of more worthy candidates. The abbots were often secular figures who never took orders and used the monasteries merely as sources of income.

The Cistercians who had dominated the monastic scene in earlier centuries had declined, and only Holy Cross and Kilcooley, both in County Tipperary, managed to revitalize their buildings in the fifteenth century. Apart from them, the only bright stars in the Irish religious firmament were the friars, in particular the Franciscans who, having played a somewhat subsidiary role during the earlier centuries of Anglo-Norman domination, now began to come into their own. It was most noticeably they who encouraged the practice of religion among the people and kept up a high level of preaching. One of them, Maurice O'Fihely, who died in 1513, was known as *Flos Mundi* ('the flower of the world'), and had a reputation as a scholar which went far beyond the bounds of his native country. The friars can also take the credit for assembling translations of many continental religious literary works, though it has been suggested that these works of piety barely compensate for the inadequacies of other clergy.

The earlier friars' foundations in Ireland had mainly been in towns during the thirteenth century, but, after the Black Death had reduced their numbers considerably in 1348-50, they tended to concentrate largely in rural Ireland. They often opted for remote locations, as they drew their

LEFT Mendicant orders other than the Franciscans were active builders in Ireland during the late Middle Ages. The Dominicans, for instance, were assisted by Richard de Burgo in 1469 in the foundation of this friary idyllically located on a sea inlet at Burrishoole in County Mayo.

RIGHT A rare example of a medieval Irish church currently used by the Catholic Church is the Augustinian priory in Fethard, Co. Tipperary, founded by Walter de Mulcote around 1320. It was dissolved at the Reformation, but the friars returned in 1820 and restored the church as the focal point of their renewed foundation.

LEFT The White Church at Adare, in County Limerick, was the only Irish priory of the Trinitarian Canons and was founded around 1230 with a dedication to St James, though the church is largely fifteenth century in date. In 1811 the second Earl of Dunraven generously gave over their, by then, long-deserted church to the Catholic population of the village to serve as their parish church, and his successor extended and partially rebuilt it. To this day it still remains one of the few medieval churches still used in Ireland by the Catholic Church.

FAR LEFT Most thirteenth-century friaries in Ireland were founded in towns and, although it is now surrounded by green fields, Ardfert Franciscan friary in County Kerry was no exception, as it lay on the edge of what was once a sizeable medieval borough, now vanished. The friary was founded and built shortly after 1250, when it consisted of an arcaded nave and a long chancel to the east, with closely spaced lancet windows. The tower, unusually located at the western end, is a fifteenth-century addition, as was also the south transept at right-angles to the long-halled church.

strength from the scattered Gaelic population, and there the Franciscans became the church builders *par excellence* of fifteenth-century Ireland. Whereas the Franciscans were strongest in Munster, the Augustinians and Dominicans were more frequently found in Connacht.

In an effort to get back to their original strict observance of the vows of poverty, chastity and obedience, the friars introduced the Observantine Reform, the Augustinians starting at Banada in County Sligo in 1423, and the Franciscans at Quin ten years later. The regular, 'Third Order' Franciscans encouraged the laity – some of whom were actually attached to the community – to be involved in prayer, good works and the organization of the liturgy. Had it not been for this zealous renewal of fervour on the part of the friars, the numbers in monastic communities would have dwindled much further than they did, and it was the friars who kept alive the flame of faith. One report in a state paper of 1515 said:

> For there is no archbishop, no bishop, abbot nor prior, parson nor vicar, nor any other person of the Church, high or low, great or small, English or Irish, that is accustomed to preach the word of God, saving the poor friars beggars; and where the Word of God do cease there can be no grace, and without the special grace of God this land may never be reformed.

Another account which emanated a decade later from Ormond territory warned that 'if the King's grace do not seek for hasty remedy, there is likely to be no more Christianity here than in Turkey'.

That was a century when not a single Gaelic bishop was of legitimate birth, suggesting that the Church was certainly in need of reform – and what it got was the Protestant Reformation as introduced by Henry VIII's Church of England, instituted when he broke with Rome in 1534. Only two years later the English-born Archbishop of Dublin, George Browne, pressed through Parliament an Act of Supremacy, declaring that the king should be supreme head of the Church of Ireland, and another act to the effect that anyone who called the king a heretic would forfeit his life. A third stated that anyone who preached in favour of the pope's claim to be head of the Church would be outlawed and his goods confiscated. The Church of Ireland now became the official Church, but there was little enthusiasm for the changes within the Pale, and none at all outside it. The monasteries which took their orders from Rome were dissolved and their lands and possessions taken during the next five years.

The Dissolution of the Monasteries meant that the education they provided suffered heavily, and the buildings gradually decayed to become the roofless ruins we see dotting the countryside today. Others were virtually demolished to provide the gentry with stones for their new residences. The native Irish were horrified, too, when some of their most sacred relics, including the staff of St Patrick known as the *Bachall Íosa* and the wonder-working statue of Our Lady of Trim, were consigned to the flames in the late 1530s. The Observantine friars campaigned vigorously in Gaelic Ireland against the new tenets of the Reformed Church, and the reign of the Catholic Queen Mary (1553-8) gave some respite to the Catholics on both

sides of the Pale, but the spread of the Reformed Church under her successor Queen Elizabeth I (1558-1603) went hand in hand with her military conquest, which was completed in the first decade of the seventeenth century. By then almost all of the church buildings and land had been taken over, and the newly established Church continued to use most of the cathedrals and large parish churches. Support for the Catholic Church was mainly – but not exclusively – confined to the Gaelic areas of the country. The links which the Catholic Church kept up with Rome might have been expected to have introduced elements of the Renaissance into Ireland during the sixteenth century, but the rural nature of the Gaelic-speaking population may have been responsible for very little of its influence getting through to Ireland, except in the highest echelons of society.

HOLY CROSS ABBEY
Co. Tipperary

The abbey of Holy Cross, nestling close to the River Suir, is one of the few good examples of a Cistercian effort to revitalize the order's Irish churches in the fifteenth century, and the quality of its carved stonework makes it the outstanding Irish church building between the Black Death (1348-50) and the Dissolution of the Monasteries (1536-40).

It gets its name from a relic of the True Cross probably donated by Dónal

LEFT Holy Cross Abbey, which got its name from a relic of the True Cross that it still treasures, was first built in the late twelfth century, but contributions from pilgrims who came to venerate the holy relic enabled it to be almost entirely rebuilt to a high standard in the fifteenth century.

ABOVE A rosette carved in relief.

RIGHT The high quality of stone carving in Holy Cross Abbey is exemplified by the triple sedilia in the choir, decorated with the arms of England, Ormond and Fitzgerald.

Mór O'Brien, King of Thomond, who gave the abbey its charter in 1185/6. The relic is still venerated in the church today. Only small sections of the church – including the north arcade of the nave, parts of the south aisle and the monks' doorway leading from it to the cloister – survive from the original late twelfth- or early thirteenth-century foundation. The remainder of what we can see now dates from the fifteenth century, and its richness is the

LEFT One of Ireland's few late medieval frescoes is preserved in the north transept at Holy Cross and represents a hunting scene, the story behind which remains obscure.

RIGHT The unique open-arcaded monument that separates the two side chapels in the south transept of Holy Cross Abbey must surely have been where the monastery's relic of the True Cross was displayed for public veneration.

product of the alms of pilgrims coming to visit the relic of the True Cross. More importantly, the patronage afforded to the abbey by various members of the Butler family and in particular James, the White Earl, who was the English king's deputy in Ireland between 1405 and 1452, enabled the church to be built to a high standard in the years of the earl's beneficence.

The monastic layout is typically Cistercian, the church with square presbytery or choir at the east end, two chapels for each transept, a low tower at the crossing and a lean-to cloister arcade surrounded by the usual conventual buildings to the south. The presbytery has fine lierne vaulting, also found in the tower vault over the crossing as well as in the north transept. Other than this vaulting and the traceried east window, the outstanding feature of the presbytery is the triple sedilia in the south wall, bearing the arms of the English king and the Earls of Ormond in the spandrels. Dividing the two chapels in the south transept is a unique structure, consisting on each side of three arches with fluted columns rising from a low decorated wall, and with miniature vaulting covering the intervening space, which probably housed the relic of the True Cross. In the north transept is one of Ireland's few surviving Gothic frescoes, depicting a hunting scene. High up on the north-west crossing pier is the charming representation of an owl, a bird which keeps its eyes open at night – perhaps a hint to the monks to do the same when singing their office in the nocturnal darkness. It is only one of a number of interesting carvings which the perceptive eye can pick out in the church interior. The cloister arcade, with an elaborate array of cusped arches, was built presumably around 1450 by the abbot Dionysius O'Congail, whose name appears beneath a crucifix on a heraldic shield at one corner of the cloister. It was partially reconstructed in the 1980s, when the west range was also converted to modern use.

The abbey escaped dissolution in 1540 by turning itself into a secular college, but this came to an end when the former abbey and its property were granted to Thomas Butler, Earl of Ormond, appropriately it would seem, as it was the patronage of his ancestor which set the monastery on its road to greatness. After centuries of subsequent decline, the abbey buildings were vested in the Commissioners of Public Works in 1880 and, by special Act of Parliament in 1969, they were empowered to hand the buildings back again to the ecclesiastical authorities for use as a Catholic parish church. Dr Morris, Archbishop of Cashel and Emly, raised funds for the reconstruction of the church, which was suitably roofed by a team of local craftsmen under the supervision of Percy le Clerc. It was ceremoniously reconsecrated in 1975, when it regained its former splendour, though its simple grandeur has been somewhat dimmed in the intervening years with over-ornate furnishing.

THE FRANCISCANS

Together with the Dominicans, the Franciscans were the most important of the new mendicant orders which had arrived in Ireland during the thirteenth century. Their founder, St Francis of Assisi, who had received the wounds of Christ (stigmata), died in 1226, and at around the same time his friars came to Ireland from England making their first landfall at Youghal. They were doubtless Englishmen, and it is not surprising that their other early foundations in Ireland were in the Anglo-Norman towns and cities such as Dublin, Kildare, Downpatrick, Kilkenny, Waterford and Cork – an urban preference common to the mendicant orders throughout thirteenth-century Europe. Among these English- or French-speaking friars, language must obviously have played a role for some in the choice of their locations, but it apparently presented no barrier to others who ventured into the rural areas of Gaelic-speaking Ireland to places like Ennis. With time, this led to a dichotomy between the friars of English inclination and those who spoke Irish. The division came to a head at a provincial chapter in Cork in 1291, when discussion of the contents of a papal Bull, which 'are disastrous to the friars and turn gentle and mild men into fighters', led to a bloody fracas in which sixteen friars were killed. The upshot of this was that a papal Bull in 1312 deprived the Irish Franciscans of the right to elect the head of their own Irish Province – and in practice they were to be loyal subjects of the English king until 1469.

The Irish Province had, in fact, become independent by 1230, and the freedom which that had given them was reinforced by the arrival of the Bruce brothers from Scotland in the second decade of the fourteenth century, as a number of Irish friars identified themselves with their Scottish brethren as communal foes of England. The crisis was defused to the disadvantage of the Irish by a chapter held in Dublin in 1324, when it was ordered that friars from the suspect Irish houses were to be distributed among other – presumably less seditious – houses. The vivid image of the Kilkenny friar John Clyn writing his Annals until the plague forced the pen to fall from his lifeless hand brings home to us how disastrously the Black Death must have affected the friaries' congregations. But, on the credit side, it did defuse much of the 'two nation' mistrust between the friars. In the following century they built up a whole new energy which must have brought them into considerable conflict not only with the episcopal hierarchy but also with the local parish clergy, whose livelihood they were filching. Nevertheless, the struggle between the Gaelic and Anglo-Norman cultures as well as the effect of the Black Death must have been taking their toll in the strictness with which the rule of the order was being obeyed.

In the early decades of the fifteenth century the new Observantine

Moyne Friary in County Mayo typifies the best of Irish Franciscan architecture of the fifteenth century – a long, halled church with switch-line tracery windows, a doorway at the western end and an added tall, slender tower dominating both the church and the adjoining domestic buildings.

movement – encouraging the friars to return to the original ideas and ideals of their founder – put down its first Irish Franciscan roots with the foundation of Quin in 1433. Within forty years the Observants received permission to elect their own Vicar Provincial, who would govern their Observantine houses, though this doubtless led to further jealousies between the original Conventual friars and the reformed Observantines, who were growing in strength and popularity all the time. With this freedom and independence from England, the number of Observantine friars swelled particularly in the Gaelic-speaking western half of Ireland and, where English power was gradually pushed back eastwards, the Observantine friars of whichever order tended to follow.

The friars' objective of preaching was severely hampered by Henry VIII's Dissolution of the Monasteries in 1536-40, which affected friaries as well. However, one of the Franciscan strengths was that they held on to their own houses and, even when expelled from their friaries, they are frequently reported as having come back again well into the seventeenth century. These difficult conditions brought out the best in the Irish Franciscans, who in the first half of the seventeenth century produced important scholars without whose efforts our knowledge of the country's past would be very much the poorer – men like John Colgan, Luke Wadding and the friars who are generally known as the Four Masters, the writers of those great Annals of ancient Ireland (1632-36) which bear their names.

The Irish Gaelic-speaking population, being largely rural, was less affected by the Black Death of 1348-50 and was able to recover more easily from it than the largely urbanized Anglo-Norman colonies. The poems of Gearóid Iarla, the translations into early modern Irish of continental religious and philosophical tracts, as well as the activity of native families in erecting large castles like Blarney and Bunratty, were all symbols of a Gaelic revival from the late fourteenth century onwards which was to be further epitomized early in the following century by the sudden rise of innovative friary architecture. One early manifestation of the new Franciscan style is Askeaton, Co. Limerick (*c.*1420), located not surprisingly in the lands of the successors of Gerald the poet (Gearóid Iarla). Quin follows in 1433 as the first of the Observantine houses, and their influence no doubt speeded up the construction of many other fine friaries in the second half of the century, of which Muckross, Adare and Ross Errilly are examples illustrated in the following pages.

Ennis is one of the few reasonably well-preserved specimens of the architecture of the early Franciscans in Ireland, but it is their fifteenth-century houses which must be singled out as the representatives of the finest Franciscan contribution to Irish architecture. Indeed, with the exception of monasteries such as Holy Cross in the fifteenth century, the Franciscans can be said to have taken over from the Cistercians of the earlier period as the builders of the best Irish ecclesiastical architecture of the later Gothic period, though some of the friaries of the other mendicant orders also shine through. In taking the Franciscans' foundations as the norm, Professor E.C. Rae was able to claim that 'as perfected in the fifteenth century, the whole friary (church and monastic buildings) shares with western work of Transitional style the honour of being probably Ireland's most significant contribution to the history of European ecclesiastical architecture of the Gothic period'.

The pattern of these Franciscan buildings is something peculiarly Irish, though they probably derived ideas from contemporary English houses now vanished and, with travel to and from the continent having been more common than we might think, their architects must have been cognizant of developments in friary architecture in Italy, France and Germany as well. Like the Dominicans, the Franciscans were mendicant preachers, and their long hall churches reflect the importance they attached to giving sermons to the public. These were uttered from pulpits facing the nave and placed next to the towers which divide it from the choir, where the friars performed their own liturgies, largely unseen by the lay faithful. These very characteristic towers were generally slender in shape, often only little more than half the breadth of the church where they rose above the roof, their broader supports unseen from outside. Their vertical emphasis was usually tempered by a number of horizontal string courses distributed throughout their height, and stepped battlements gave added interest to the top of their skyline silhouette. It should be pointed out, however, that other orders borrowed the scheme, as exemplified by the Dominicans at Kilmallock (p. 178), and even Clonfert Cathedral (p. 131) adopted the idea too. Conversely, however, the Franciscans were not averse to using the squat, lower towers of the Cistercians, as at Muckross. In the case of the foundations of earlier centuries, the towers we see today were later additions of the fifteenth and possibly even of the sixteenth century.

Another characteristic feature of the Franciscan friaries is the presence of a cloister, usually placed north of the church. Whereas most of the earlier monasteries had lean-to cloister arcades, the fifteenth-century Franciscan friaries had cloister walks on the ground floor with domestic buildings above them, which gave greater width to the first-floor rooms. The twin-shafted piers of the cloister arcades occasionally offered the opportunity for sculptural embellishment, usually involving the figure of the founding father, St Francis. The well-preserved windows in the churches, as well as in the transepts and chapels attached to them, offer an interesting variety of traceried designs and contribute to the pleasure of viewing these friaries, many of which still stand in open countryside, where they fitted well into the rural society of late medieval Gaelic Ireland.

ENNIS FRIARY
Co. Clare

Ennis friary, located near the River Fergus and close to the vanished palace of the Kings of Thomond at Clonroad, is alleged to have been founded by Donnchad Cairbreach O'Brien, who died in 1242. But it is more likely that the earliest of the surviving buildings were erected more towards the close of the century by Torlough O'Brien who, before he died in 1306, had filled the friary 'with monks, and . . . sweet bells, crucifixes and a good library, embroidery, veils and cowls'. He also filled the east window with coloured glass 'painted with blue'. Composed of three central lancets, flanked on each side by a further window separated by a wall pier, this east window – now sadly minus its glass – is one of the joys of the choir, which was among the first parts of the church to have been completed, presumably by Torlough. The unusual vaulted room of uncertain use to the north of the choir is known to have been erected shortly afterwards by the blind Maccon Macnamara. The entire nave, however, dates from later in the fifteenth century, when the tower and south transept were probably also erected, though the cloister may be somewhat earlier. Ennis is notable, among other things, for the quality of its tomb-sculpture (p. 220).

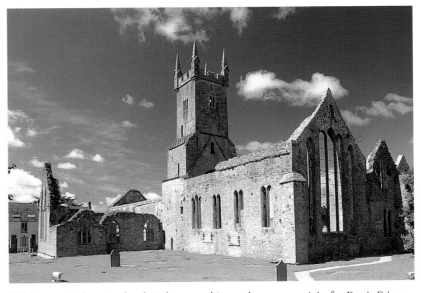

Tall lancet windows in the choir betray a thirteenth-century origin for Ennis Friary, a good example of early Franciscan architecture in Ireland. The transept on the left is a fifteenth-century addition, as was the tower, which had pinnacles added in the nineteenth century.

QUIN FRIARY
Co. Clare

There is something very appropriate about the fact that the Franciscan Friary built at Quin in 1433 should be sited on the foundations of a Norman de Clare castle of *c.*1280, for it rises symbolically like a phoenix from the ashes of Norman Ireland and heralds the revival of Irish church architecture after the devastating effects of the Black Death almost a century before. It is significant, too, that this revival came not in the old Norman towns but in the rural areas of the western half of Ireland where the Franciscans had been warmly welcomed. Founded for the Observantines by Maccon Macnamara, little is known of the friary's history until its suppression at the Reformation. The friars reoccupied the buildings intermittently throughout the seventeenth century, when a number of them are known to have been put to death by Cromwell's forces.

The finely moulded west doorway giving access to the church is located directly beside one of the rounded corner towers of the Norman castle, and the roughly square plan of the friary derives its shape from that of the castle, whose walls it uses for much of its foundations. The quality of both the stone and the workmanship has ensured the preservation of the friary buildings. The church has the long, hall shape typical of the Franciscans, and off it opens a transept to the south, which still preserves its medieval stone altars, as do also the nave and choir. The arcade of the cloister is particularly well preserved, with richly moulded dumbbell piers, and having what may be a chapter room on the first floor. The slender fifteenth-century tower located almost in the middle of the church can be climbed to the top, where there is a fine view of how the friary sits on the foundations of the de Clare Castle.

RIGHT Cloisters are among the most attractive features of the Irish Franciscan friaries of the later Middle Ages. As here at Quin, domestic quarters on the first floor gained more space by being built over the attractive cloister arcades on the ground floor, which were supported by buttresses.

BELOW The Franciscan Friary at Quin in County Clare was the first Irish house specifically founded for the Observantine friars, who strove for a return to the original spirit of the rule of their founder, Saint Francis. It also symbolizes the rebirth of Gaelic Ireland after the Black Death of 1348-50, as it rises phoenix-like from the rubble of a Norman castle upon whose foundations the friary was built in 1433.

MUCKROSS FRIARY
Killarney, Co. Kerry

Muckross is one of the best known of the Irish Franciscan friaries, beautifully situated as it is near the Lakes of Killarney in the Bourn-Vincent National Park. From a distance, it could be taken for a Cistercian foundation because of its squat tower, but it was founded for the Franciscans probably around 1440 by Donal MacCarthy, who restored it in the year of his death, 1468. A papal Bull of the same year granted an indulgence for its completion, which probably did not have to wait for long. Except for its missing roof, the friary is in a remarkably good state of preservation. The tower is vaulted above the arch which constricts the passage between nave and choir, both of which are cluttered with many modern tombs. Leading off the nave is a south transept which, like the nave and choir, is enlivened by a considerable variety of window shapes. But the most attractive part of the friary is the cloister, which, as was the custom with the Franciscans, has a cloister-walk with dumb-bell piers and rooms above – the whole enclosing a romantic old yew tree. After the suppression around 1540, the friars occupied the friary again, and two of them were tortured and stoned to death within its walls in 1586. The buildings were restored in 1602 but apparently abandoned again for the last time shortly afterwards.

ABOVE Muckross Friary near the Lakes of Killarney has a much stouter and more Cistercian-style tower than most Irish Franciscan friaries of the fifteenth century.

RIGHT The golfers in Adare must marvel at the nobility of the ruined fifteenth-century Franciscan friary, which stands beside their fourteenth green.

RIGHT AND BELOW The numerous gables of Ross Errilly in County Galway are like the crest of a crown, which this extensive friary certainly is in the canon of fifteenth-century Franciscan architecture in Ireland. Ross is not only picturesque, it is also built in high-quality masonry, as can be seen in the well-preserved cloister arcade, dating like the rest of the building from late in the fifteenth century.

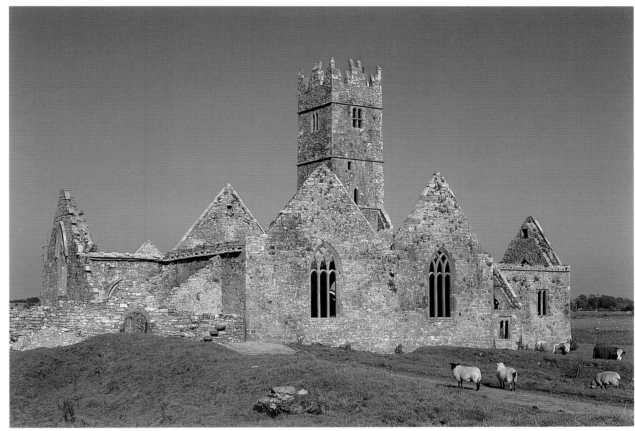

ADARE FRIARY
Co. Limerick

During the last century successive Earls of Dunraven made Adare into one of the prettiest villages in Ireland, blending old and new into a harmonious mix. Their success was assured because of the wonderful material they had to work on, for scattered in and around the village is one of the country's finest collections of medieval buildings, both religious and secular. Two of the friaries were renovated to become parish churches; a third, still roofless, is more romantic, if less utilitarian, standing in parkland which is now a golf course. Dedicated to St Michael the Archangel, the friary was Observantine from its start in 1464. In Thomas Fitzgerald, Earl of Kildare, and his wife Johanna, a daughter of the Earl of Desmond, it had patrons from the highest echelons of society, who donated the church, one wing of the cloister and glass for the windows. This generosity must have prompted others to do the same, for we have lists of donors and what they paid for, such as Margaret Fitzgibbon, wife of the poet Cú-Uladh O'Daly, who built a large chapel; Johanna's brother, who built a small chapel; and Marianus O'Hickey, who, having contributed towards a part of the refectory and wooden choir stalls, later came to enjoy them himself when he entered the community. Thanks to this host of benefactors, the friary was largely completed within a decade or two – the church with large south transepts accompanied by three small chapels, and the cloister with details on each side varying slightly, reflecting perhaps the individual whims of the benefactors who contributed a side apiece. The friary was suppressed in 1539-40.

ROSS ERRILLY FRIARY
Co. Galway

The friary of Ross Errilly, or Ross to give it its more colloquial name, is the largest and best preserved of all the Franciscan houses of Ireland. Some sources give a foundation date of 1351, but others suggest that it was founded some time before 1470 for the friars of the strict observance. In the seventeenth century the great historian Sir James Ware was probably closest to the truth in saying that the friary was built in 1498 by the otherwise obscure Gannard family. Picturesquely sited beside the Black River which separates Galway from Mayo, it presents an integrated design, suggesting that most of it was built all at one time. The church is unusual for its double transept, with later chapels opening off it. The tower standing midway along the church has an unusually low arch, and above this is another arch which looks towards the nave and probably housed a crucifix originally. The domestic buildings are particularly extensive, because north of the normal cloister there is another square courtyard, which is only slightly smaller. Opening off its north-western corner is a kitchen with its own built-in water- or fish-tank. Beside the choir, but not accessible from it, is a three-storey tower known locally as 'Burke's Castle', which was probably a later addition. The amount of space available in the domestic buildings implies a Franciscan community of considerable size here around 1500, but it is no longer possible to establish how the individual rooms were used. After the friary was suppressed in 1540, the friars were expelled a total of seven times, but they always returned – except in 1753, after which they returned no more.

CREEVELEA FRIARY
Co. Leitrim

Situated on the outskirts of Dromahaire village, Creevelea was one of the last Franciscan houses to be founded in Ireland before the Reformation hammer fell. Its benefactors were the local O'Rourke chieftain, Eoghan, and his wife Margaret, daughter of Conor O'Brien – both of whom were later interred there. Created for the Observantine Franciscans in 1508 and consecrated three years later, it was gutted by fire in 1536. Although the friary was presumably suppressed around 1540, the friars managed to stay on until 1598, and returned on at least three subsequent occasions, only to have to leave again some time later.

The buildings conform to the usual Franciscan plan with a church consisting of nave and choir, to which a transept was attached, and the cloister garth placed to the north of the church. The cloister, irregular in shape, bears the most unusual and attractive features in the friary – small carvings of St Francis on one of the pillars near the centre of the north side. One shows the order's founder with cord and stigmata, and another St Francis preaching in a pulpit to the birds in a tree beside him – whose language he is said to have understood.

SLANE FRIARY
Co. Meath

The Hill of Slane, it is alleged, was where St Patrick lit the Paschal Fire at Easter in the year 433, in defiance of Loegaire, King of Tara. Thereby he symbolically introduced the light of Christianity to Ireland in what subsequently transpired to be a successful contest with the dark powers of paganism. It matters little how reliable this ancient tradition is; what is significant is that it has established a special niche in the history of Ireland for this dominant hill which provides a view across to Tara, seat of the High Kings of Ireland, as well as a wonderful panorama over the landscape north and south of the River Boyne flowing past its foot. With the exception of two stones of an Early Christian reliquary shrine in the churchyard, the earliest remains surviving on the hill are those of a Norman motte, dating from shortly before 1200. What are much more obvious from both land and air are, however, the tower and church of a friary of the Third Order of Franciscans, started by the Fleming family, Lords of Slane. Christopher Fleming, who founded it in 1512, also instituted in the same year a college for four priests, four clerics and four choristers, the buildings of which now stand to the north of the church and bear a carving of the quartered arms of France and England.

ABOVE Creevelea in County Leitrim pays homage to the order's founder in illustrating St Francis twice on its cloister arcade. The carving seen here clearly demonstrates the stigmata wound in his side.

RIGHT Wall-builders made an irregular ring around the cemetery enclosing the Franciscan friary on the Hill of Slane and its dominant tower at the western end, but the college founded in the same year – 1512 – is left free to stand on its own to the north of the friary.

MURRISK FRIARY
Co. Mayo

It was apparently necessary to found the friary at Murrisk in 1456 because 'the inhabitants of those parts have not hitherto been instructed in the faith', which would not have pleased poor St Patrick who had done his best to christianize the Irish a thousand years before. In fact, tradition says (rightly or wrongly) that the national apostle fasted for forty days and nights on top of Cruachan Aigle, or Croagh Patrick, which rises right beside Murrisk, in order to plead the cause of the Irish to the Almighty above. In the later Middle Ages pilgrims started their climb to the summit from the 'abbey' of Murrisk, which preserved the

Since its foundation more than five hundred years ago, Murrisk Friary on the shores of Clew Bay in County Mayo has always been the starting point for the pilgrimage to Croagh Patrick, in whose lee it lies.

saint's tooth and his 'Black Bell' among its relics. It was the O'Malleys who encouraged the Augustinian hermits (or 'Austin friars') to found Murrisk from Banada in the neighbouring county of Sligo, and it was the transmission of the more rigorous Observant spirit to foundations like Murrisk that ensured the order's survival in Ireland.

The remaining friary is L-shaped, consisting of a church and, at right angles to it, two-storey claustral buildings, which include a chapter room and a sacristy on the ground floor. These latter may have been intended as one side of a quadrangular cloister but there is no sign of the other sides ever having been built, probably due to lack of funds. The church is long and narrow, and originally had a tower over the west end, which fell many centuries ago, leaving merely some traces of the vaulting. The friary's most unusual feature is the embattled parapet which sits on top of the western end of the south wall.

While the friary was probably closed at the Dissolution around 1540, the friars must have clung on till driven out in 1578. But they had returned by 1603, and gifts of chalices – in 1635, 1648 and 1724 respectively – show the foundation to have continued, its last prior being recorded in 1795-9. One of the community, who had been ordered by the

prior to leave his beloved Murrisk some time around 1740, was so displeased that he wrote a poem in Gaelic in protest and praise, which was later set to music and became a famous folk song known as 'The Abbey of Murrisk'. A part of it written down by the celebrated folk-song collector, Edward Bunting, runs as follows:

Céud slán don teach úd ann a mbin uair
Ar mo thráthuibh mhór fhada láimh leis a ccruaich
Bheadh na ceólta bin ó fhlaithios gabháil chuguin a mias
Agas na sléibhte cur meala ó dheas's ó thuaigh.

(A thousand farewells to the Abbey where they read
The long matins and hours by the side of the Cruach,
Where the sweetest music sounds from heaven coming down,
And the mountains yield honey from the South and the North.)

CRAFTSMANSHIP

In architecture the transition from Romanesque to Gothic can be seen to bring in a whole new wave of ideas strongly influenced by the West of England, and it was not until the advent of friary architecture early in the fifteenth century that a characteristically Irish style re-emerges as part of the Gaelic revival. We can glimpse something of the same tendency occurring in the world of Irish craftsmanship in the later Middle Ages, but to paint even the broad brush strokes of development may not present a true picture because it is based on such a small quantity of surviving material – doubtless only a fraction of what once existed.

Stained glass, for instance, is only preserved in tiny fragments, and frescoes or line-paintings only survive in a few instances – Cormac's Chapel, Abbeyknockmoy, Clare Island, Holy Cross and Jerpoint (all, but the first, Cistercian) – but even they are far from complete and lack much of their ancient freshness. The Synod of Cashel in 1453 prescribed that each parish church should possess three statues – a crucifix, the Virgin and one of the local saint to whom the church was dedicated. But how many statues resulting from the synod have survived? Little more than a handful, one may surmise, though the large wooden statues from Fethard (now in the National Museum) do give us an inkling of what a group of parish statues would have looked like. These are just competent works of sculpture, but the misericords in Limerick Cathedral demonstrate what high standards of woodwork could be achieved – and only make us wince at how much Irish religious art must have been destroyed at the time of the Reformation.

In Gaelic Ireland a reduction in quality and quantity is certainly noticeable in the aftermath of the Norman invasion, as more money was poured into war than art, and it is not until after the Black Death that a revival of Irish craftsmanship began to manifest itself. It first emerges in metalwork, where attention was focused on repairs made to embellish reliquary shrines many centuries old. New and better-quality work is evident in the O'Dea crozier and mitre of 1418 and the Ballymacasey cross of 1479, objects that stand in a pan-European tradition and show Ireland conforming to an international norm rather than trying to reinvent its own national identity.

The Charter of the City of Waterford of *c.*1381 shows the Anglo-Norman population emulating the standards of manuscript painting in England, whereas the Irish did try to revive something of the ornamental spirit of the earlier codices, without ever reaching their skilled standards.

In contrast to the relative fragility of wood and fresco-painting, which can be so ephemeral, and metalwork and manuscripts, which can be so easily melted down or destroyed, stone is really the only permanent material that can provide anything approaching a more complete picture in the history of at least one branch of Irish medieval craftsmanship. The end of the 'School of the West' around 1230, combined with the effects of the Norman invasion, caused a long interruption in the Gaelic mason's craft, but in the eastern part of the country the stone-carving tradition introduced by the early Norman invaders was continued, and even at times enriched, with the import of ready-made sculpture from England. But the Black Death delivered it a mortal blow, from which it never recovered.

The revival of stone sculpture started in a small way in the western half of Ireland through representations of St Francis in the cloisters of some of his orders' friaries, perhaps as early as the first third of the fifteenth century. Just before the middle of the century, some of the aristocratic families of the Pale erected free-standing table-shaped, or *mensa*, tombs to their dead. In the third quarter of the century the emphasis moved to the midlands of Ireland, where fine doorways were carved with saints and fabulous animals, as at Clonmacnoise. Vibrant schools of sculpture developed too in the Gaelic-speaking areas of the west of Ireland, as witnessed by the tomb-sculpture at Ennis and Strade. The south-east of Ireland jumped to the fore in the late fifteenth and early sixteenth century with a fine series of tombs bearing effigies supported by 'weepers', often in the form of apostles and other saints. Perhaps the earliest of these is the James Rice tomb of 1482 in Waterford Cathedral, showing the deceased as a decaying cadaver. By the early sixteenth century, two sculptural workshops emerged in Kilkenny – one comprising the O'Tunney family, and the other an anonymous 'school' working for the Butler Earls of Ormond. Both concentrated on producing fine effigies of knights and their ladies, borne by attractive if slightly squat weeper figures. Examples of the work of both teams can be seen to advantage in St Canice's Cathedral in Kilkenny, though their influence also extended to the neighbouring county of Tipperary.

Also in the late fifteenth and early sixteenth century, a number of baptismal fonts bear testimony to the continuing liveliness of the sculptural tradition in County Meath, as seen in the fine example (now white-

LEFT This carving of St Francis at Ennis Friary bearing the signs of his stigmata is a reminder of the contribution made by the Franciscan friaries to the revival of the stonemason's craft in the west of Ireland during the fifteenth century.

BELOW Later alterations to the cathedral at Clonmacnoise included the addition around 1459 of a beautifully carved Gothic doorway in the north wall. Weird and wonderful products of the medieval bestiary can be found lurking among the foliage around the doorway – a splendid example of the late medieval, Irish stonemason's craft — while above its arch stand the figures of Saints Francis, Patrick and Dominic.

Despite a thick coating of whitewash, the carving on the fifteenth-century baptismal font in the parish church at Curraha, Co. Meath, shines through as being of high quality. The font was moved there from Crickstown in the same county around 1904 and, in addition to the apostles seen here, it bears representations of the Annunciation and the Crucifixion.

washed) in Curraha Church and the slightly more naive example in Clonard. The zenith of late medieval carving comes with the County Kildare effigy of Bishop Walter Wellesley of 1539, now in Kildare Cathedral, which displays incipient Renaissance influence, and, as it has no parallels or antecedents in Ireland, the suspicion must arise that its sculptor may have been imported. Being a period of both secular and religious warfare, the later sixteenth century reflects a gradual decline in quality, though the Johnstown Crucifixion at least shows that a personal and idiosyncratic style could still produce surprises.

THE O'DEA MITRE AND CROZIER
Limerick

Fifteenth-century Limerick was a town with a fine artistic tradition in various media – stone, wood and metalwork, as well as jewellery. Other cities doubtless had equally talented craftsmen, but Limerick was fortunate in that its craftwork survived the Reformation, whereas so much else disappeared in flames ardently fanned by religious fervour. Together with the wooden misericords, Limerick's unique survivals are a mitre and crozier, which, as John Hunt pointed out, are the only medieval Irish art treasures remaining in their ancient custody (the Bishop of Limerick), and 'the most valued and important objects of Irish metalwork which have come down to

us from the later middle ages'. Both were commissioned by the same prelate, Cornelius O'Dea, in 1418. He was a member of a County Clare family and became Bishop of Limerick in 1400 (though not before he had apparently married and had offspring). He resigned his bishopric in 1425, when he retired to his native heath at Dysert O'Dea, but he must have been buried in St Mary's Cathedral in Limerick, as Thomas Dineley records having seen his tombstone there in 1681.

The mitre consists of silver-gilt plates attached to a leathern backing, and decorated with jewels and pearls. One inscription states that the mitre was made by Thomas O Carryd, a craftsman about whom we otherwise know nothing, and another stating that it was made for Cornelius O'Dea. At the base of the central orphrey there are figures in two niches, one showing a bishop – presumably none other than Cornelius himself – offering a gift to the Virgin and Child in the other niche. The crozier consists of two separate parts, the staff and the decorated head, with a combined height of 6 feet 6 inches (2m). At the bottom of the head is an inscription stating that 'Conor O'Dea, Bishop of Limerick had me made in the year of Our Lord 1418, in the 18th year of his consecration'. Somewhat above this comes a tower with two superimposed rows of figures. Those in the lower row are larger, placed in niches with crocketed and pinnacled canopies, and represent the Trinity, the Virgin and Child, Saints Peter and Paul, St Munchin (patron of the diocese) and St Patrick. The upper row, with smaller figures,

Bishop Cornelius O'Dea's mitre and crozier are outstanding works of art in any context, the mitre being the only full example of its period to survive anywhere in Britain or Ireland. It seems like a miracle that they have been preserved so intact since they were first created in 1418.

shows St John the Evangelist, St Margaret of Antioch, St Catherine of Alexandria, St Barbara, St Brigid of Kildare and St Bridget of Sweden. The whole is topped by a charming representation of the Annunciation.

MISERICORDS IN ST MARY'S CATHEDRAL
Limerick

St Mary's Cathedral, Limerick, founded by Dónal Mór O'Brien in the later twelfth century, still retains elements of the original structure, as in the west doorway. But it has undergone many alterations and additions in the meantime, including the creation of the wooden misericords both in the choir and nave – the only ones of their kind surviving in Ireland. In earlier times the clergy had to stand for long periods during the performance of the liturgy, something which caused considerable discomfort, particularly to the older clerics. Their choir-stools, however, were provided with 'tip-up' seats on which they were permitted to rest, the name for these supports being misericord, from the Latin word for 'mercy' – which, under the circumstances, was more than just a gift from God. In their upright position, the vertical face of the misericords frequently displayed carvings which could puzzle, enlighten or distract, for many of the sculpted subjects were more allegorical than obvious – symbols which require contemplation for their meaning to be revealed.

Between leaved stems which fall from either side of the seat of the Limerick misericords are numerous animals taken from the medieval bestiary – fantastic creatures imbued with certain characteristics, both good and bad. They include the amphisbaena, which has two heads so that it can move forwards or backwards with equal ease, and the manticora with a human face, body of a lion, wing of an eagle and the tail of a scorpion. Another was the griffin, sometimes interpreted as Christ because its leonine body was taken to embody Christ as King of the Earth, and the eagle head to show him as Lord of the Skies. A more natural lion is seen to overcome a wyvern, symbolizing the victory of good over evil. An eagle appears by itself, and other 'normal'

animals add further to the menagerie – the swan, recalling martyrs because it is said to sing with its dying breath, and a boar, of less certain significance. An angel may have helped to raise devotional thoughts heavenwards, while two men are shown wearing 'chaperons' – wind-blown hats in the style of the later fifteenth century, to which period the misericords probably belong. The quality of carvings such as the angel, the swan and the griffin are particularly fine, and Edwin C. Rae pointed out that while the foliage flanking the main motifs is characteristically British, 'the fine linear patterns on the surfaces and the almost metallic effect are fully in tune with Irish ideals'.

TOMB-SCULPTURE IN ENNIS FRIARY
Co. Clare

The tomb erected around 1843 by the Creagh family against the north wall of the chancel of Ennis friary includes a number of fifteenth-century Passion scenes and individual figures, which may once have formed part of the tomb of More Ní Bhriain, the wife of Terence MacMahon. The details of the biblical carvings reveal that they were copied from Nottingham alabaster tables of the kind produced between 1420 and 1460. These were often assembled in groups to form an altar reredos, and exported to many parts of Europe, including France, the eastern Baltic and as far away as Iceland, but also Ireland, where a handful have survived, though not those which acted as the model for the Ennis carvings.

The sculptures in the main front of the tomb are in two registers, the upper one containing figures of Christ and his twelve apostles. The lower register consists of three separate panels, that on the left illustrating the Flagellation of Christ; in the centre is the Crucifixion and on the right the Entombment of Christ, with figures of Joseph standing beside the head of Christ and Nicodemus at his feet, as well as Mary Magdalen kneeling with the pot of ointment. Around the corner, on the western end, are an archbishop and the Betrayal of Christ, while the eastern end contains the Resurrection and a female figure possibly representing More Ní Bhriain, the founder of the original tomb.

St Mary's Protestant cathedral in Limerick is fortunate in preserving the only surviving medieval Irish wooden misericords, which are a *tour-de-force* of the woodcarver's craft.

RIGHT AND BELOW RIGHT Copied from Nottingham alabaster tables of around 1460, these carved panels show the Betrayal and Resurrection of Christ, and now decorate a tomb of 1843 in the north wall of Ennis Friary. This was precisely where the Easter Sepulchre was located in medieval churches, sculpted in wood or stone with representations of the Death, Burial and Resurrection of Christ, and the presence of these scenes among the associated carvings surviving in Ennis could suggest that they may have formed an elaborate Easter Sepulchre if the panels did not, as is usually presumed, form part of the tomb of a lady named More Ní Bhriain, possibly seen on the right of the Resurrection panel.

Imaginative style and choice of subject
characterize the later fifteenth-century
carvings at Strade Friary in County
Mayo, where the figure groupings are
unique in Ireland.

figures into separate niches, but has them forming a continuous panel. The figure on the left, seemingly pulling off a hood, may represent the unknown founder of the tomb, as he kneels in front of an archbishop, followed by St Peter and his keys and St Paul with a sword. It has been suggested that the whole composition illustrates pilgrimages undertaken by the donor: the Magi, whose shrine is in Cologne; the archbishop perhaps representing Thomas Becket murdered in Canterbury; and St Peter and St Paul symbolizing Rome.

TOMBS IN ST CANICE'S CATHEDRAL
Kilkenny

Since it was constructed in the thirteenth century, St Canice's Cathedral (p. 156) has been the burial place of many prominent personages, of whom Bishop de Ledrede (p. 150) was only one. It can also claim to have the best representative collection of Irish tomb-sculpture dating from the fifteenth and sixteenth centuries, as the city had two very active stone-masons' workshops operating there during this period. One of these was

Carved by craftsmen of an anonymous workshop active in Kilkenny during the sixteenth century, the armoured effigy of the slender eighth Earl of Ormond (d.1539) and the more voluminously robed figure of his wife Margaret (d.1542) rest in peace in the south transept of St Canice's Cathedral in the town.

SCULPTURES AT STRADE FRIARY
Co. Mayo

The friary at Strade was originally founded for the Franciscans by one of the MacJordan sept in the early thirteenth century, but it was transferred to the Dominicans in 1252. The chancel of the church dates from the period of foundation, but it contains fifteenth-century carving which is among the most unusual and lively to be found in the west of Ireland in the later Gothic period. Unlike some of the more aristocratic tomb-monuments in the east of Ireland which were free-standing, the west of Ireland inserted the tombs in church walls and provided a carved tomb-front surmounted by an elaborately decorated canopy. The Strade monument belongs to the latter category, but lack of any inscription prevents us from knowing who erected it. The main focus of attention is the imaginatively selected figures on the tomb-front, which are spread over two separate stones. The left-hand one has four figures, each standing in its own niche. Three of these represent the Magi from the east – Caspar, Melchior and Balthasar – bearing their gifts of gold, frankincense and myrrh, while the fourth niche is occupied by Christ, with his wounded hands raised and with the upper part of his garment laid open to reveal his pierced side. In contrast, the right-hand stone does not divide the

associated with the O'Tunney family, whose members sometimes signed their names on monuments they had carved; the other was a more anonymous workshop, which was probably in the employ of the Earl of Ormond, and used a slightly different style to produce much the same kind of memorial – a box tomb with effigy on top, supported by 'weepers' (usually apostle figures), Crucifixion scenes and armorial bearings.

The Butler Earls of Ormond used St Canice's practically as a family vault after they had acquired Kilkenny Castle (p. 144) in 1391/2, and it is their effigies in the south transept which are among the most striking. Piers Butler, the eighth earl, lies beside his long-robed wife Margaret, both portrayed in the prime of life, suggesting that the double effigy – though not the inscription – may have been prepared long before his death in 1539. His successor, James, the ninth earl, is normally taken to be the subject of the adjacent effigy, this time unaccompanied. Common to both is not only the Ormond workshop which produced them, but also the sad fact that the weepers and other sculptured stones now supporting them did not necessarily do so originally. The Cromwellians apparently wrought havoc among the monuments in the cathedral and what we see today is the result of efforts to present the tombs in the best way possible, with whatever stones survived intact from the blows of the iconoclasts' hammers. This helps to explain why the naively attractive Crucifixion supporting the south side of the double effigy is not by the Ormond workshop, but carved by one of the O'Tunneys. By contrast, the 'weepers' – apostle figures – supporting the side of the single effigy are by the same Ormond workshop which carved the armed figure of the presumed Butler earl above it.

CARVINGS AT KILCOOLEY ABBEY
Co. Tipperary

Kilcooley was a Cistercian monastery near Urlingford which owed its foundation to Dónal Mór O'Brien, King of Thomond, in 1184 – being a daughter-house of Jerpoint. Like Holy Cross Abbey in the same county, it was one of the few Cistercian churches which underwent considerable rebuilding in the fifteenth century. The Butler family must have contributed generously to the building fund, as one of their number was probably buried in the chancel, where his tomb-effigy now occupies a niche on the gospel side, though this was not its original position. He was Pierce fitz Oge Butler, who died in c.1526, and the effigy shows all the intricate detail of his plate armour, covered at the shoulders with a pisane, but with his face sadly damaged. The inscription states that it was carved by Rory O'Tunney, one of a family of sculptors who were responsible for much tomb-sculpture in the area in and around Kilkenny during the sixteenth century, and this is his earliest signed work. The tomb-supports, though not signed, are also a product of his workshop, as the apostle figures show the characteristics of the O'Tunneys' cap-like hair-do, detailed beards and garments, which fall in folds directly to the ground, as well as crisp foliage in the spandrels above the figures.

As they stand, these 'weeper' figures occupy two separate stones. One, with seven apostles, is likely to have formed the long side of the tomb as originally installed, the other with three figures probably having acted as

LEFT The apostle figures now acting as the tomb-front for the effigy of Pierce fitz Oge Butler (d.c.1526) in the Cistercian abbey of Kilcooley, Co. Tipperary, show that the Kilkenny-based O'Tunney workshop was active outside its own county.

RIGHT The alluring mermaid with her comb and mirror being ogled at by a well-fed fish beside the sacristy door in the Cistercian abbey of Kilcooley may well have been intended as a visual warning to the monks not to nibble at the sins of the flesh.

the narrow foot-end of the tomb, showing that it was originally free-standing. Reading from left to right, the saints identified by their names above, are as follows:

1. Peter with two keys
2. Andrew with saltire cross
3. James Major with wallet and scallop shell
4. John the Baptist, clean-shaven, with chalice and dove
5. Thomas holding a spear
6. James Minor with saw
7. Philip bearing a cloth with five loaves
8. Bartholomew with book and flesher's knife
9. Simon with a sparth
10. Thaddeus holding a weapon with scythe-like blade – normally the attribute of St Matthew, which this figure should represent.

Kilcooley has another, more remarkable, complex of carvings which – after the Jerpoint cloisters (pp. 164-7) – represents the most ambitious sculptural project undertaken by the Irish Cistercians in the later Middle Ages. This is the screen surrounding the door leading from the south transept into the sacristy, with a seemingly disjointed series of panels, well-carved in limestone, randomly distributed across its surface. In addition to the Ormond coat of arms, the subjects represented are a Crucifixion, a bishop or abbot beneath an angel and a pelican piercing its breast (symbol of the church feeding its flock), St Christopher bearing the Christ Child and – unexpected in such company – a mermaid.

EFFIGY OF BISHOP WELLESLEY
Kildare Cathedral

Probably the finest sixteenth-century effigy surviving in Ireland is that of Walter Wellesley, Bishop of Kildare from 1529 until his death ten years later. His family had held land in the county from the thirteenth century and, as a supporter of the English population, he had gone to Oxford, where he obtained a degree in Canon Law in the early years of the sixteenth century. He later became 'Commendatory Prior' of the Augustinian house of Greatconnell near Newbridge, a post he held concurrently with his bishopric. It was at Greatconnell that he was buried, but in 1971 his effigy was transferred for safety to St Brigid's Cathedral in Kildare, where it was erected in the south transept. The effigy is a masterly one, showing the prelate in full pontificals – bejewelled mitre, crozier, amice and chasuble,

The dignified and tranquil effigy of Bishop Walter Wellesley (d.1539), brought to Kildare Cathedral from his priory at Greatconnell, is the most outstanding stone carving of late medieval Ireland.

223

this last finely incised to display the patterns of contemporary Italian velvet. The attention is focused on the youthful but earnest face of the bishop, untroubled by the disturbances of the Reformation which took place during his episcopate. He is shown as if very much alive under a canopy supported by a pair of protective angels. Though some of the tomb-supports with their putti are amongst the earliest traces of Renaissance decoration in Ireland, the noble high-relief effigy is still anchored in the Gothic tradition in which, one suspects, the bishop felt most at home. This is an effigy in the best European tradition which has no equals in Ireland, raising the question as to where its master-craftsman originated – a problem which has yet to find a satisfactory solution.

CRUCIFIX AT JOHNSTOWN
Co. Kilkenny

Let into a niche in the wall on the left-hand side leading up to the Catholic church at Johnstown in County Kilkenny, on the Dublin–Cork road is a stone figure of the crucified Christ. It originally came from Fertagh, not far away, where it probably formed part of the tomb of a member of the FitzPatrick family around the late sixteenth century. It was brought to Johnstown some time after 1800, along with archi-

tectural fragments from the old monastery there. For its period, or indeed for any period, it is an extraordinary carving, one of the most gripping representations of the Crucifixion to survive from late medieval Ireland. The figure of Christ is set against a cross, and he is shown wearing a loin-cloth with flowing folds gathered up into a large knot on his left side. The intensely dramatic expression of the face is made more poignant by the disfiguring gap left where a new nose (now lost) was inserted after the original was broken in antiquity. The schematized arms and hands are made up of grooved planes, as are the ribs, which would do honour to any modern sculptor, and the angularly laid legs and feet beneath the loin-cloth give added asymmetrical treatment to the lower part of the figure.

SHEELA-NA-GIG AT KILLINABOY CHURCH
Co. Clare

In addition to the double-armed cross in the west gable (p. 62), the church at Killinaboy preserves another interesting piece of stonework over the south doorway – the carved figure of a sheela-na-gig. The origin of the name is somewhat obscure, one of the better suggestions being that the first part is a personal name and that the latter two words come from the Gaelic *na gcíoch*, meaning 'of the breasts'. For these, mostly grotesque, carvings represent unclad females who expose their breasts and sometimes even point to their naked genitalia as they splay their legs widely. These figures make their first appearance in Ireland on a Romanesque church of the twelfth century, and continued to be carved well into the sixteenth century if not later, more than half of the examples being built into the exterior walls of castles. One of them even decorates the underside of the effigy of Bishop Walter Wellesley of c.1539, now in Kildare Cathedral, so that the word erotic sometimes applied to these figures might seem to be misplaced. They are, with few exceptions, of execrable quality and scarcely carved by the same masons who sculpted tomb-monuments. Their position high up on the walls of tower-houses, and over the doors of churches, not to mention ornamenting the tomb of a bishop, would suggest rather that these crude figures – about which the historical record is entirely silent – may have had an apotropaic function, i.e. warding off evil.

LEFT Late medieval Ireland's most compelling representation of the Crucifixion must surely be that with a stylized, grimacing Christ at Johnstown, Co. Kilkenny.

RIGHT Sheela-na-gigs – those mysterious and intriguing figures of naked women openly displaying their pudenda – are occasionally found on churches, as here at Killinaboy, Co. Clare, but the majority are found on castle walls, perhaps to ward off evil from those who lived inside.

CHAPTER SIX

THE SEVENTEENTH CENTURY

THE POLITICAL SCENE

The seventeenth century saw Ireland emerge from the 'blinkered' Middle Ages to a more enlightened modern period, but it was also a century which at the start, middle and end brought sadness and disaster to the Irish. The opening year 1601 saw the culmination of Queen Elizabeth's campaign to subdue Ireland when a combined Irish and Spanish force was defeated at Kinsale. The Irish nobility realized that the game was up for them; fighting against greater odds was no longer practicable, and in 1607 the flower of the Gaelic aristocracy in the north – the O'Neills and O'Donnells – sailed off down Lough Swilly to exile in Spain, leaving their people powerless and without a spirit or rudder to guide them.

Effigies of Roger Boyle, Earl of Cork, and his wife Katherine are the most prominent among the four generations of his family represented on the memorial that he had erected in St Patrick's Cathedral, Dublin, around 1631. King Charles I's Lord Deputy in Ireland, Thomas Wentworth, Earl of Strafford, objected to its all too conspicuous position near the high altar and forced Boyle to move it to a less obtrusive location, but Boyle later got his revenge by helping to bring about Wentworth's impeachment and eventual execution ten years later. Perhaps it was this that earned Boyle praise from none other than the regicide Oliver Cromwell, who said that if there were an Earl of Cork in every province in Ireland, it would be impossible for the Irish to rebel – an interesting comment on the methods of a man who started off as an adventurer buying 42,000 acres (17,000 ha) from Sir Walter Raleigh for £1500 and ending up as owner of lands stretching from Waterford to the Shannon. Perhaps it was pique which led the Earl to erect a somewhat similar tomb in St Mary's Church in Youghal, where he died and was buried in 1643 – making this monument a cenotaph for himself, but not for his wife, who was buried in St Patrick's.

The plantations which Elizabeth instigated in the midlands and south were continued under her Stuart successor, James I (1603-25), in the north. There, lands of the defeated Irish were confiscated and granted instead to industrious planters brought in from England and Scotland to set up new colonies in Ulster. It was at this time that the town of St Columba's monastic foundation at Derry got its London prefix for the first time. The new settlers entrenched themselves in a new style of Plantation castle over many parts of the north of Ireland.

With the Plantation of Ulster the last bastion of Gaelic Ireland had fallen, and the old Brehon Laws which had guided the Irish since the seventh century were abolished in 1606. In the second quarter of the century the English King Charles I (1625-49) came under increasing pressure from Parliament, which sought more independence, and the struggle had its knock-on effects in Ireland when the Old Catholics banded together at the Confederation of Kilkenny in 1642 to combat the Parliamentary roundheads. It needed the Lord Protector, Oliver Cromwell himself, to come to Ireland in order to subdue the Catholic population in the name of religion. The slaughter and destruction which Cromwell and his generals brought about in Ireland in a few short years, between 1649 and 1652, has left an indelible and long-lasting memory in the Irish psyche, and makes it difficult for some Irish to understand how the English honour Cromwell by having his statue outside the Mother of Parliaments at Westminster.

But even England had its fill of the Commonwealth, and after Cromwell's death, the monarchy was restored when Charles II mounted the throne of his decapitated father in 1660. After the horrors of Cromwell Ireland settled down to a period of peace, and, on the cultural front at least, Dublin began to make its mark by contributing to the world of literature in English for the first time – but by no means the last! Meanwhile, the planters had become masters of Ulster, and late in the reign of Charles II (1660-85) the Catholic Irish began to experience hope that the practice of their religion might be liberalized with the prospect of the Catholic-friendly Duke of York mounting the throne as his successor. This hope was expressed in the re-erection of earlier High Crosses, such as Dysert O'Dea and the Market Cross of Kells in the 1680s. But things turned sour for the Irish when the new king, as James II, was threatened through the invasion of England by his staunchly Protestant son-in-law William of Orange, and the two monarchs fought out their destinies on Irish soil. After the city of Londonderry had successfully withstood a Jacobite siege in 1689, William defeated James's forces in successive encounters in 1690-91 at the Boyne, Aughrim and Limerick. James departed for the continent, defeated and with the opprobrium of the Irish in his ears for having deserted them when they most needed him. There was nothing left for the fighters who had supported him but to agree to the Williamite terms, sail off to France and seek military careers in the service of the King of France and the Emperor of Austria.

With the Treaty of Limerick Ireland reached its nadir point, and what followed was a dark century for the Gaelic-speaking population. The poets kept up the spirits of the numerically increasing Catholic inhabitants in a period of religious and cultural repression, with the majority living penniless in mud-huts, eking out a precarious existence, which came to depend more and more on the potato as a means of survival. But for those who were now the new lords of the land things were different, and with their growing affluence they were able to introduce Ireland to a flourishing new classically inspired culture in the eighteenth century which was to bring out once more the best

in Irish craftsmanship and architecture – but that is a story which is covered in Jacqueline O'Brien's companion volume, *Great Irish Houses and Castles*.

TUDOR, STUART AND PLANTATION ARCHITECTURE

While the traditional tower-house architecture managed to live on into the seventeenth century, a new breeze was already beginning to be felt in the Elizabethan period with the occasional appearance of a gracious style of Tudor architecture in Ireland. This was spear-headed in the south-east by the Earl of Ormond's manor house at Carrick-on-Suir, but it also expressed itself in merchants' urban buildings such as Rothe House in Kilkenny. While these structures show a desire to be liberated from the trammels of defence, the Elizabethan wars nevertheless brought with them the necessity for the English to create fortifications to protect themselves, as at Duncannon Fort.

The gradual preference for style over defence during the Elizabethan period is evident in buildings such as Rathfarnham Castle of *c.*1583 and Kanturk Castle two decades later. This led the way for the development early in the following century of fortified houses in the Jacobean style, put up very much now with comfort in mind, while not entirely neglecting the possibility of having to fire the occasional musket from within, as can be seen at Coppinger's Court or Portumna Castle.

Such architecture was not confined to the English elements of the population, but was copied in time by the leaders of Gaelic society, as was the case at Kanturk. One fine example is Leamanegh Castle of 1643, where a

LEFT Jacobean swags and swagger characterize the overmantel which the planter Sir Basil Brooke inserted into the first-floor hall of the older O'Donnell Castle in Donegal town to impress visitors with his new-found wealth.

RIGHT Surprisingly for an early Jacobean manor house, Kanturk Castle was built by a native Munsterman, Dermot MacDonagh, a circumstance reflected in its blend of Irish tower-house and Renaissance architecture. But the castle was never finished because his jealous planter neighbours got a Privy Council order to have the building stopped.

fine three-storeyed manor was attached to an earlier tower-house. A parallel case, but with different players, can be seen at Donegal Castle, where an O'Donnell tower was adapted by one of the Ulster planters who added to it a grandiose Jacobean mansion. Feeling threatened by the Gaelic population whose land they had appropriated, these new settlers fortified themselves behind town walls like those of Derry, but also built their own defensive bawns, as at Parke's Castle or Monea, which frequently betray their English or Scottish architectural origins.

The remainder of the seventeenth century was too troubled a time in Ireland to be able to continue the development of domestic architecture, though detective work of the kind carried out by Dudley Waterman and Maurice Craig reveals the existence of a considerable number of houses of the period still surviving in Ireland. The closing years of the century are marked particularly by two works erected for the state by Sir William Robinson. One of these was Charles Fort, Kinsale, which – with the exception of the Napoleonic defences – was to remain the last great fortification to be erected in Ireland. The second was his Royal Hospital at Kilmainham, the first in a series of public buildings culminating in the eighteenth-century masterpieces of the capital city so beautifully covered in the other companion volume on Dublin by Jacqueline O'Brien with Desmond Guinness.

CARRICK-ON-SUIR CASTLE
Co. Tipperary

The first and finest of the Tudor manor houses in Ireland was built at Carrick-on-Suir by 'Black Tom', the tenth Earl of Ormond, *c.*1565/75. Using the two towers of a fifteenth-century castle as one side of

a courtyard, Black Tom built the other three sides, of which the main Tudor front faces north. The triple-gabled facade is entered by a projecting central door which is flanked on each side by three sets of windows, two-light on the ground floor and three-light on the floor above, with scarcely a hint of fortification to be seen anywhere. In the hallway are two mural paintings – one of Black Tom and the other of Queen Elizabeth I. She was not only his queen but also his cousin, for one of his ancestors as Earl of Ormond was grandfather to Elizabeth's mother, Anne Boleyn, who is claimed by unsubstantiated tradition to have been born in the older portion of the castle. Black Tom had been brought up with the young Prince Edward at the court of Henry VIII, when he would have had ample opportunity to see the latest architectural style common in England before building his own Irish response at Carrick-on-Suir.

Black Tom is said to have had a flirtation with 'good Queen Bess' who called him her 'Black Husband' just to annoy her other suitors. His affection for her is further demonstrated in the 63-foot (19.2m)-long gallery which takes up the whole first floor of the north front, where her bust decorates a partially reconstructed plaster frieze, flanked by allegorical figures of Justice and Equity, and accompanied by her initials 'ER' and those of the builder, 'TO' (Thomas of Ormond). The plastered ceiling is divided by richly moulded ribs into panels enclosing arms and mottoes of the Ormond family. The other notable feature of the hall is a grandiose limestone fireplace, including a finely carved overmantel with an ornate armorial bearing and an inscription stating that it was erected by Thomas Butler, Earl of Ormond, in 1565, the seventh year of Elizabeth's reign. While this would appear to give us the year in which the castle was built, Maurice Craig has suggested that it was a second visit to England in 1572

LEFT Carrick-on-Suir Castle started a fashion in Ireland for Tudor-style manor houses when it was built around or shortly after 1565.

RIGHT AND BELOW On the first floor of Carrick Castle is this splendid long gallery with notable overmantel of 1565 and a stucco frieze incorporating the bust of Queen Elizabeth I, cousin of the castle-builder 'Black Tom', the tenth Earl of Ormond, who is said to have flirted with the virgin queen.

which may have provided Black Tom with the inspiration for the mansion. Percy Le Clerc put forward a date of 1573 for the stucco decoration – perhaps applied in the vain hope that Elizabeth might one day pay a visit. The whole complex, towers and Tudor buildings, was restored by the state between 1948 and 1960 – just in time to save it from falling into complete and undeserved decay.

The dark oak panelling, tapestries and other furnishings of the hall and mansion have long since disappeared, but the splendour of the original interior is still vividly recalled for us in some stanzas of a Gaelic poem written in honour of the Court of Black Tom by his own house poet, Eoghan Mac Craith, which may be rendered in English as follows:

> A court without torch-light, yet illumined
>   Court of the light of wax tapers.
> A plentiful mansion so artistically stuccoed,
>   with sun-lit gables and embroidery-covered walls.
> A mansion where banquets abound, a neatly-tiled house
>   replete with lances . . . where richly-carved horns and goblets are
>   found . . .
> A delightful habitation, celebrated, superby finished,
>   handsome, rustic-planned, whitewashed.

LEFT The south front of Portumna Castle, built around 1620, had the rounded hallway and entrance added to it in the late eighteenth century, doubtless to facilitate access to the waters of Lough Derg nearby.

RIGHT AND BELOW RIGHT In 1643 Conor O'Brien and his wife Máire built a stately mansion up against the narrow pre-existing fifteenth-century tower-house at Leamanegh, Co. Clare, and in front of it they placed a monumental entrance gate, which his descendants removed to Dromoland Castle in 1907 to act as a garden ornament.

RIGHT Business must have been flourishing greatly in Cork during the 1620s for Sir Walter Coppinger to have built this mansion for his family some 30 miles (50km) west of the city.

He was Richard de Burgo, fourth Earl of Clanricarde, Lord President of Connacht from 1604 to 1616, and it was shortly after this period that he set about building his castle by 'remote control' from his permanent home in England, probably completing the construction before his death in 1635. The gateways of two formal garden enclosures led in to the main entrance, Jacobean in style, while the back of the castle, though less ornate, had the advantage of having a long gallery on the first floor which provided a splendid view southwards across the lawn to the waters of Lough Derg on the Shannon. By all accounts, the castle was richly furnished within, but an accidental fire in 1826 consumed the lot, leaving the ruin we see today which has been sensitively conserved in recent decades by the Office of Public Works.

COPPINGER'S COURT
Co. Cork

Coppinger's Court is the name given to a splendid semi-fortified house at Ballyvireen near Rosscarbery in west Cork. Its builder, Sir Walter Coppinger, was one of the 'old English' Catholics and a merchant in Cork whose business was successful enough for him to build this large pile 30 miles (50km) west of the city. With four storeys over the basement, the castle has a rectangular plan with square towers projecting forward from each end of the north wall, and giving ample protection to the main doorway recessed between them. The staircase was housed in a tower outside the centre of the south wall. At parapet level there are 'machicolations' at various points around the building, where they may have served more decorative than military purposes, Mark Samuel suggesting that they may have acted as 'rainwater heads'. Further features include numerous two-, four- and six-light windows as well as tall eight-sided chimneys, which gave rise to the tradition that the house had a window for every day in the year, a chimney for every week and a door for every month! The castle was probably built c.1620-30 and was sacked and partially burned in 1641, but the Coppingers managed to continue living in the castle until around 1698, after which it gradually fell into ruin.

LEAMANEGH CASTLE
Co. Clare

The composite Leamanegh Castle neatly illustrates the symbolic contrast between the narrow mind of the Middle Ages and the more open aspect of the Age of Enlightenment. The eastern end consists of a tall and slender tower-house with thin arrow-slits, which Westropp dates to around 1480, whereas the remainder is a more grandiose manor or 'strong-house' of the 1640s. Its broad, mullioned windows are larger on the ground floor than above, letting in much more light, and are more commodious than defensive. Typical of the west of Ireland is the bartizan at second-floor level on the south-eastern corner. The house was entered through a round-headed doorway at the centre of the south wall, in front of which there was an impressive courtyard gateway, but Lord Inchiquin moved it in 1907 to his castle at Dromoland some 20 miles (32km) away, where it now serves as a garden feature. Above the doorway in Dromoland are two coats of arms, one of Sir Donat O'Brien of c.1690, the other, earlier, of his father, bearing beneath it the inscription: 'This was built in the yeare of our Lord 1643 by Conor O'Brien and by Mary Ní Mahon, wife of the said Conor.' Conor, descended from Brian Boru, was the builder of the castle, and his wife was the famous Máire Rua (Red Mary), around whose person many fabulous tales grew up – all unjustified, as Máire Mc Neill makes clear in her wonderful book *Máire Rua, Lady of Leamaneh*. To the east of the castle the couple built a large walled garden (the 'deer park'), now largely on the opposite side of the road, with a rounded turret at one corner, and a fish pond in the middle (now dried up). Conor died after a skirmish with the Parliamentarian General Ludlow in 1651, and Máire later married a Cromwellian, cornet Cooper, in order to save the lands for her younger son. The O'Briens remained in occupation of the castle until the end of the seventeenth century when they moved to Dromoland, where the present building of 1826 functions as a luxury hotel.

CITY WALLS AND ST COLUMB'S CATHEDRAL
Derry

When James I granted the old town of Derry to the citizens of London in 1613 and gave royal approval for the name to be changed to Londonderry, he set in train what is probably the first real piece of urban town planning in Ireland. Over the following fifteen years a new town was built on what was largely virgin territory laid out on the grid system associ-

ated with the name of the ancient Greek planner Hippodamus of Miletus, then revitalized and idealized in the Renaissance and used in most of the major cities of North America today. The new planters who had come to build the town needed protection and got one of their own, Sir Edward Doddington, to design ramparts 12-foot (3.7m) thick and with a circumfer-

ABOVE St Columb's Cathedral in Derry nestles for protection close to the massive early seventeenth-century town walls seen in the foreground.

ABOVE Among the many gates that provide access to the city of Derry through the town walls, Ferryquay Gate has an especially hallowed place as it was the one that the small band of Apprentice Boys closed on 7 December 1688, thereby denying access to the forces of James II, who subsequently besieged the town without success for 105 days.

LEFT AND RIGHT The Protestant St Columb's Cathedral in Derry was built by the Corporation of London between 1628 and 1633 on the highest ground in the city and was intended to resemble a medieval English parish church.

ence of 1700 yards (1554m) around the town. These ramparts took five years to complete and were the last circuit of town walls to have been built in Ireland, and perhaps even anywhere in Europe. The ditch outside the ramparts was filled in within a century, but Brian Lacy's excavations in the city during the 1970s recovered much seventeenth-century pottery which, interestingly, found some of its best parallels in the early colonial towns of North America. The walls have been altered somewhat over the centuries, but were strong enough to withstand their famous siege when the 'apprentice boys' supporting King William closed the doors of the town and, along with other citizens, held out successfully against the forces of King James for 105 days in 1688-9. Since then, the walls and their guns – particularly the famous 'Roaring Meg' – have become symbols of the Unionist attachment to the British crown.

Just inside the walls is the Protestant cathedral of St Columb, the saint who founded a monastery at Derry more than a thousand years ago. It was erected on the highest ground in the city and was built between 1628 and 1633 by the City of London for the new settlers which it had sent there within the previous two decades. In the Gothic style of an English medieval parish church, the cathedral has an aisled nave and a western tower raised 21 feet (7m) in 1778 by the city's eccentric travelling bishop, the Earl of Bristol. There have, however, also been a number of important additions in the meantime, including the Chapter House of 1910, which houses relics of the siege of 1689.

PARKE'S CASTLE
Co. Leitrim

Lough Gill, whose waters lap the shores of counties Sligo and Leitrim, is the idyllic setting of Yeats's Lake Isle of Inisfree – the place where 'peace comes dropping slow'. Four hundred years ago, peace may – in a somewhat different sense – have been slow to come, for the native Irish were locked in battle with the Elizabethan forces. The O'Rourke lords of Breifne had built a tower-house on a tongue of land at the eastern end of the lake, and it was probably there that succour was given to Captain Francisco Cuellar, the only survivor of the Spanish Armada to have written a detailed account of his experiences. He describes Sir Brian O'Rourke as being always at war 'with the heretics', who won out in the end by bringing Brian to London and hanging him there in 1591. Only the foundations of his tower-house remain, discovered in Claire Foley's archaeological excavations in the 1970s, which showed it to have stood off-centre in a tall-walled five-sided bawn next to the lake, but enterable through a surviving gate-house on the eastern side.

When the Ulster Plantation got under way, its effects reached as far as Lough Gill, and it appears that Captain Robert Parke was able to gain possession of 'Newtowne', as the castle became known. It was probably in the 1620s that Parke demolished the O'Rourke tower-house and built for himself instead a strong-house within the old bawn, which conformed more to

Captain Robert Parke built himself a fine, strong house on the shores of Lough Gill around the 1620s, one of the few notable 'planter castles' in the Republic.

the Plantation style in vogue at the time. This was a manor house incorporating the old gate house, and provided with a wooden stair leading to the hall above. The interior of this manor house has recently been restored by the Office of Public Works using woodcraft of a very high quality. The Office has also rebuilt an old forge dating from Parke's time and provided tourist facilities within the bawn. The Parkes lost the castle for a while in the 1640s and 1650s – first to the Irish and then to Cromwell's Parliamentarians – but after the Restoration of Charles II it was returned to the family and descended through marriage to, among others, the Gore-Booth family of Lissadell.

ENNISKILLEN CASTLE
Co. Fermanagh

The Enniskillen of today is essentially a creation of the early seventeenth century, when Captain William Cole built a 'fair strong wall' and a house for himself. But this strategic location commanding the top end of Lower Lough Erne had already been fortified by the Maguires of Fermanagh, who had built a castle there early in the fifteenth century. It was probably not until the Maguires had to yield to the Jacobean planter Cole that the castle took on its present form. Its centrepiece is the building now housing the Fermanagh County Museum and the regimental museum of the Royal Inniskilling Fusiliers, which was presumably built

by Cole on top of what remained of the old Maguire tower-house, though its roof was truncated about two centuries ago.

But the castle is known, above all, for its Water Gate, fronting on to the banks of the River Erne. Some of its fabric may be the work of Connacht Óg Maguire in the later sixteenth century, but the rounded corner bartizans projecting at the corners from the first story upwards suggest that it owes much of its present character to Cole, who is the most likely candidate to have included this peculiarly Scottish architectural feature found in slightly later Planter castles in Ulster, such as Ballygalley (pp. 238-9).

MONEA CASTLE
Co. Fermanagh

Monea Castle, some miles north-west of Enniskillen, is the largest and best-preserved of those castles erected by the planters in County Fermanagh who had been granted lands there after the collapse of Gaelic Ulster in the first years of the seventeenth century. It is, however, also the most unusual in appearance because of the two massive round bastions standing at the western end of the three-storey rectangular tower. These provided protection for the sole entrance doorway which was located in the more northerly of the two towers. There is a gabled 'caphouse' on top of each tower, placed at a diagonal to the main building, and these give a very Scottish appearance to the building,

Enniskillen's best-known 'logo' is the early seventeenth-century Water Gate, built probably by Captain William Cole as part of a castle that controlled communications between Upper and Lower Lough Erne in County Fermanagh.

LEFT Castles in Scotland, the land of
Malcolm Hamilton's birth, must have
inspired the two unusually topped
rounded bastions at the western end
of the castle he built at Monea,
Co. Fermanagh, shortly before 1619.

RIGHT Ballygalley Castle is a fine
Scottish planter's house of 1625, now
functioning as a hotel on the Antrim
coast road.

indicating the land of origin of the man who built the castle. When
Captain Nicholas Pynnar was sent by the government of the time to
inspect the progress of the new planters' buildings in 1619, he reported
on Monea that Malcolm Hamilton had built a 'strong castle of lime and
stone', and he recommended that a bawn should be built – a suggestion
followed up three years later. The castle occupies one corner of the
bawn, the walls of which still stand to a height of 12 feet (3.7m), and on
its northern flank there are turrets, one of which has probably been
rebuilt. The castle was occupied briefly by the Maguires during the
Rebellion of 1641, but retaken shortly afterwards by the Hamiltons, who
defended it successfully in 1688.

BALLYGALLEY CASTLE
Co. Antrim

The Ulster planters used contrasting architectural styles, depending on
the land of their origin, and this is well demonstrated in County
Antrim, where Dalway's Bawn near Carrickfergus shows the square-walled
bawn with corner towers constructed by the English settlers, while the much
better-preserved Ballygalley Castle is more unashamedly Scottish in origin.
Ballygalley, which is now incorporated into a splendid hotel, was built by
James Shaw who hailed from Greenock in western Scotland. The original
doorway, now approached through the hotel, bears a date and an inscription:

1625
GODIS . PROVIDENS . IS . MY INHERITANS

The doorway provided access to what was a square tower with one or two rooms for each of its three storeys over basement, all connected by a spiral staircase in one corner of the tower. The features which betray its Scottish origin are the dormer windows with decoration in the pediment, and the small corner turret projecting at third-floor level which we have come to associate with the 'Scottish baronial' style of the last century. Originally, the castle stood in a roughly square bawn fronting onto the sea, but the only well-preserved stretch of its wall is seen bordering Carrickcastle Road, where it leads off at right angles to the sea, and has a round turret surviving at the landward end.

The castle was thus a combination of a residence and a fortification, and the latter aspect became more relevant when the castle was briefly and unsuccessfully besieged in 1641. But it fared worse in 1680, when it was temporarily occupied by the 'Tories of Londonderry', though it managed to survive the Williamite wars unscathed.

Two buildings were added in the middle of the eighteenth century to accommodate the families and retinues of two of the sisters of the then Mrs Shaw, who had come to live at Ballygalley – one of whom is said to have haunted the castle by knocking on the doors of the various rooms. After the Shaws lost possession early in the nineteenth century, a series of different owners occupied the castle before it was turned into a hotel in our own day. It is perhaps the only Planter castle which is both still occupied and accessible to the general public today.

CHARLES FORT
Kinsale, Co. Cork

Charles Fort is the most imposing of those star-shaped forts erected in Ireland during the course of the seventeenth century, getting its name from Charles II (1660-85), in whose reign it was built. It commands a strategic position at Ringcurran Point, on the eastern shore of Kinsale harbour, which provided a safe anchorage for British warships vulnerable to attack from overseas vessels. In building this mighty defence, the English were showing their determination to learn from sad experience earlier in the same century when an English fleet, having arrived at the mouth of the harbour during the siege of Kinsale in 1601, was denied access by water to the town through the presence of a Spanish force occupying a small outpost where Charles Fort now stands. After they had defeated the Irish on land, and their artillery had driven the Spaniards out of Ringcurran, the English decided to fortify both sides of the harbour approaches. On the west bank they built a star-shaped fort in 1602-4, now known as James Fort. However, it was not until after the royalist Prince Rupert had used it as a base to attack Cromwellian vessels in 1649, and a Dutch fleet had frightened England with a devastating descent on the Thames in 1667, that the English realized how easily the south coast of Ireland could be attacked from the same quarter and decided to strengthen the defences of Ringcurran on the east bank.

At first an earthenwork fortification was created by Roger Boyle, the first Earl of Orrery, who was responsible for the defence of Munster. He had prepared a design for a star-shaped fort on the hill just inland from the back of the present fort. But plans were changed so that the fort could be built directly beside the shore, doubtless to enable its cannon to get closer to any intruding ships. By 1678 work was underway, directed by Sir William Robinson, 'engineer and surveyor general of all fortifications, buildings, etc. in Ireland', and he concentrated his endeavours initially on the seaward defences. The angular design of the walls, with pointed bastions giving greater fire-power in various directions, was one which was being constantly improved and subsequently brought to its greatest perfection by Louis XIV's great military engineer Vauban. To suit the lie of the land, various changes were made during the course of construction, and the final version provided for two levels of batteries overlooking the sea, and long stretches of wall on the landward side, where the entrance was protected by three further bastions.

Work had been completed by the time the fort was visited in 1685 by a military engineer, Thomas Philipps, during the course of a royal mission to inspect the country's harbours and defences. He was impressed by the quality of the workmanship, but he pointed out that the weakness of the fort was that it was overlooked by the rising ground on the landward side.

The massive fortifications of Charles Fort, Kinsale, could not save it from being taken in 1690 – all because its ill-chosen site allowed it to be bombarded from the high ground behind. But it still remains the supreme piece of military architecture surviving in Ireland from the seventeenth – or indeed any other – century.

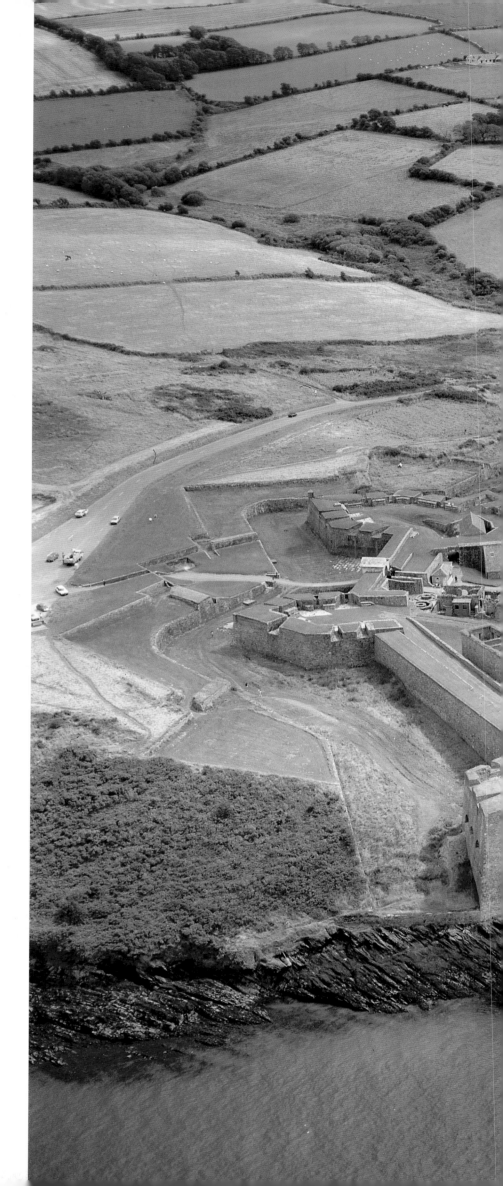

His fears were all too well founded for when, five years later, the fort was attacked by Williamite forces in the one and only time it underwent a siege, cannon firing from that small hillock caused the garrison loyal to King James II to capitulate and abandon the fort, thereby revealing the mistake of not having carried out Orrery's original intention to locate the fortification on the hillock rather than down by the shore.

During the following century the extensive barrack buildings were constructed in the interior, but by this time Kinsale's star was waning. The possibility of a naval attack from across the Atlantic during the American War of Independence and the fear of an invasion from the continent of Europe in the aftermath of the French Revolution led the government of the time to make Cork harbour the centre of its south coast defences. While the strategic importance of Charles Fort was thereby lessened, it still remained an English militia depot throughout the nineteenth century. It was only in 1921 that the British garrison withdrew after the setting up of the Irish Free State, with the sad consequence that the Irregular forces which took it over destroyed the barracks and other buildings, leaving them in a state of ruin. However, after the Commissioners of Public Works had scheduled the fort as a national monument in 1973, they set about conserving the fort and rendering it safe for all to enjoy and marvel at today.

KILLYLEAGH CASTLE
Co. Down

Killyleagh Castle adjoining the County Down village of the same name looks as if it might have come straight out of a fairy tale, perhaps because its present facade derives not from the unsettled period of Irish history when it was first built, but from the romance of the High Victorian period. The whole exterior is the work of the architect Sir Charles Lanyon, who placed 'candle-snuffers' on top of each tower, recalling the medieval miniatures of the Duke of Berry in order to please the francophile passion of his patron, Archibald Rowan Hamilton.

But, in providing the whole new exterior casing, Lanyon successfully united different parts of the earlier castle behind it which had been built in two separate stages during the seventeenth century. The older section, on the left, was built in the Scottish style by James Hamilton, Lord Clandeboye, shortly after 1610, and was described by a contemporary as 'ane vere stronge Castle, the lyk is not in the Northe'. When repairs had to be carried out in 1666 after a Cromwellian siege eleven years earlier, Henry, second Earl of Clanbrassil, added an almost mirror image of it on the right. He it was, possibly, who also built the walls flanking the long bawn leading

Killyleagh Castle in County Down was built in two separate stages in the seventeenth century but was given its romantic fairy-tale appearance in the 1850s.

the eye – and the twin avenues – up to the castle door. Shortly after Lanyon's restoration was completed in 1860, a two-century old feud within the family was brought to a happy end when the two sides were united in marriage, on the agreement that one would pay the other a pair of silver spurs and a golden rose of equal value on alternate years – a custom felicitously observed until the outbreak of the First World War.

BEAULIEU
Co. Louth

Beaulieu, near the banks of the Boyne estuary, was built in the 1660s by Sir Henry Tichborne, who had successfully defended the town of Drogheda, 2 miles (3km) away, in 1642. The house is still occupied by his descendants: Mrs Nesbit Waddington is the ninth generation to inherit the house. It fits snugly into its rural sylvan surroundings today, but it must have seemed quite an innovation in an Ireland recovering during the Restoration period from the havoc created by the whirlwind of the Cromwell era. It is not surprising that a mansion built by such an ardent supporter of King Charles II should be virtually an English home transplanted into Ireland, for Beaulieu has many parallels in the English coun-tryside, though built more by regicides than royalists, as it happens. It shares with them the hipped roofs, the deep eaves, the dormer windows, the heavy mouldings around doors and windows, and the happy mixture of red brick and plaster. Within, the most striking room is the hall, its fireplace two-storeyed like itself, and with fine deeply carved wooden panels in the tympana above the doors.

Beaulieu is, in the words of Mark Girouard, 'one of the earliest surviving examples of an Irish country house, excluding castles and semi-fortified buildings'. As such, it represents a new beginning in Irish architecture, the large undefended classical house, which was to lead to more sophisticated heights – a story taken up to great effect in the companion volumes, *Great Irish Houses and Castles* and *Dublin: A Grand Tour*. Though this book appears as the last in the trilogy, its subject-matter precedes those of the other two, and Beaulieu makes an appropriate conclusion – an architectural watershed that leaves behind the turbulent Middle Ages and portends the classical Georgian grace that was to come.

Beaulieu House in County Louth, built in the 1660s, is the most interesting of the rare Irish houses of the period, and an early forerunner of the great series of Irish country houses that were to follow in the ensuing centuries.

SELECT BIBLIOGRAPHY

This is not a complete bibliography but one in which some basic and/or recent works have been chosen so as to facilitate further research on the monuments featured in the text. After the general books and guides the order follows the sequence of subjects covered in the book (with some exceptions), and the publications cited under each heading are arranged chronologically according to date of publication.

ABBREVIATIONS
DOENI: Department of the Environment, Northern Ireland

HMSO: Her Majesty's Stationery Office

JRSAI: Journal of the Royal Society of Antiquaries of Ireland (and its predecessors with differing titles)

n.d.: No date of publication given

n.p.: No place of publication given

OPW: Office of Public Works

PRIA: Proceedings of the Royal Irish Academy

UJA: Ulster Journal of Archaeology

GENERAL
Ó Ríordáin, Seán P., *Antiquities of the Irish Countryside* (Cork 1942; 5th edn. London 1979).

Moody, T.W. and F.X. Martin (eds), *The Course of Irish History* (Cork 1967, latest edn 1994).

Evans, E. Estyn, *The Personality of Ireland* (Cambridge 1973; enlarged and revised Belfast 1981).

De Breffny, Brian (ed.) *The Irish World: The History and Cultural Achievements of the Irish People* (London 1977, reprinted 1986).

Harbison, Peter, Homan Potterton and Jeanne Sheehy, *Irish Art and Architecture* (London 1978; reprinted 1993).

Craig, Maurice, *The Architecture of Ireland from the Earliest Times to 1880* (London/Dublin 1982).

Moody, T.W., F.X. Martin and F.J. Byrne, *A New History of Ireland*, Vol. VIII, *A Chronology of Irish History to 1976, A Companion to Irish History, Part I* (Oxford 1982).

De Paor, Liam, *The Peoples of Ireland: From Prehistory to Modern Times* (London/Notre Dame 1986).

Mitchell, Frank, *The Shell Guide to Reading the Irish Landscape* (Dublin 1987).

Foster, R.F. (ed.), *The Oxford History of Ireland* (Oxford/New York 1989).

Mallory, J.P. and T.E. McNeill, *The Archaeology of Ulster from Colonization to Plantation* (Belfast 1991).

Ryan, Michael (ed.), *The Illustrated Archaeology of Ireland* (Dublin 1991, paperback edn entitled *Irish Archaeology Illustrated* 1994).

O'Brien, Jacqueline and Desmond Guinness, *Great Irish Houses and Castles* (London 1992).

O'Brien, Jacqueline with Desmond Guinness, *Dublin: A Grand Tour* (London 1994).

GUIDES
Killanin, Lord and Michael V. Duignan, *The Shell Guide to Ireland* (London 1962, 3rd edn revised by Peter Harbison, 1989).

Evans, E. Estyn, *Prehistoric and Early Christian Ireland: A Guide* (London 1966).

Weir, Anthony, *Early Ireland: A Field Guide* (Belfast 1980).

Harbison, Peter, *Guide to National and Historic Monuments of Ireland* (Dublin 1992).

IRELAND BEFORE HISTORY
Herity, Michael and George Eogan, *Ireland in Prehistory* (London 1977, reprinted 1989).

Harbison, Peter, *Pre-Christian Ireland* (London 1988).

O'Kelly, Michael J., *Early Ireland: An Introduction to Irish Prehistory* (Cambridge 1989).

Twohig, Elizabeth Shee, *Irish Megalithic Tombs*, Shire Archaeology Series (Princes Risborough 1990).

Brindley, Anna, *Irish Prehistory: An Introduction* (Dublin 1994).

Cooney, Gabriel and Eoin Grogan, *Irish Prehistory: A Social Perspective* (Dublin 1994).

Eogan, George, *The Accomplished Art: Gold and Gold-working in Britain and Ireland during the Bronze Age (c. 2300-650 BC)* (Oxford 1994).

Raftery, Barry, *Pagan Celtic Ireland: The Enigma of the Irish Iron Age* (London 1994).

The Stone Age
SITES
Newgrange and Knowth, Co. Meath
O'Kelly, Michael J., *Newgrange: Archaeology, Art and Legend* (London 1982).

Sweetman, P. David, 'A Late Neolithic/Early Bronze Age Pit Circle at Newgrange, Co. Meath', *PRIA* 85 C, 1985, 195-221.

Eogan, George, *Knowth and the Passage Tombs of Ireland* (London 1986).

Eogan, George, 'Prehistoric and Early Historic Culture Change at Brugh na Bóinne', *PRIA* 91 C, 1991, 105-32.

Creevykeel, Co. Sligo
Hencken, H. O'Neill, 'A long cairn at Creevykeel, Co. Sligo', *JRSAI* 59, 1939, 53-98.

Ó Nualláin, Seán, *Survey of the Megalithic Tombs of Ireland*, Vol. V, *County Sligo* (Dublin 1989), 9-10.

Dolmens and Wedge-Tombs
Ó Nualláin, Seán, 'The Megalithic Tombs of Ireland: Neolithic Tombs and their Art', *Expedition* (Philadelphia) 21(3), Spring 1979, 6-14

O'Kelly, Michael J., 'The Megalithic Tombs of Ireland', in Renfrew, Colin (ed.), *The Megalithic Monuments of Western Europe* (London 1983), 113-26.

Ó Nualláin, Seán, 'Irish Portal Tombs: Topography, Siting and Distribution', *JRSAI* 113, 1983, 75-105.

Lynch, Ann, 'Poulnabrone – A Stone in Time', *Archaeology Ireland* 2(3) 1988, 105-7.

Twohig, Elizabeth Shee, *Irish Megalithic Tombs*, Shire Archaeology Series (Princes Risborough 1990), 27-36 and 53-9.

The Bronze Age
SITES
Stone Circles
Fahy, E.M., 'A Recumbent-Stone Circle at Drombeg, Co. Cork', *Journal of the Cork Historical and Archaeological Society* 64, 1959, 1-27.

Burl, Aubrey, *The Stone Circles of the British Isles* (New Haven and London 1976), esp. 213-53.

Ó Nualláin, Seán, 'A Survey of the Stone Circles in Cork and Kerry', *PRIA* 84 C, 1984, 24-5.

Ó Nualláin, Seán, *Stone Circles in Ireland* (Dublin 1995).

Standing Stones
Leask, H.G., 'The Long Stone, Punchestown, Co. Kildare', *JRSAI* 67, 1937, 250-52.

Ó Ríordáin, S.P., *Antiquities of the Irish Countryside*, 3rd edn (London 1953), 81-3.

Evans, E. Estyn, *Prehistoric and Early Christian Ireland: A Guide* (London 1966), 20-21.

Weir, Anthony, *Early Ireland: A Field Guide* (Belfast 1980), 27-8.

Céide Fields, Co. Mayo
Caulfield, Seamus, *Céide Fields* (n.p., n.d.).

Dún Aengus and Dún Conor, Co. Galway
Cotter, Claire, '1. Western Stone Fort Project, Interim Report', in *Discovery Programme Reports 1, Project Results 1992* (Dublin 1993), 1-19.

Cotter, Claire. 'Atlantic Fortifications – the Dúns of the Aran Islands', *Archaeology Ireland* 8(1), 1994, 24-8.

Waddell, John, 'The Archaeology of Aran', in Waddell, J., J.W. O'Connell and A. Korff (eds.) *The Book of Aran* (Kinvara 1994), 84-90.

Cotter, Claire, '1. Western Stone Fort Project, Interim Report', in *Discovery Programme Reports 2, Project Results 1993* (Dublin 1995), 1-11.

Dunbeg, Co. Kerry
Barry, T.B., 'Archaeological Excavations at Dunbeg Promontory Fort, County Kerry, 1977', *PRIA* 81 C, 1981, 295-329.

Doon Fort, Co. Donegal
Rowan, Alistair, *The Buildings of Ireland – North West Ulster* (Harmondsworth 1979), 457.

Lacy, Brian *et al.*, *Archaeological Survey of County Donegal* (Lifford 1983), 136-7.

Grianán of Aileach, Co. Donegal
Petrie, George (aided by John O'Donovan), 'Section 2. – Antiquities. – Pagan. Grianán of Aileach', in Colby, Thomas (Superintendent), *Ordnance Survey of the County of Londonderry, Volume the First* (Dublin 1837), 217-34.

Rowan, Alistair, *The Buildings of Ireland – North West Ulster* (Harmondsworth 1979), 312-13.

Lacy, Brian *et al.*, *Archaeological Survey of County Donegal* (Lifford 1983) 111-12.

Lacy, Brian, 'The Grianán of Aileach', *Donegal Annual* 36, 1984, 5-24.

Rynne, Etienne, 'Grianán Oiligh (The Grianán of Aileach), Co. Donegal', *Donegal Annual* 41, 1989, 54-6.

Staigue Fort, Co. Kerry
'Proceedings', *JRSAI* 27, 1897, 316-18.

O Loingsigh, Pádraig, *Cathair na Stéige, Staigue Fort* (n.p., 1989).

The Arrival of the Celts
SITES
The Turoe Stone, Co. Galway
Duignan, Michael, 'The Turoe Stone: Its Place in Insular La Tène Art', in Duval, Paul-Marie and Christopher Hawkes (eds.), *Celtic Art in Ancient Europe: Five Proto-historic Centuries* (London 1976), 201-17.

Waddell, John, 'From Kermaria to Turoe?', in Scott, B.G. (ed.), *Studies on Early Ireland, Essays in Honour of M. V. Duignan* (1982), 21-8.

Raftery, Barry, *La Tène in Ireland: Problems of Origin and Chronology* (Marburg 1984) 291-3.

Kelly, Eamonn P., *Early Celtic Art in Ireland* (Dublin 1993).

Navan Fort, Co. Armagh
Mallory, J.P. and T.E. McNeill, *The Archaeology of Ulster from Colonization to Plantation* (Belfast 1991), 115-79.

Lynn, C.J., 'Hostels, Heroes and Tales: Further Thoughts of the Navan Mound', *Emania, Bulletin of the Navan Research Group* 12, 1994, 5-20 (with latest bibliography).

Mallory, J.P. and Gerard Stockman (eds), *Ulidia* (Belfast, 1994,).

Dún Ailinne, Co. Kildare
Wailes, B. *et al.*, various articles in *Emania, Bulletin of the Navan Research Group* 7, 1990, 10-36.

The Hill of Tara, Co. Meath
Petrie, George, 'On the History and Antiquities of Tara Hill', *Transactions of the Royal Irish Academy* 18, 1839, 25-232.

Macalister, R.A.S., 'Temair Breg: A Study of the Remains and Traditions of Tara', *PRIA* 34 C, 1919, 231-404.

Macalister, R.A.S., *Tara: A Pagan Sanctuary of Ancient Ireland* (London 1931).

Ó Ríordáin, Seán P., *Tara, The Monuments on the Hill*, 3rd edn (Dundalk 1960).

Swan, D.L., 'The Hill of Tara, County Meath: The Evidence of Aerial Photography', *JRSAI* 108, 1978, 51-66.

Newman, Conor, Edel Bhreathnach *et al.*, 'Tara Project', in *Discovery Programme Reports 1, Project Results 1992* (Dublin 1993), 69-103.

Newman, Conor and Edel Bhreathnach, '4. Tara Project', in *Discovery Programme Reports 2, Project Results 1993* (Dublin 1995) 62-76.

Bhreathnach, Edel, *Tara: A Select Bibliography*, Discovery Programme Reports 3 (Dublin 1995).

THE EARLY MIDDLE AGES
Historical Background to 1169 (including works relevant to the following chapter)
Kenney, James F., *The Sources for the Early History of Ireland. I. Ecclesiastical. An Introduction and Guide* (New York 1929, 2nd edn. revised by Ludwig Bieler, 1966).

Dillon, Myles (ed.), *Early Irish Society* (Dublin 1954).

Bieler, Ludwig, *Ireland, Harbinger of the Middle Ages* (London 1963).

McNally, Robert (ed.), *Old Ireland* (Dublin 1965).

Hughes, Kathleen, *The Church in Early Irish Society* (London 1966).

Gwynn, Aubrey, *The Twelfth-Century Reform*, A History of Irish Catholicism Vol. II (1) (Dublin and Sydney 1968).

Byrne, Francis John, *The Rise of the Uí Néill and the High-Kingship of Ireland*, O'Donnell lecture (Dublin 1970).

MacGearailt, Gearóid (pseudonym of Donncha Ó Corráin), *Celts and Normans* (Dublin 1969).

Ryan, John, *The Monastic Institute*, A History of Irish Catholicism Vol. I (2) (Dublin 1972).

Corish, Patrick J., *The Christian Mission*, A History of Irish Catholicism Vol. I (3) (Dublin 1972).

Mac Niocaill, Gearóid, *Ireland before the Vikings*, Gill History of Ireland I (Dublin 1972).

Ó Corráin, Donncha, *Ireland before the Normans*, Gill History of Ireland 2 (Dublin 1972).

Byrne, Francis John, *Irish Kings and High-Kings* (London 1973, reprinted 1987).

Lexikon des Mittelalters (Munich/Zurich 1977 – ongoing).

Löwe, Heinz (ed.), *Die Iren und Europa im früheren Mittelalter*, 2 vols (Stuttgart 1982).

Ní Chatháin, Próinséas and Michael Richter (eds.) *Irland und Europa: Die Kirche im Frühmittelalter/Ireland and Europe: The Early Church* (Stuttgart 1984).

Sharpe, Richard, 'Some Problems Concerning the Organization of the Church in Early Medieval Ireland', *Peritia, Journal of the Medieval Academy of Ireland* 3, 1984, 230-70.

Hughes, Kathleen, *Church and Society in Ireland, A.D. 400-1200* (ed. David Dumville), Variorum Reprint (London 1987).

Kelly, Fergus, *A Guide to Early Irish Law* (Dublin 1988).

Erichsen, Johannes (ed.), *Kilian, Mönch aus Irland, aller Franken Patron*, Veröffentlichungen zur Bayerischen Geschichte und Kultur 19/89 (Munich 1989).

Mackey, James P. (ed.) *An Introduction to Celtic Christianity* (Edinburgh 1989).

Bitel, Lisa M., *Isle of the Saints: Monastic Settlement and Christian Community in Early Ireland* (Ithaca and London 1990; reprinted Cork 1993).

Gwynn, Aubrey, *The Irish Church in the Eleventh and Twelfth Centuries* (ed. Gerard O'Brien) (Blackrock 1992).

Mytum, Harold, *The Origins of Early Christian Ireland* (London/New York 1992).

De Paor, Liam, *St. Patrick's World: The Christian Culture of Ireland's Apostolic Age* (Blackrock/Notre Dame 1993).

Dumville, David *et al.*, *Saint Patrick A.D. 493-1993* (Woodbridge/Rochester N.Y. 1993).

O Cróinín, Daibhí, *Early Medieval Ireland 400-1200*, Longman's History of Ireland Vol. 1 (London 1995).

METALWORK

Henry, Françoise, *Irish Art*, 3 vols (London 1965-70).

Ryan, Michael (ed.), *Treasures of Ireland: Irish Art 3000 B.C.-1500 A.D.* (Dublin 1983).

Ryan, Michael (ed.), *Ireland and Insular Art A.D. 500-1200* (Dublin 1987).

Youngs, Susan (ed.), *'The Work of Angels': Masterpieces of Celtic Metalwork, 6th-9th Centuries AD* (London 1989).

Ryan, Michael, *Metal Craftsmanship in Early Ireland* (Dublin 1993).

Spearman, R. Michael and John Higgitt (eds), *The Age of Migrating Ideas: Early Medieval Art in Northern Britain and Ireland* (Edinburgh/Stroud 1993).

Bourke, Cormac (ed.), *From the Isles of the North: Early Medieval Art in Ireland and Britain* (Belfast 1995).

SITES

Reconstructed Crannog, Craggaunowen, Co. Clare

Healy, Elizabeth, *Craggaunowen and the Hunt Museum* (n.p., n.d.).

Ogham

Macalister, R.A.S., *Corpus Inscriptionum Insularum Celticarum*, Vol. 1 (Dublin 1945).

MacManus, Damian, *A Guide to Ogam*, Maynooth Monographs (Maynooth 1991).

St Gall and other manuscripts

Duft, Johannes and Peter Meyer, *The Irish Miniatures in the Cathedral Library of St Gall* (Berne 1954).

Alexander, J.J.G., *Insular Manuscripts 6th to the 9th century* (London 1978).

Roth, Uta, 'Studien zur Ornamentik frühchristlicher Handschriften des insularen Bereichs: Von den Anfängen bis zum Book of Durrow', *Bericht der Römisch-Germanischen Kommission* 60, 1979, 5-225.

The Book of Kells, MS 58, Trinity College Library Dublin: Facsimile with Commentary, edited by Peter Fox (Luzern 1990).

Nees, Lawrence, 'The Irish Manuscripts at St Gall and their Continental Affiliations', in King, J.C. (ed.), *Sangallensia in Washington, The Arts and Letters in Medieval and Baroque St Gall Viewed from the Late Twentieth Century* (New York 1993), 95-132.

Meehan, Bernard, *The Book of Kells* (London 1994; reprinted 1996).

Ochsenbein, Peter, Karl Schmuki and Anton von Euw, *Irische Buchkunst: die irischen Handschriften der Stiftsbibliothek St Gallen und das Faksimile des Book of Kells* (2nd edn, St Gall 1994).

O'Mahony, Felicity (ed.), *The Book of Kells* (Dublin/Aldershot 1994).

Meehan, Bernard, *The Book of Durrow* (Dublin and Boulder 1996).

Croagh Patrick, Co. Mayo

Ó Lochlainn, Colm, *Cruach Phdraic: Ireland's Holy Mountain* (Dublin 1961).

MacNeill, Máire, *The Festival of Lughnasa* (Oxford 1962), 71-84.

Hughes, Harry, *Croagh Patrick: An Ancient Mountain Pilgrimage* (Westport 1991).

Walsh, Gerry, 'Preliminary Report on the Archaeological Excavations on the Summit of Croagh Patrick, 1994', *Cathair na Mart* 14, 1994, 1-10.

Architecture to 1200 (including works relevant to the following chapter)

Olden, T., 'On an early Irish Tract in the Leabhar Breac Describing the Mode of Consecrating a Church', *Transactions of the St. Paul's Ecclesiological Society* 4, 1900, 98-104 and 177-80.

Champneys, Arthur, *Irish Ecclesiastical Architecture* (London/Dublin 1910; reprinted Shannon 1970, with Introduction by Liam de Paor).

Leask, Harold G., *Irish Churches and Monastic Buildings*, Vol. I, *The First Phases and the Romanesque* (Dundalk 1955).

Henry, Françoise, *Irish Art*, 3 vols (London 1965-70).

De Paor, Liam, 'Cormac's Chapel: the Beginnings of Irish Romanesque', in Rynne, Etienne (ed.), *North Munster Studies, Essays in Commemoration of Monsignor Michael Moloney* (Limerick 1967), 133-45.

Gwynn, Aubrey and R. Neville Hadcock, *Medieval Religious Houses Ireland, with an Appendix to Early Sites* (London 1970; reprinted Blackrock 1988).

Laing, Lloyd, *Late Celtic Britain and Ireland, c.400 – 1200 AD* (London 1975).

De Breffny, Brian, *The Churches and Abbeys of Ireland* (London 1976).

Hughes, Kathleen and Ann Hamlin, *The Modern Traveller to the Early Irish Church* (London 1977; reprinted New York 1981 under the title *Celtic Monasticism*).

Radford, C.A. Ralegh, 'The Earliest Irish Churches', *UJA* 40, 1977, 1-11.

Harbison, Peter, 'Early Irish Churches', in Löwe, Heinz (ed.), *Die Iren und Europa im früheren Mittelalter*, Vol. 2 (Stuttgart 1982), 618-29.

Hamlin, Ann, 'The study of Early Irish churches', in Ní Chatháin, Próinséas and Michael Richter (eds), *Irland und Europa: Die Kirche im Frühmittelalter/Ireland and Europe: The Early Church* (Stuttgart 1984) 117-26.

Doherty, Charles, 'The Monastic Town in Early Medieval Ireland', in Clarke, H.B. and Anngret Simms (eds) *The Comparative History of Urban Origins in Non-Roman Europe*, BAR International Series 255(i) (Oxford 1985), 45-75.

Hamlin, Ann, 'The Archaeology of the Irish Church in the Eighth Century', *Peritia, Journal of the Medieval Academy of Ireland* 4, 1985, 279-99.

Henry, Françoise, *Studies in Early Christian and Medieval Art*, Vol. III, *Sculpture and Architecture* (London 1985).

Hare, Michael, 'The Study of Early Church Architecture in Ireland: an Anglo-Saxon Viewpoint', with an appendix by Ann Hamlin on documentary evidence for round towers, in Butler, L.A.S. and R.K. Morris (eds), *The Anglo-Saxon Church: Papers on History, Architecture, and Archaeology in Honour of Dr. H.M. Taylor*, Council for British Archaeology Research Report 60 (London 1986), 131-45.

Richter, Michael, *Medieval Ireland: the Enduring Tradition* (London/Dublin 1988).

Edwards, Nancy, *The Archaeology of Early Medieval Ireland* (London 1990).

Harbison, Peter, *Pilgrimage in Ireland: The Monuments and the People* (London/Syracuse 1991).

Karkov, Catherine, 'The Decoration of Early Wooden Architecture in Ireland and Northumbria', in Karkov, Catherine and Robert Farrell (eds), *Studies in Insular Art and Archaeology*, American Early Medieval Studies 1 (Oxford, Ohio 1991), 27-40.

Berger, Rainer, 'Radiocarbon Dating of Early Medieval Irish Monuments', *PRIA* 95 C, 1995, 159-74.

Herity, Michael, *Studies in the Layout, Buildings and Art in Stone of Early Irish Monasteries* (London 1995).

Manning, Conleth, *Early Irish Monasteries* (Dublin 1995).

SITES

Clonmacnoise, Co. Offaly

Petrie, George, *Christian Inscriptions in the Irish Language* (ed. Margaret Stokes), Vol. I (Dublin 1872).

Westropp, Thomas Johnson, 'A Description of the ancient buildings and crosses at Clonmacnois, King's County', *JRSAI* 37, 1907, 277-306.

Macalister, R.A. Stewart, *The Memorial Slabs of Clonmacnois, King's County: with an Appendix on the Materials for a History of the Monastery* (Dublin 1909).

Macalister, R.A.S., *Corpus Inscriptionum Insularum Celticarum*, Vol. II (Dublin 1949), 43-71.

Ryan, John, *Clonmacnois: A Historical Summary* (Dublin 1973).

Corkery, John, *Cluan Chiaráin, The City of Ciaran* (n.p., n.d. but c.1979).

Doherty, Charles, 'The Monastic Town in Early Medieval Ireland', in Clarke, H.B. and Anngret Simms (eds.) *The Comparative History of Urban Origins in Non-Roman Europe*, BAR International Series 255, Part I (Oxford 1985) 63-7.

Ó Murchadha, Domhnall and Giollamuire Ó Murchú, 'Fragmentary Inscriptions from the West Cross at Durrow, the South Cross at Clonmacnois, and the Cross of Kinnitty', *JRSAI* 118, 1988, 53-66.

Manning, Conleth, *Clonmacnoise* (OPW, Dublin 1994).

Manning, Conleth, 'Clonmacnoise Cathedral – The Oldest Church in Ireland', *Archaeology Ireland* 9 (4) 1995, 30-33.

Ó Floinn, Raghnall, 'Clonmacnoise: Art and Patronage in the Early Medieval Period', in Bourke, Cormac (ed.), *From the Isles of the North, Early Medieval Art in Ireland and Britain* (Belfast 1995) 251-60.

Glendalough, Co. Wicklow

Leask, H.G., *Glendalough, Co. Wicklow: Official Historical & Descriptive Guide* (Dublin, n.d. but c.1950).

Leask, Harold G., *Irish Churches and Monastic Buildings*, Vol. I (Dundalk 1955).

Barrow, Lennox, *Glendalough and St. Kevin* (Dundalk 1972).

Mac Shamhráin, A.S., 'Prosopographica Glindelachensis: The Monastic Church of Glendalough and its Community Sixth to Thirteenth Centuries', *JRSAI* 119, 1989, 79-97.

Mac Shamhráin, A.S., 'The Uí Muiredaig and the Abbacy of Glendalough in the Eleventh to Thirteenth Centuries', *Cambridge Medieval Celtic Studies* 25, 1993, 55-75.

Manning, Con, 'The Nave of Glendalough Cathedral', *IAPA Newsletter (Bulletin of the Irish Association of Professional Archaeologists)* 22, 1996, 6.

Kells, Co. Meath

Simms, Anngret and Katharine Simms, *Kells*, Irish Historic Towns Atlas – 4 (Dublin 1990).

Berger, Rainer, '[14]C Dating Mortar in Ireland', *Radiocarbon* 34(3), 1992, 880-89.

Casey, Christine and Alistair Rowan, *The Buildings of Ireland – North Leinster* (Harmondsworth 1993) 328-9.

Skellig Michael, Co. Kerry

De Paor, Liam, 'A Survey of Sceilg Mhichíl', *JRSAI* 85, 1955, 174-87.

Lavelle, Des, *Skellig: Island Outpost of Europe* (Dublin 1976).

Horn, Walter, Jenny White Marshall and Grellan Rourke, *The Forgotten Hermitage of Skellig Michael* (Berkeley 1990).

Inishmurray, Co. Sligo

Wakeman, W.F., *A Survey of the Antiquarian Remains on the Island of Inismurray* (Dublin 1893).

Heraughty, Patrick, *Inishmurray, Ancient Monastic Island* (Dublin 1982).

Meehan, Denis Molaise, *Molaise of Inishmurray* (Tralee 1989).

Sweetman, P. David, 'Archaeological Excavations at King John's Castle, Limerick', *PRIA* 80 C, 1980, 207-29.

Spellissy, Sean and John O'Brien, *Limerick, The Rich Land* (Limerick 1989), 17-18.

Harbison, Sheelagh, 'The Castle of Limerick', *The Irish Sword* 18 (No. 72), 1991, 199-204.

Hill, Judith, *The Building of Limerick* (Cork 1991).

Wiggins, Kenneth, 'Strange Changes at King John's Castle', *Archaeology Ireland* 5(3), 1991, 13-15.

Thomas, Avril, *The Walled Towns of Ireland*, Vol. 2 (Blackrock 1992) 142-53.

Wiggins, Kenneth, 'King John's Castle . . . Revisited', *Archaeology Ireland* 7(3), 1993, 26-8.

Cunningham, George, *King John's Castle, Limerick, Ireland – A Superb Attraction Not to Be Missed* (Shannon, n.d.).

Dunamase Castle, Co. Laois

Leask, Harold G., *Irish Castles and Castellated Houses* (Dundalk 1964), 64-5.

McNeill, T.E., 'The Outer Gate House at Dunamase Castle, Co. Laois', *Medieval Archaeology* 37, 1993, 236-9.

Hodkinson, Brian, 'The Rock of Dunamase', *Archaeology Ireland* 9(2), 1995, 18-21.

Kilkenny Castle

Lanigan, Katherine M., *Kilkenny Castle* (n.p., n.d. but 1966).

Lanigan, Katherine M., 'The Castle is Open Again', *Old Kilkenny Review*, New Ser., 1(4), 1977, 248-53.

Sweetman, P. David, 'Some Late Seventeenth- to Late Eighteenth-Century Finds from Kilkenny Castle', *PRIA* 81 C, 1981, 249-66.

Bradley, John, 'The Early Development of the Medieval Town of Kilkenny', in Nolan, William and Kevin Whelan (eds.), *Kilkenny: History and Society, Interdisciplinary Essays on the History of an Irish County* (Dublin 1990), 63-73.

Anon., *Kilkenny Castle*, OPW (Dublin, n.d. but 1991).

Adare Castle, Co. Limerick

Dunraven, Caroline, Countess of, *Memorials of Adare Manor* (Oxford 1865).

O'Callaghan, Kate (ed.), *Adare* (Limerick 1976).

Sweetman, P. David, 'Archaeological Excavations at Adare Castle, Co. Limerick', *Journal of the Cork Historical and Archaeological Society* 85 (Nos. 241 & 242), 1980, 1-6.

Barry, T.B., *The Archaeology of Medieval Ireland* (London 1987), 49.

Spellissy, Sean and John O'Brien, *Limerick, The Rich Land* (Limerick 1989), 93-4.

Athenry Castle, Co. Galway

Knox, H.T. and a colleague, 'Notes on the Burgus of Athenry, its First Defences and its Town Walls', *Journal of the Galway Archaeological and Historical Society* 11, 1920-21, 1-26 (see also C. McNeill on pp. 132-41).

Papazian, Cliona, 'Excavations at Athenry Castle', *Journal of the Galway Archaeological and Historical Society* 43, 1991, 1-45.

Reginald's Tower, Waterford

Downey, Edmund, *A Brief History of Reginald's Tower* (Waterford, n.d.).

Mackey, Pat, *Reginald's Tower and the Story of Waterford* (Waterford 1980).

Carroll, J.S., 'Reginald's Tower', *Decies* 26, 1984, 22-7.

Thomas, Avril, *The Walled Towns of Ireland*, Vol. 2 (Blackrock, Co. Dublin 1992), 200-210.

St Laurence's Gate, Drogheda, Co. Louth

Bradley, John, 'The topography and layout of medieval Drogheda', *Co. Louth Archaeological and Historical Journal* 19(2), 1978, 118.

Buckley, Victor M. and P. David Sweetman, *Archaeological Survey of Co. Louth* (Dublin 1991), 356-9.

Thomas, Avril, *The Walled Towns of Ireland*, Vol. 2 (Blackrock 1992), 72-9.

Casey, Christine and Alistair Rowan, *The Buildings of Ireland – North Leinster* (Harmondsworth 1993), 236-7.

Roscrea Castle, Co. Tipperary

Cooke, Thomas, *The Early History of the Town of Birr or Parsonstown* (Dublin 1875; reprinted Tullamore 1990).

Gleeson, Dermot F., *Roscrea* (Dublin 1947).

Cunningham, George, *Roscrea and District* (Roscrea 1976), 39-45.

Stout, Geraldine, 'Trial Excavations at Roscrea Castle, Co. Tipperary', *Éile, Journal of the Roscrea Heritage Society* 2, 1983-4, 29-42.

Stout, Geraldine, *Archaeological Survey of the Barony of Ikerrin* (Roscrea 1984), 116-21.

Cunningham, George, *The Anglo-Norman Advance into the South-west Midlands of Ireland 1185-1221* (Roscrea 1987), 124-5.

Town Walls of Youghal, Co. Cork

Buckley, M.J.C., 'The Town Walls of Youghal', *Journal of the Cork Historical and Archaeological Society*, 2nd ser. 6, 1900, 156-61.

C. (J)., 'The Walls of Youghal in the 17th Century', *Journal of the Cork Historical and Archaeological Society*, 2nd ser. 12, 1906, 103-4.

Barry, John, 'The Military History of Youghal', *The Irish Sword* 4 (No. 15), 1959, 114-19.

Fethard, Co. Tipperary

Thomas, Avril, *The Walled Towns of Ireland*, Vol. 2 (Blackrock 1992), 102-3.

Bradley, John, *Walled Towns in Ireland* (Dublin 1995), 31-3.

The Norman Church and New Monastic Orders (including works relevant to the following chapters)

Corish, P.J., 'The Church in Ireland in the Fifteenth Century, V., Summing up', *Irish Catholic Historical Committee Proceedings* 1956, 14-16.

Martin, F.X., 'The Irish Friars and the Observant Movement in the Fifteenth Century', *Irish Catholic Historical Committee Proceedings* 1960, 10-24.

Hand, Geoffrey, *The Church in the English Lordship 1216-1307*, A History of Irish Catholicism II (3) (Dublin and Sydney 1968).

Gwynn, Aubrey, *Anglo-Irish Church Life: Fourteenth and Fifteenth Centuries*, A History of Irish Catholicism II (4) (Dublin and Sydney 1968).

Mooney, Canice, *The Church in Gaelic Ireland: Thirteenth to Fifteenth Centuries*, A History of Irish Catholicism II (5) (Dublin and Sydney 1969).

Mooney, Canice, *The First Impact of the Reformation*, A History of Irish Catholicism III (2) (Dublin and Melbourne 1967).

Watt, J.A., *The Church and the Two Nations in Medieval Ireland*, Cambridge Studies in Medieval Life and Thought, Third Series (Cambridge 1970).

Watt, John, *The Church in Medieval Ireland*, Gill History of Ireland 5 (Dublin 1972).

Gothic Cathedrals and Parish Churches

Fallow, T.M., *The Cathedral Churches of Ireland* (London 1894).

Day, J. Godfrey F. and Henry E. Patton, *The Cathedrals of the Church of Ireland* (London 1932).

Clapham, Alfred, 'Some Minor Irish Cathedrals', *The Archaeological Journal* 106, Supplement, Memorial Volume to Sir Alfred Clapham, 1952, 16-39.

Jackson, Robert Wyse, *Cathedrals of the Church of Ireland* (Dublin 1971).

Stalley, Roger, 'Irish Gothic and English Fashion', in Lydon, James (ed.), *The English in Medieval Ireland* (Dublin 1984), 65-86.

Galloway, Peter, *The Cathedrals of Ireland* (Belfast 1992).

SITES

Christ Church Cathedral, Dublin

Street, George Edmund, *The Cathedral of the Holy Trinity Commonly Called Christ Church Cathedral, Dublin: An Account of the Restoration of the Fabric, with an Historical Sketch of the Cathedral by Edward Seymour* (London 1882).

Leask, Harold G., 'The Architecture of Christ Church Cathedral', *Christ Church Cathedral Yearbook* 1956, 17-21.

Stalley, Roger, *Christ Church, Dublin: The Late Romanesque Building Campaign*, Gatherum Series 2 (Ballycotton 1973).

Stokes, A.E., *Christ Church Cathedral, Dublin*, The Irish Heritage Series 12 (Dublin 1978).

Stalley, Roger, 'The Medieval Sculpture of Christ Church Cathedral, Dublin', *Archaeologia* 106, 1979, 107-22.

Stalley, Roger, 'Three Irish Buildings with West Country Origins', in Coldstream, N. and P. Draper (eds.), *Medieval Art and Architecture at Wells and Glastonbury* (London 1981), 71-5.

Eames, Elizabeth S. and Thomas Fanning, *Irish Medieval Tiles* (Dublin 1988), 62.

Clarke, Howard (ed.), *Medieval Dublin*, 2 vols (Dublin 1990).

St Patrick's Cathedral, Dublin

Mason, W.M., *The History and Antiquities of the Collegiate and Cathedral Church of St Patrick near Dublin, from its Foundation in 1190, to the Year 1819* (Dublin 1820).

Jackson, Victor, *St Patrick's Cathedral, Dublin*, Irish Heritage Series 9 (Dublin 1976).

Bethell, Denis, 'Dublin's Two Cathedrals', in Clarke, H. (ed.), *Focus on Dublin: Dublin Arts Festival* 1978, supplement (Dublin 1978), 27-34.

Rae, Edwin C., 'The Medieval Fabric of the Cathedral Church of St Patrick in Dublin', *JRSAI* 109, 1979, 29-73.

O'Neill, Michael, 'Marks of Unheeded Dilapidations': The Nineteenth and Early Twentieth Century Restorations, St Patrick's Cathedral 800 Series (Dublin 1991).

O'Neill, Michael, 'The Architecture of St Patrick's Cathedral, Dublin', *Irish Arts Review Yearbook* 11, 1995, 140-41.

St Canice's Cathedral, Kilkenny

Graves, J. and J.G.A. Prim, *The History, Architecture and Antiquities of the Cathedral Church of St Canice, Kilkenny* (Dublin 1857).

Stalley, R.A., *Architecture and Sculpture in Ireland 1150-1350* (Dublin 1971), 71-80.

Barry, Siuban, John Bradley and Adrian Empey, in Empey, A. (ed.), *A Worthy Foundation. The Cathedral Church of St Canice, Kilkenny, 1285-1985* (Mountrath 1985).

Tietzsch-Tyler, Daniel, *Building Stones of St Canice's Cathedral, Kilkenny* (Dublin, n.d. but 1995).

St Brigid's Cathedral, Kildare

Comerford, M., *Collections relating to the Dioceses of Kildare and Leighlin* II (Dublin), 1-21.

Cowell, George Young, 'St Brigid and the Cathedral Church of Kildare', *Journal of the County Kildare Archaeological Society* II(4), 1897, 235-52.

Craig, H.N., *Some Notes on the Cathedral of St. Brigid* (Naas 1946).

Buchanan, A.D., *St Brigid's Cathedral* (Newbridge 1972).

Barrow, George Lennox, *The Round Towers of Ireland* (Dublin 1979), 118-23.

Paterson, John, *Kildare: The Cathedral Church of St. Brigid* 1982.

Andrews, J.H., *Kildare: Irish Historic Towns Atlas No. 1* (Dublin 1986).

Costello, Con, *Looking Back: Aspects of History, County Kildare* (Naas 1988), 31-2.

King, Heather A., 'The Medieval and Seventeenth-Century Carved Stone Collection in Kildare', *Journal of the County Kildare Archaeological Society* 17, 1987/91, 59-95 – with detailed references.

St Nicholas of Myra Collegiate Church, Galway

Fahey, J., 'The Collegiate Church of St Nicholas, Galway', *Irish Ecclesiastical Record*, 3rd ser., 16, 1895, 700-10.

Berry, J. Fleetwood, *The Story of St Nicholas' Collegiate Church, Galway* (Galway 1912).

Leask, Harold G., 'The Collegiate Church of St Nicholas, Galway', *Journal of the Galway Archaeological and Historical Society* 17, 1936, 1-23.

Anon., *The Collegiate Church of St Nicholas, Galway* (Galway 1961).

St Mary's Church, Youghal, Co. Cork

Hayman, Samuel, *The Guide to Saint Mary's Collegiate Church, Youghal* (Cork 1869).

Hayman, Canon, *Memorials of Youghal, Ecclesiastical and Civil* (Youghal 1879, reprinted 1971).

Hallessy, J.V., *A History of Youghal and a Guide to its Most Interesting Ancient Foundations* (Cork c. 1949).

Anon., *St Mary's Collegiate Church*, Youghal (c. 1968).

Thomas, Avril, *The Walled Towns of Ireland*, Vol. 2 (Blackrock 1992), 215-20.

St Mary's Cathedral, Limerick

Meredyth, Francis, *A Descriptive and Historic*

Guide ThroughSt Mary's Cathedral, Limerick (Limerick 1887).

Westropp, Thomas J., 'St Mary's Cathedral, Limerick: its Plan and Growth', *JRSAI* 28, 1898, 35-48 and 112-25.

Dowd, James, *History of St Mary's Cathedral, Limerick* (Limerick 1899).

Westropp, Thomas Johnson, 'A Survey of the Ancient Churches in the County of Limerick', *PRIA* 25, 1904, 356-57 – with earlier references.

Westropp, T.J., R.A.S. Macalister and G.U. Macnamara, *The Antiquities of Limerick and its Neighbourhood*, Royal Society of Antiquaries of Ireland, Antiquarian Handbook Series VII (Dublin 1916), 10-20.

Day, J. Godfrey F. and Henry E. Patton, *The Cathedrals of the Church of Ireland* (London 1932), 153-9.

Hewson, R.F., 'St Mary's Cathedral, Limerick, its Development and Growth', *North Munster Antiquarian Jn.* 4, 1944-5, 55-67.

Clapham, Sir Alfred, 'Some Minor Irish Cathedrals', *Archaeological Jn.* 106, Supplement 1952, 28-30.

Talbot, M.J., *A Pictorial Tour of Limerick Cathedral* (Limerick c. 1966).

Hill, Judith, *The Building of Limerick* (Cork 1991), 13-20.

Galloway, Peter, *The Cathedrals of Ireland* (Belfast 1992), 157-61.

The Cistercians

Stalley, Roger, *The Cistercian Monasteries of Ireland: An Account of the History, Art and Architecture of the White Monks in Ireland from 1142 to 1540* (London and New Haven, 1987) – essential reference work with extensive bibliography to which the following may be added:

SITES
Mellifont Abbey, Co. Louth
Casey, Christine and Alistair Rowan, *The Buildings of Ireland – North Leinster* (Harmondsworth 1993), 387-93.

Baltinglass Abbey, Co. Wicklow
Carville, Geraldine, *Baltinglass: Abbey of the Three Rivers* (Moone 1984).

Jerpoint Abbey, Co. Kilkenny
Leask, H.G., *Jerpoint Abbey, Co. Kilkenny* (Dublin, n.d.).

Rae, Edwin C., 'The Sculpture of the Cloister of Jerpoint Abbey', *JRSAI* 96, 1966, 59-91.

Hunt, John, *Irish Medieval Figure Sculpture, 1200-1600* (Dublin/London 1974), 172-80.

Dunbrody Abbey, Co. Wexford
Doyle, Ian, 'The Foundation of the Cistercian Abbey of Dunbrody, Co. Wexford and its Historical Context', *Journal of the Old Wexford Society* 14, 1992-3, 81-91.

Culleton, Brendan (compiler), *Treasures of the Landscape: County Wexford's Rural Heritage* (Wexford 1994), 88-9.

Pierce, John W., *Dunbrody Abbey, Co. Wexford: Monastery and Monument* (Arthurstown 1994).

St Mary's Abbey, Dublin
Luddy, Ailbe J., *St. Mary's Abbey, Dublin* (Dublin 1935).

Ó hÉilidhe, 'The cloister arcade from Cook Street, Dublin', in Bradley, J. (ed.), *Settlement and Society in Medieval Ireland: Studies presented to F.X. Martin, O.S.A.* (Kilkenny 1988), 379-95.

Duiske Abbey, Graiguenamanagh, Co. Kilkenny
Hughes, Edward W., 'Duiske Abbey, Graignamanagh – Abbey Triumphant', *Old Kilkenny Review*, New Ser. 1(4) 1977, 254-60.

Bradley, J. and C. Manning, 'Excavations at Duiske Abbey, Graiguenamanagh, Co. Kilkenny', *PRIA* 81 C, 1981, 397-426.

Swayne, Seán, *Duiske Abbey, Graignamanagh* (1988).

Corcomroe Abbey, Co. Clare
Nelson, E. Charles and Roger A. Stalley, 'Medieval Naturalism and the Botanical Carvings at Corcomroe Abbey (County Clare)', *Gesta* 28/2, 1989, 165-74.

Boyle Abbey, Co. Roscommon
Hills, Gordon M., *Boyle Abbey and the Architecture of the Cistercian Abbeys of Ireland* (n.p., n.d.).

Sharkey, P.A., *The Heart of Ireland* (Boyle c.1927), 104-27.

Wheeler, H.A., *Boyle Abbey, Boyle, Co. Roscommon: A Short Descriptive and Historical Account* (National Parks and Monuments Service, n.d.).

Stalley, Roger, 'Saint Bernard, His Views on Architecture and the Irish Dimension', *Arte Medievale* II Serie, VIII (1), tomo 2, 1994, 13-19.

The Augustinians – and the School of the West

Dunning, P.J., 'The Arroasian Order in Medieval Ireland', *Irish Historical Studies* 4, 1944/5 (1948), 297-315.

Martin, F.X., 'The Augustinian Friaries in Pre-Reformation Ireland 1282-1500', *Augustiniana* (Louvain) 6, 1956, 346-84.

Leask, Harold G., *Irish Churches and Monastic Buildings*, Vols. II-III (Dundalk 1966).

Gwynn, Aubrey, and R. Neville Hadcock, *Medieval Religious Houses Ireland* (London 1970), 146-200 and 293-305.

Harbison, Peter, 'Twelfth and Thirteenth Century Irish Stonemasons in Regensburg (Bavaria) and the End of the "School of the West" in Connacht', *Studies* 64 (No. 256), Winter 1975, 333-46.

Stalley, Roger, *The Cistercian Monasteries of Ireland* (London and New Haven 1987), 91-2 and 107-9.

SITES
Ballintober Abbey, Co. Mayo
Egan, Thomas A., *The Story of Ballintubber*, 3rd edn (Ballintubber 1967).

Lewis, C. Day, *The Abbey that Refused to Die* (Ballintubber 1967).

Stalley, Roger, *Architecture and Sculpture in Ireland 1150-1350* (Dublin 1971), 110-17.

Stalley, Roger, *The Cistercian Monasteries of Ireland* (London and New Haven 1987), 184-7.

Cong Abbey, Co. Mayo
Leask, H.G., 'The Augustinian Abbey of St. Mary the Virgin, Cong, Co. Mayo', *Journal of the*

Galway Archaeological and Historical Society 19, 1941, 107-17.

Harbison, Peter, 'Twelfth and Thirteenth Century Irish Stonemasons in Regensburg (Bavaria) and the End of the "School of the West" in Connacht", *Studies*, Winter 1975, 333-46.

Adare Priory and Friary, Co. Limerick
Dunraven, Caroline, Countess of, *Memorials of Adare Manor* (Oxford 1865).

Hewson, George J., 'Adare and Some of its Ancient Buildings', *Limerick Field Club Journal* I(2), 1897-1900, 19-37.

Foran, E.A., 'Historical Notes on Augustinian Abbey of Adare', *Irish Ecclesiastical Record*, 5th ser., 3, 1914, 584-93.

Westropp, T.J., R.A.S. Macalister and G.U. Macnamara, *The Antiquities of Limerick and its Neighbourhood*, Royal Society of Antiquaries of Ireland, Antiquarian Handbook Series VII (Dublin 1916), 62-83.

Wyse Jackson, R., *Adare Church* (c. 1970).

O'Callaghan, Kate (ed.), *Adare, A Short Guide to the Village* (Limerick 1976) – with further references.

Athassel Priory, Co. Tipperary
Anon., 'The Abbey of Athassel', *Clonmel Historical and Archaeological Society* 1(4) 1955-6, 61-3.

Stalley, Roger, *Architecture and Sculpture in Ireland 1150-1350* (Dublin 1971), 125-30.

Craig, Maurice, *The Architecture of Ireland: From the Earliest Times to 1880* (London 1982), 28-30.

Brennan, Peggy, 'Incised Effigial Slab at Athassel Priory', *Tipperary Historical Journal* 1990, 193-5.

Kells Priory, Co. Kilkenny
Lahert, Richard, *The History and Antiquities of the Parish of Dunnamaggan in the Diocese of Ossory, Including a Full History of the Great Monastic Foundation of Kells in Ossory* (Tralee 1956).

Stalley, Roger, 'Monastery on the Defensive, Kells Priory, Co. Kilkenny', *Country Life* 157 (No. 4064), May 22, 1975, 1344-6.

Empey, C.A., 'A Case Study of the Primary Phase of Anglo-Norman Settlement: the Lordship of Kells', *Old Kilkenny Review* New Series 3, 1984, 32-40.

Empey, C.A., 'The Sacred and the Secular: the Augustinian Priory of Kells in Ossory, 1193-1541', *Irish Historical Studies* 24 (No. 94), November 1984, 131-51.

Harbison, Peter, 'The Other Kells – County Kilkenny', *Ireland of the Welcomes* 42(3), May/June 1993, 26-9.

Tietzsch-Tyler, Daniel, *The Augustinian Priory of Kells, Co. Kilkenny* (Kells 1993).

The Benedictines and Fore Abbey, Co. Westmeath

Leask, H.G., *Fore* (Dublin, n.d. but c.1938).

De Varebeke, Hubert J., 'The Benedictines in medieval Ireland', *JRSAI* 80, 1950, 92-6.

Casey, Christine and Alistair Rowan, *The Buildings of Ireland – North Leinster* (Harmondsworth 1993), 293-9.

The Dominicans

Mould, Daphne D.C. Pochin, *The Irish Dominicans: The Friars Preachers in the History of Catholic Ireland* (Dublin 1957).

Leask, Harold G., *Irish Churches and Monastic Buildings*, Vols II-III (Dundalk 1966).

Gwynn, Aubrey and R. Neville Hadcock, *Medieval Religious Houses Ireland* (London 1970), 218-34.

SITE
Kilmallock Priory, Co. Limerick
Hogan, Arlene, *Kilmallock Priory* (Kilmallock 1991).

The Carmelites and Loughrea Friary, Co. Galway

O'Dwyer, Peter, 'The Carmelite Order in Pre-Reformation Ireland', *Irish Ecclesiastical Record* 110, 1968, 350-63.

Monahan, Phelim, *The Old Abbey, Loughrea 1300-1650* (c.1982).

LATE MEDIEVAL IRELAND 1400-1600
Castles and Tower-Houses

Leask, Harold G., *Irish Castles and Castellated Houses* (Dundalk 1941).

Leask, H.G., 'The Irish Tower-House Castle', *Belfast Natural History and Philosophical Society, Proceedings and Reports*, 2nd ser. 3, 1945-50, 28-34.

Ó Danachair, Caoimhín, 'Irish Tower Houses and their Regional Distribution', *Béaloideas, The Journal of the Folklore Society of Ireland* 45-47, 1977-9, 158-63.

O'Callaghan, John, 'Fortified Houses of the Sixteenth Century in South Wexford', *Journal of the Old Wexford Society* 8, 1980-81, 1-51.

Cairns, C.T., *Irish Tower Houses: A Co. Tipperary Case Study*. Irish Settlement Series 2 (n.p., 1987).

McCarthy, Judith, 'The Importance of the Tower House in the Late Medieval Society of Breifne', *Breifne* 8, 1989-90, 118-35.

Jordan, A.J., 'Date, Chronology and Evolution of the County Wexford Tower House', *Journal of the Old Wexford Society* 13, 1990-91, 30-81.

Cairns, Conrad, 'The Irish Tower House – a military view', *Fortress* 11, 1991, 3-13.

McNeill, T.E., 'The Origins of Tower Houses', *Archaeology Ireland* 6(1) Spring 1992, 13-14.

Barry, Terry, 'The Archaeology of the Tower House in the Late Medieval Ireland', in Anderson, Hans and Jes Wienberg (eds), *The Study of Medieval Archaeology, European Symposium for Teachers of Medieval Archaeology, Lund 11-15 June 1990*, Lund Studies in Medieval Archaeology 13 (Stockholm 1993), 211-17.

Kerrigan, Paul, *Castles & Fortifications in Ireland 1485-1945* (Cork 1995).

Reeves-Smyth, Terence, *Irish Castles* (Belfast 1995).

Sweetman, David, *Irish Castles and Fortified Houses* (Dublin 1995).

Donelly, Colm J., 'Frowning Ruins: The Tower Houses of Medieval Ireland', *History Ireland* 4(1), 1996, 11-16.

See also publications cited under 'Norman Castles and Earthworks' above p. 247.

SITES
Cahir Castle, Co. Tipperary
Lanigan, Katherine M., 'Cahir Castle', *Journal of the Butler Society* 4, 1972, 237-44.

Johnson, D. Newman, 'A Contemporary Plan of the Siege of Caher Castle, 1599, and Some Additional Remarks', *The Irish Sword* 12 (No. 47), 1975, 109-15.